Dedication ...

To my family and friends who spurred me
on to write about Driftwillow and The Flying N,
And to Nancy who looked after the final
round-up of recipes.

When members of the International Wine and Food Society travel around the world, sampling as they go, Fr. Charles Depiere is often called upon to ask the blessing. He's a pastor from Spokane, Washington, who is known for his nice blend of "grace and grape".

When he heard about Jean Hoare's book, he sent along another kind of blessing:

Jean's book will once more bring us near
To wine and dine and share good cheer.
Give us the grace of moderation
To keep us all in circulation
So we'll enjoy the celebration!

Best Little Cookbook in the West

Written by: Jean Hoare, Claresholm, Alberta
Published by: Deadwood Publishing Ltd.
Box 564, Stn. G, Calgary, Alberta, Canada T3A 2G4

Copyright 1983
ISBN 0-920109-00-4

First Edition: September 1983

Design: Dianne Bersea, Calgary, Alberta
Photography: Steve Wendelboe of The Studio Ltd., Calgary, Alberta
Typesetting: Duffoto Process Company Ltd., Calgary, Alberta
Printing: Centax of Canada, Regina, Saskatchewan

Food Consultant: Carolann Johnson, B.H.Ec. Calgary

Canadian Cataloguing in Publication Data
Hoare, Jean, 1914-
Best little cookbook in the West

Includes index.
ISBN 0-920109-00-4

Cookery, Canadian. 2. Flying N (Restaurant).
Title.

715.H62 1983   641.5971   C83-090114-0

A Note About Metric Conversions ...

Recipes in the BEST LITTLE COOKBOOK IN THE WEST are given in both standard and metric measurements. All have been tested in the standard measurements but have not been tested specifically with the metric conversions.

The standard measurements have been converted to metric by a method known as common metric replacement, a method that does not produce exact equivalents but comes close. Exact conversions sometimes result in awkward fractions and sizes, so the replacement method rounds up or down for ease in measuring.

Foreword ... or How a Cookbook was Born

In 1956, Jean Hoare decided to turn her lifetime dream into a reality. Besides, she needed the money.

So she opened a restaurant and called it the Driftwood Room.

It wasn't quite the stuff of which her dreams were made. For that, she would have needed a big old mansion in the midst of a bustling city, fixed up with the best of everything. Instead, she lived in the foothills of Alberta in a big old country ranchhouse that needed just about everything, especially a well that didn't go dry everytime you turned around!

Still and all, she bought three big round oak tables and put them into a rearranged living and dining room. She hauled water to supplement the stingy well and she figured out a way to get a sign out on the highway so that customers had half a chance of finding their way over the miles of gravelled road, over the Texas gate, down the coulee and up the hill.

Many people predicted doom. Where in the world would this crazy lady find customers, and how in the world would they find her?

However, as it turned out, the combination of good food, friendly service and a drive in the country proved to be an irresistible combination ... especially after Ken Liddell of the Calgary Herald found her place one day and wrote a glowing story about Jean Hoare and her "Steak in the Country".

Thus was a restaurant born.

For the next ten years, the Driftwood Room grew steadily, spilling over into rooms that had to be added onto the original house, spreading its reputation further and further afield.

Jean introduced the idea of a fruit salad with the main meal, fresh fruit at that! Remember, this was at a time when most fruit came canned or not at all in restaurants. She also introduced the idea of dining, rather than eating. Because the main courses had to be prepared from scratch and therefore took longer than many customers were used to, Jean filled the time with appetizers and good cheese and salads and the best bread she could find in the country. Somehow, customers found they didn't mind the wait.

Still, for all the successes, there was still that well that failed at the very worst times. Water had to be hauled from Claresholm, 8 miles away, three and four times a night. The signs on the bathroom door that asked, "Do not flush unless absolutely necessary" were no laughing matter.

So in 1966, Jean bought an old supply depot located in what had been a NATO training centre at the Claresholm RCAF base. It was located about 2 miles from the town.

The building was rather big and bleak looking compared to the cozy clutter of the ranchhouse but it had a walk-in refrigerator and freezers, a hardwood maple floor perfect for dances, a paved road right to the door and best of all ... water without end.

Thus was the restaurant reborn in a new location with a new name.

Some of the warmth and western flavour was transferred to the new location by filling the walls with western memorabilia, using the big round tables again, building various hitching posts and chuckwagon pieces around the rooms.

Business boomed what with regular customers who kept on coming back for more, plus a host of special parties and catering jobs. One year, there was a wedding reception every weekend from March until October.

"I never wanted to see another bride or bride's mother as long as I lived," she said later.

In 1972, Ann Hardy who put out restaurant guides in Canada picked The Flying N as one of Canada's ten best restaurants. It was picked again in the 1973/74 guide, Where To Eat in Canada.

Jean and the staff were pleased, of course, but the resulting crowds were such that they wished they'd never been picked. It got to be difficult to maintain the high quality of food and service that earned the awards in the first place. People poured in from all over southern Alberta, often without reservations, thinking that a country restaurant would never be that busy, or that businesslike.

The hassles finally outweighed the pleasures so in 1975, Jean Hoare sold lock, stock and hitching post to a Calgary restaurateur who promised to maintain The Flying N in the manner to which customers had become accustomed. Four years later, he folded his tent, leaving Jean with a useless mortgage and a rundown restaurant.

She went back once again to try to get The Flying N on its feet for another buyer but on December 31, 1981, she called it quits. The banks hadn't found a buyer and she couldn't keep up the pace any longer. She was in her late 60's, after all.

It was at her retirement party that a group of loyal friends and fans started a cookbook fund. If Jean couldn't run the restaurant, then she'd have to write a cookbook, they said.

I met Jean early in 1983. She was in the midst of her favourite activities — cooking and entertaining. I was soon in the midst of two of my favourite activities — eating and being entertained.

We got on like a house on fire, and went on from there. Would she get busy and write up her recipes of a lifetime if I got busy and published them?

So she did and I did, and here's the Best Little Cookbook in the West.

(Nancy Millar)
Deadwood Publishing

Table of Contents

Table of Contents

A Love Story ...

This is a love story ... a lifelong love affair with food. It started when I was just young — preparing food for my long suffering (but not always silent) parents, planning parties in minute detail for adolescent friends, always dreaming of the "someday" when I might have a restaurant of my own.

Even before I moved with my husband to a small ranch in the foothills of Alberta, I had a notion that "country" and "cooking" went together. "Farm fresh" always sounded good; hand lettered signs on gate posts promising "Chicken dinners" always beckoned to me. But never in my wildest fantasies did country enter into my thinking as much as it eventually did in reality.

When the day finally arrived and I officially opened the door of my restaurant to the public, a more unlikely location would have been nigh-on impossible to find. We were located at the end of four miles of gravel road, the access to which was an unmarked turn-off on the nearest pavement. We were ten miles from the nearest town, 80 miles from the nearest city.

The restaurant had only two things going for it: my appalling ignorance of the basics of normal restaurant operations and the curiosity of people who couldn't resist checking out this crazy lady who lived in the middle of nowhere and had the audacity to serve six course meals that took up to three hours to eat.

It was not an overnight success — my ranchhouse restaurant — but that fact turned out to be a fortunate break. It gave me time to work gradually into one of the world's most difficult business ventures, that of feeding the public. Having a dinner party for 20 guests is one thing; catering to 20 customers is — to put it mildly — another kettle of fish.

However, my confidence and the clientele grew and eventually we were said to be "halfway to everywhere" rather than in the middle of nowhere.

This book includes recipes, of course; my favorites scrounged from relatives and friends (sometimes one and the same). But it's also the story behind the Driftwillow Ranch and The Flying N restaurants, with reminiscences of how this fascination with food has widened my horizons, and given me so much more than what a reporter friend used to call — Jean's Steak in the Country.

FRESH FRUIT

It was the fresh fruit that did it. It made our reputation at the restaurant and contributed to our selection as one of Canada's top ten restaurants in 1972, 1973 and 1974.

When planning the very first menu, I made three decisions: to serve fruit instead of vegetables with the main course, to stay away from jellied fruit salads and to serve fresh fruit only.

That final decision presented some problems, especially during the winter months when the variety of fresh fruit dwindled to rock bottom — apples, winter pears, oranges, bananas and the pineapples that doubled as containers for the salad. I desperately wanted some colour variety for the fruit boats so I picked up some pomegranates at the wholesale one day, thinking the bright red seeds would perk up the winter fruits.

Later when I went to make up the fruit boats, I couldn't find the precious pomegranates. After watching me dig around in all manner of improbable spots, one of the helpers that night said, "I don't know what it is you're looking for. The only things I saw were some rotten apples and I threw them out." She had never seen pomegranates before.

I had never seen kiwi fruit when it was first listed by a wholesale house, so I asked the clerk what they looked like. "Like a lot of little brown mice without tails," he told me. Fortunately, I took a chance on the taste and discovered one of the nicest additions to our fruit boats in years!

The Famous Flying N Fruit Boat

1	pineapple	1

melon balls (honeydew, cantaloupe, watermelon)
berries (strawberries, blueberries, raspberries)
fruits (peaches, cherries, apricots, pears)
exotic fruit (kiwi, mango, papaya)
grapes for the top

Cut the pineapple in half, cut out the fruit, leaving the shell intact to serve as the fruit boat container. Discard the hard pineapple core. Mix the rest of the pineapple fruit with melon balls, whole and cut up berries, sliced fruit, a smattering of exotic fruit. Put the combination back into the pineapple shell and top everything with a topknot of grapes — either the green seedless or the attractive blue grapes when they're in season. The trick of this is to use fresh fruits of the season arranged in an attractive way.

If pineapple is hard to come by, use a cantaloupe or honeydew melon as the fruit container. Somehow, fruit tastes so much better in a natural container than in a dish. Scallop the edges of the melon and it will do very nicely.

To make a large fruit boat for a buffet, use a watermelon as the container. They can be turned into long boats, tall ships, whales, just about anything your imagination can dream up. They are also very attractive with designs carved along the sides. Use a slender pointed knife and create a masterpiece or simply write, "Happy Birthday, Mom".

The fruit boats were always accompanied by the minted cream sauce, the recipe for which was requested so often that we finally included it in our restaurant newsletter.

Minted Cream Sauce

1 cup	whipping cream	250 mL
1 cup	salad dressing	250 mL
1 tbsp.	creme de menthe	15 mL
few drops	green food colour	few drops

Whip the cream. The secret of this recipe is to have equal amounts of whipping cream and salad dressing. Don't use mayonnaise.

Mix together the whipped cream and salad dressing. Fold in the creme de menthe (add more if you'd like it stronger) and shake in enough green food colour to make the sauce a light mint green. Use mint jelly if you're not keen on creme de menthe. If you have access to mint leaves, put a tiny sprig on the very top of the sauce. Spoon into an attractive dish and serve alongside the fruit boats.

Sometimes, fruit salads were ordered for special functions and we got even fancier.

Fruit Filled Melon

1	large melon	1
2 cups	fresh strawberries	500 mL
1½ tsp.	unflavoured gelatin	7 mL
¼ cup	cold water	50 mL
½ cup	white wine	125 mL
2 tsp.	orange liqueur	10 mL
2 tsp.	frozen orange juice	10 mL
1 pkg. (8 oz.)	cream cheese	1 pkg. (250 g)
2 tsp.	creme de menthe	10 mL

Note: Use a large honeydew or Persian melon. Orange liqueur refers to Triple Sec or Grand Marnier.

Peel the melon making sure all the rind is removed. Cut a hole in one end, large enough to get inside with a spoon to remove the seeds. Reserve the cut out piece. Wash and hull the strawberries, keeping the largest with the green stems and tops still on them for garnish.

In a small pan, combine gelatin and cold water, stirring well. Add wine and orange liqueur, stirring over heat until gelatin is completely dissolved. Remove from heat and stir in frozen orange juice concentrate and 3 ice cubes. This will speed up the cooling and setting.

Put peeled melon into a small bowl that will hold it upright and put the hulled strawberries in, a few at a time, pouring the syrupy gelatin over them as they go in. This will ensure that the melon is completely filled up. Chill until firmly set.

To serve, cut a thin slice off the side or bottom so that the melon will stand on a plate. Whip the cream cheese and creme de menthe together well, and cover the melon with the mixture, like an icing. Seal the cut out piece back into place and cover it up with icing as well. Garnish with the reserved strawberries and fresh mint. Chill until served.

For a real exercise in contradictions, try my favourite use of avocados ... in an ice cream, of all things!

Avocado Lime Surprise

2	ripe avocados	2
1	lime	1
1 cup	icing sugar	250 mL

equal amts. lime sherbet or vanilla ice cream

Peel and slice ripe avocados. If properly ripened, the stone will drop out easily. Put into food processor or blender. Squeeze the juice from the lime and add to the avocado meat along with the icing sugar. Process until the mixture is creamy. Now, add as much sherbet or ice cream as is contained in the avocado mixture — cup for cup, but you don't have to measure exactly. Process again. Serve at once, garnished with mint leaves.

My mother always used to keep a good supply of bananas in our house in anticipation of a little cousin who lived nearby and often dropped in with the words, "I love you, Auntie Eva. Do you have any bananas?"

As a child, I liked them sliced generously over warm spicy gingerbread, topped with whipped cream. Sometimes I put pureed applesauce in there as well, the better to keep the banana slices from falling off the gingerbread!

Since then, I've gotten a bit more sophisticated and can whip up things like Bananas Foster.

Bananas Foster

6	bananas	6
¼ cup	lemon juice	50 mL
¾ cup	brown sugar	175 mL
⅓ cup	butter	75 mL
¼ cup	orange liqueur	50 mL
ice cream		

Note: Bananas should be under ripe. Suitable orange liqueurs are Grand Marnier, Triple Sec, Curacao. If you want to make this at the table with a suitable amount of pomp and circumstance, use a chafing dish or electric skillet or electric wok.

Peel the bananas, cut in half lengthwise and brush with lemon juice to keep them from browning. In the heated dish, melt brown sugar and butter. Add bananas and cook about 3 minutes, turning them so they get coated with the sugar mixture. Add orange liqueur and heat through.

Spoon bananas with a fair share of sauce over individual servings of ice cream.

Fresh Fruit

When those lovely seedless green grapes are available, try this for something entirely different.

Bake Me a Grape, Beulah

½ lb.	green grapes	250 g
1 cup	sour cream	250 mL
½ cup	brown sugar	125 mL

Wash grapes, remove stems and place in a deep pie plate or shallow casserole dish. Spread the sour cream over top, and sprinkle with the brown sugar.

Put under a preheated broiler and watch carefully until the sugar bubbles and boils. Serve at once. The fruit will still be cold; the crust of cream and sugar will be hot and irresistible.

Almost any fresh fruit should work in this recipe.

For a special breakfast or brunch, serve grapefruit or oranges in new ways. For instance, you can top grapefruit halves with maple syrup, brown sugar or honey and then broil until bubbly. Or you can make a Grapefruit Soufflé.

Grapefruit Soufflé

2	grapefruit, halved	2
¾ cup	citrus marmalade	175 mL
4	egg whites	4
¼ cup	sugar	50 mL

Halve the grapefruit, remove core and tough fibre between the sections.

If marmalade is very chunky, whirl it briefly in the blender or mash lightly. Heat in a small saucepan until warm.

Beat egg whites until very stiff, fold in sugar and warm marmalade. Pile soufflé mixture onto grapefruit halves and bake in 425°F (215°C) for about 8 minutes or until soufflés are puffed up and brown.

Sprinkle with icing sugar and serve at once.

This is equally good done with oranges. Cut a generous cap off the top of each orange and save for garnish. Use orange marmalade in the soufflé and proceed as above.

APPETIZERS

I learned very quickly when my first restaurant became a reality that my customers were by and large "meat and potato" people, but once they learned that they could get a good steak, cooked to order, with potatoes that looked like potatoes, they relaxed enough to try some of the "extras".

Today, it is the "extras" that folks remember ... like the famous onion soup mix dip.

I thought everybody knew about this particular dip—the manufacturer of the onion soup mix certainly advertised it, even included a description on the box—but apparently it was a new taste to many of our customers. Some asked for the recipe—which I readily gave. Others tried to figure it out for themselves, seeking out what they were sure must be "secret" ingredients!

Another customer asked for the recipe and I repeated, as I had so many other times, "Just combine sour cream and onion soup mix." She phoned me later to say that I hadn't told her whether the soup should be added when it was hot or cold. She had made the soup first, complete with 4 cups of water, and was understandably baffled about what to do next!

We got tired of preparing (and tasting) the same old dip so occasionally we'd branch out to something entirely different. Inevitably, however, someone would ask for the "onion dip" which they had enjoyed on a previous visit. So we gave in and made the onion dip a permanent feature.

My mother would have approved of our famous dip. It didn't require any fussing at all.

The Flying N Dip, No Relation of Mine

1 envelope	onion soup mix	1 envelope (39 g)
2 cups	sour cream	500 mL

Note: Creamed cottage cheese can be used instead of or along with sour cream. Blend it thoroughly first.

Mix the two ingredients together and serve with chips or light crackers.

The basic dip can be dressed up with various additions: drained cut-up clams or tuna fish or salmon—adding a bit of celery and lemon juice to any of the above; ½ cup (125 mL) corned beef, thinly sliced and chopped, with ½ cup (125 mL) pimiento stuffed olives; crumbled bacon; chopped red or green pepper; crushed garlic or ¼ tsp. (1 mL) garlic powder; curry powder to taste; 1 tsp. (5 mL) dill weed; 1 tbsp. (15 mL) minced parsley; worcestershire sauce; green or black olives.

My mother would not have been so fond of this dip—it does take a bit of fussing, there's no getting around it! But it is my favourite by far.

A Dilly of a Dip

10 oz. pkg.	frozen spinach	300 g pkg.
2 cups	sour cream	500 mL
1 pkg.	dry leek soup mix	1 pkg. (74 g)
1 cup	blender mayonnaise	250 mL
½ cup	green onions	125 mL
½ cup	fresh parsley	125 mL
½ cup	fresh dill	125 mL
2 tsp.	beau monde seasoning	10 mL

Note: Fresh spinach may be used in place of frozen. Cook for about 1 minute to approximate state of frozen. Also, ordinary mayonnaise may be used, but recipe for blender mayonnaise is on page 70. Beau monde seasoning is available in spice sections of most supermarkets. Dry parsley and dill can be used in place of the fresh, but cut down amounts to 1 tsp. (5 mL) of each.

Drain spinach, whether fresh or frozen, on paper towel. Chop onions, parsley and dill.

Put everything into a blender or food processor and mix until smooth, usually less than a minute. Scrape down the sides and give it another whirl.

Serve with any or all of the following: celery, mushrooms, cherry tomatoes, broccoli, cauliflower, zucchini, radishes, carrots, turnips, cucumber, edible pea pods, red and green peppers, frilly leaf lettuce and parsley. Try to find a basket or bowl or some interesting way to present the vegetables—that's half of the success of fresh vegetable dips. They can look so bright and appealing if presented well.

I got this dip recipe from the Evans Farm Inn in the southern U.S.A. and from my neighbour Audrey, who lives just down the way from me. Goes to show that good food gets around. Also, that the grass is no greener in Virginia!

Crab Anything

1 can (5 oz.)	crab meat	1 can (142 g)
1 pkg. (8 oz.)	cream cheese	1 pkg. (250 g)
1	green onion	1
1 tsp.	grated horseradish	5 mL

Drain crabmeat and lay on paper towels to absorb excess liquid. Soften cream cheese. Mix together all ingredients.

Use as a dip with crackers and vegetables or spread on toast and heat in oven as canapes. Also use to fill tiny pastry shells or small cream puffs. Also freezes well.

Guacamole is a wonderfully smooth dip, but requires some special treatment to keep the bright green colour.

Guacamole That Stays Green

2	large ripe avocados	2
1	small onion	1
1	large tomato	1
3 tbsp.	lime or lemon juice	50 mL
1 tbsp.	olive oil	15 mL

salt, tabasco and/or chopped chili peppers to taste

Mash the avocados to a puree. Chop up the onion and add. Peel, seed and chop the tomato and add. Add lime or lemon juice and small amount of olive oil to thin the mixture to dipping consistency. (Thickness depends somewhat on juiciness of tomato and so on. Use your judgment.) Season with salt, tabasco and/or chopped chili peppers.

To keep the avocado mixture from turning black, bury the avocado pit in the guacamole and refrigerate until ready to serve. Also, cover the guacamole with a thin coating of mayonnaise, sealing right to the edges. Then stir in the mayonnaise when it comes time to eat. Serve with corn chips.

Variations on the guacamole theme can include the addition of a minced garlic clove, a small grated cucumber or crisp bits of bacon.

Green Goddess Dip was another favourite with customers, and is still a favourite today with family and friends.

Green Goddess Dip

1/2 cup	mayonnaise	125 mL
1/2 cup	sour cream	125 mL
1 clove	garlic	1 clove
1 tsp.	anchovy paste	5 mL
1/2 tsp.	onion salt	2 mL
2 tsp.	lemon juice	10 mL
1 tsp.	tarragon	5 mL
1/4 cup	green onion	50 mL
1/4 cup	fresh parsley	50 mL

Note: If you can get it, add 1/4 cup chopped fresh watercress as well.

Chop the green onion and parsley. If using dried parsley, cut amount to 1 tbsp. (15 mL).

Put all ingredients into blender and puree until smooth. Makes 1 1/2 cups (375 mL).

Tostados are small cocktail size tortillas, which can be purchased fresh, frozen or canned. After thawing, if necessary, cut into small chip-size pieces and fry in shallow oil about 2 minutes a side. Drain on paper towels and serve with the following dip. You can also use the various flavoured corn chips available.

Mexican Bean Dip with Tostados

½ lb.	ground beef	250 g
¼ cup	chopped onion	50 mL
¼ cup	extra-hot catsup	50 mL
1½ tsp.	chili powder	7 mL
½ tsp.	salt	2 mL
1 can (14 oz.)	red kidney beans	1 can (398 mL)
½ cup	sharp cheddar cheese	125 mL
¼ cup	stuffed olives	50 mL
¼ cup	chopped raw onion	50 mL

Note: Olives can be green or black. If you can't get extra-hot catsup, increase the chili powder. Increase it anyway if you like your chili hot.

In heavy skillet, brown ground beef and ¼ cup onion. Spoon out excess fat and add catsup, chili powder and salt.

Leave the liquid on the kidney beans and puree both in a blender or food processor. (By hand, mash them up a bit.) Add to meat mixture and heat through.

Spoon into a chafing dish (or some other container that will keep the dip hot) and garnish with grated cheddar cheese, chopped olives and raw onion. As people help themselves, the garnish will gradually mix into the dip—which is exactly what was intended! Optional seasonings for added taste could include garlic salt, vinegar, worcestershire sauce, liquid smoke or crumbled bacon bits.

A seafood dip is special no matter where you live, but it's extra special for prairie people!

Seafood Dip Elegante

1 pkg. (8 oz.)	cream cheese	1 pkg. (250 g)
¼ cup	mayonnaise	50 mL
1 clove	crushed garlic	1 clove
1 tsp.	grated onion	5 mL
1 tsp.	prepared mustard	5 mL
1 tsp.	sugar	5 mL
dash	seasoned salt	dash
1 can (5 oz.)	flaked lobster	1 can (140 g)
3 tbsp.	sauterne wine	50 mL
melba toast or assorted crisp, not sweet, crackers		

Note: Flaked crabmeat or tuna will also work in this recipe. Any white wine will work as well, and if you don't have wine, use a bit of cream.

Melt the cream cheese over low heat, stirring constantly. Blend in mayonnaise, garlic, onion, mustard, sugar and salt. Heat thoroughly. Fold in lobster (or other fish), saving out some nice pieces for garnish. Add the sauterne or cream. Serve hot with melba toast or crackers.

Baba Gannoujh began its life as a Lebanese salad but has emerged in this country as a dip for flat bread or raw vegetables. The name means "spoiled old daddy". It seems that a certain toothless old gentleman couldn't manage his usual meal and threw such a fit that the kitchen finally came up with a mashed dish that he liked. Thus — Baba Gannoujh.

Baba Gannoujh

1	large eggplant	1
2 cloves	garlic	2 cloves
1 tsp.	salt	5 mL
1/3 cup	lemon juice	75 mL
1/3 cup	sesame or olive oil	75 mL

parsley sprigs and pomegranate seeds, if desired

Cut eggplant in half and broil, skin side up, until the skin is black and crackling. Let cool a bit, then pull the charred skin off. Discard the skin. Put the rest of the eggplant into a blender or food processor.

Crush garlic cloves. In a small bowl, mix garlic with salt and 1 tsp. (5 mL) lemon juice. Add to eggplant. Add remaining lemon juice alternately with oil, blending well after each addition. Taste and add additional lemon juice and salt, if needed. Pour into a serving dish and chill.

When serving, sprinkle a little oil on top, garnish with parsley sprigs and pomegranate seeds. Supply flat bread (pita bread) or fresh vegetables for dipping.

Seafood cocktails have almost become predictable — which is a shame because they offer such limitless possibilities! Teamed with the right sauce, they can be just the right beginning to a terrific meal.

Lobsters, prawns, crab and Alaskan king crab go well with Lemon Butter Mayonnaise. Arrange the fish in suitable small dishes, sit them in ice or otherwise, and serve with a generous helping of the following.

Lemon Butter Mayonnaise

3	egg yolks	3
1 tsp.	grated lemon peel	5 mL
2 tbsp.	lemon juice	25 mL
1 tbsp.	white wine vinegar	15 mL
3/4 tsp.	sugar	4 mL
2 tsp.	strong mustard	10 mL
1/2 tsp.	salt	2 mL
1/2 cup	salad or olive oil	125 mL
1/2 cup	melted butter	125 mL

Note: Strong mustard refers specifically to a Dijon-style mustard, heavier and spicier than regular prepared mustard.

In a blender, combine egg yolks, lemon peel, lemon juice, vinegar, sugar, mustard and salt. Blend at high speed for 30 seconds. With motor turned on at high speed, add oil and butter in a slow steady stream until mayonnaise is smooth and thick.

Serve at room temperature.

Appetizers

Shrimp, oysters and clams are generally teamed up with spicy tomato cocktail sauces when they are served up as appetizers.

Spicy Cocktail Sauce

2 cups	chili sauce	500 mL
¼ cup	lemon juice	50 mL
¼ cup	ground horseradish	50 mL
½ tsp.	salt	2 mL
1 tbsp.	worcestershire sauce	15 mL
dash	tabasco	dash

Note: Instead of 2 cups (500 mL) chili sauce, you may also use 1 cup (250 mL) chili sauce, 1 cup (250 mL) ketchup.

Mix all ingredients together, cover and chill.

Green mayonnaise is the best accompaniment for appetizers made with lobster and crab.

Green Mayonnaise

¼ cup	mayonnaise	50 mL
½ cup	sour cream	125 mL
2 tsp.	lemon juice	10 mL
½ tsp.	dried tarragon	2 mL
1 clove	crushed garlic	1 clove
¼ cup	chopped watercress	50 mL
¼ cup	chopped spinach	50 mL
¼ cup	chopped parsley	50 mL

Note: The watercress, spinach and parsley should all be fresh.

Mix ingredients together, cover and chill.

Remoulade sauce is the most versatile of all. It complements all seafood except oysters and clams.

Remoulade Sauce

1 cup	mayonnaise	250 mL
1 tbsp.	chopped capers	15 mL
1 tbsp.	chopped green pickle	15 mL
1 tbsp.	chopped parsley	15 mL
1 tbsp.	chopped chives	15 mL
1 tsp.	strong mustard	5 mL
½ tsp.	anchovy paste	2 mL

Note: Blender mayonnaise on page **70** would be a good choice for this recipe. Parsley and chives must be fresh, not dried. Strong mustard refers to European style mustard sometimes called Dijon.

Blend all ingredients together, cover and chill.

People often ask, "What did we ever do before we had ...?" and they name off such modern marvels as zippers, cellophane, panty hose and scotch tape.

I never ask that question. I know what I did before I bought my first clothes dryer.

I chased our clothes all over the countryside, that's what. The winds of southern Alberta not only dried our clothes; they stole them, twisted them, lost them and ruined them.

On a visit from Toronto, my dad watched my struggles with the clothesline and the wind, and finally announced he couldn't stand it anymore. He would buy me a clothes dryer.

When we went into Calgary to buy this lifesaver, the salesman in a big department store explained they didn't really have many in stock. "We don't expect they will sell in Alberta. With all this wind, who needs one?"

Recipes illustrated overleaf

Fruit makes a very welcome appetizer, especially if it's made of fresh fruit and served up in something grand—like a stemmed glass or cut glass serving bowl. You can always dress fruit with its own juice or with a bit of white wine or champagne. A honey dressing is also good.

Honey Dressing for Fruit

½ cup	vinegar	125 mL
¼ cup	honey	50 mL
¼ cup	sugar	50 mL
1 tsp.	dry mustard	5 mL
1 tsp.	paprika	5 mL
1 tsp.	celery seed	5 mL
1 tsp.	celery salt	5 mL
1 tsp.	onion juice	5 mL
1 cup	vegetable oil	250 mL

In a small saucepan, mix first five ingredients and boil for 3 minutes. Add celery seed, celery salt and onion juice. Mix well.

Put into a bottle with a secure lid, add the vegetable oil and shake well before using.

Cheese balls are fun because they offer so many possibilities for decorating. When taking some goodies into the senior citizens' lodge one day, I decided to shape a cheese ball like a porcupine and stick round toothpicks all over it for quills. After all, the lodge is named after the famous range of hills to the west of us, the Porcupine Hills.

Many times, I shaped cheese balls into pine cones and decorated them with almonds still in their red coats. The resemblance is remarkable.

I've used many different recipes for cheese balls but this is my all time favourite!

The Best of the Bunch Cheeseball

24 oz.	cream cheese	750 g
1 jar (8 oz.)	preserved ginger	1 jar (250 mL)
1 tsp.	curry powder	5 mL
1 cup	chopped nuts	250 mL

Note: If you can get bulk cream cheese, preferably Winnipeg cream cheese, do so. Otherwise, get 3 pkgs. (8 oz. each or 250 g each). If you use the packages, allow the cheese to soften to room temperature. Do not use a blender on this. You want the ginger to stay in pieces large enough to talk back.

Also note: Use any kind of nut except peanuts. Pecans, almonds, walnuts, cashews, macadamia—all are fine.

Drain the ginger but reserve the syrup. Cut ginger into small pieces and mix with the cream cheese until the mixture is fluffy. If it needs more moisture, add some of the ginger syrup. Add curry powder to taste.

Shape into a ball, wrap in foil and refrigerate. About 10 minutes before serving, remove foil, reshape if necessary and roll in coarsely chopped nuts until completely coated.

Rumaki is a traditional hot hors d'oeuvre, Japanese in origin but international in appeal!

Rumaki

½ lb.	chicken livers	250 g
2 tbsp.	dry vermouth	25 mL
16	water chestnuts	16
½ lb.	bacon	250 g
2 tbsp.	soy sauce	25 mL

Cut chicken livers into 16 bite sized pieces, rinse and drain on paper towels. Heat vermouth in a frying pan over medium heat: add liver pieces and cook, stirring until lightly browned but still pink inside. (Cut a gash to check.) Drain the livers but save the vermouth in the pan.

Cut 16 water chestnuts in half. Cut bacon strips in half, crosswise. Sandwich a piece of chicken liver between 2 water chestnut halves; wrap with bacon and fasten with a toothpick.

Add soy sauce to the vermouth remaining in the frypan. Pour over skewered livers in a shallow pan and let stand at least an hour, basting occasionally, or cover and refrigerate as long as 8 hours.

Remove rumaki from marinade and place on a rack 6″ (15 cm) below a preheated broiler unit. Broil until the bacon is crisp—about 6 minutes. Makes 16 appetizers. Can also be grilled on a barbecue 6″ (15 cm) above the coals.

When we put together a meal featuring foods native to the new world, I couldn't resist trying to create an equivalent for pemmican. What I ended up with was a pate, not quite what the Indians and fur traders had in their packsacks, but a product that kept to the spirit, if not the fact, of pemmican.

Originally, pemmican consisted of meat dried very thoroughly and then pounded into tallow and flavoured with berries. The tallow acted as a preservative in much the same way that early pioneer homemakers used to "put down" meats with a thick covering of lard. The berries added colour and nutrition.

Pemmican Pate

6 oz.	dried beef or buffalo	170 g
⅓ cup	berries	75 mL
½ cup	unsalted butter	125 mL

liquid smoke, worcestershire, salt and pepper to taste

Note: Dried beef and/or buffalo may be used. Berries may include saskatoons (probably the most authentic) or blueberries or cranberries. Unsalted butter may be replaced by bacon drippings—the pate will be a little sturdier.

Grind meat and berries with the fine blade of a food chopper or food processor. Mix with melted butter and press into a mold. Chill for 24 hours and serve with crackers.

Although I realize a hungry voyageur did not concern himself with details like presentation, I like to cover the mold with a thin layer of mayonnaise and sprinkle finely chopped chives over top.

We used hard cooked eggs in so many ways at the restaurant. In the process, we learned the lesson very early that new eggs do not peel. Only eggs that have aged a week or so will yield easily to peeling.

Some of the most popular items on the buffet table, in among much more glamorous offering, were the plain old devilled eggs. They disappeared as fast as we could make them.

Plain Old Devilled Eggs, in Case You've Forgotten

6	hard cooked eggs	6
3 tbsp.	mayonnaise	50 mL
1 tsp.	prepared mustard	5 mL

salt and pepper to taste
radishes, onion stems, parsley, olives for garnish

Cut the eggs in half lengthwise—a knife with a corrugated blade makes a nice job of this. Remove the yolks, mash them with the mayonnaise, mustard, salt and pepper. Put them back into the whites. Garnish with radish bits, circles from onion stems, bits of parsley or slices of olive.

A good garnish should be edible as well as ornamental. That's why eggs were so nice to work with—they could be colored and they could be cut to suggest all sorts of things, frogs and penguins to name just two!

Colored Pickled Eggs

Don't throw out the pickle juice after you've finished a jar of sweet or dill pickles. Instead, add a bit of green color and fill the jar with peeled hardboiled eggs. In a few days, they'll be an interesting green color, and ideal for salad garnish or for eating out of hand.

Do the same thing with beet pickle juice.

To get a marbled effect, hardboil the eggs but do not peel. Simply roll the eggs to crackle the shells and then put them into the green or red pickle juice.

There's a Penguin in My Soup, Not to Mention a Frog

Use a peeled white hardboiled egg and turn it into a penguin by adding slices of carrot for feet and beak, ripe black olives for head, wings and bib.

To make the frog, start with an egg that's been in green pickle juice for several days. Set the frog/egg on its wider bottom and cut out a mouth in the top part by cutting a wedge in the egg about ⅓ the way down from the top. With toothpicks, stick on eyes made from stuffed olives, and give the frog a lily pad made of lettuce or sorrel.

Both the penguin and frog are good additions to a buffet table—the frog looks particularly good with a dressed fish and the penguin can strut his stuff wherever the table needs a bit of class!

Appetizers

Hummus has become popular in the last few years, and rightfully so. It's a delicious dip served with pieces of pita bread.

Hummus Dip

1 can (15 oz.)	garbanzo beans	1 can
½ cup	sesame seeds	125 mL
1 clove	garlic, halved	1 clove
3 tbsp.	lemon juice	50 mL
1 tsp.	salt	5 mL

Note: Garbanzo beans are also known as chick peas. You can start from dried chick peas (sometimes known as ceci) in which case you should soak the dried beans overnight, then simmer until tender—about 3 hours—the following day. Whether using canned or home processed dried, save 1 cup of the liquid.

Drain the beans and reserve 1 cup liquid. Put the liquid into a blender along with the sesame seeds and garlic. Cover and blend on high speed until well mixed. Add beans, lemon juice and salt. Blend again until a uniform consistency.

Apple Bird

I can't leave the appetizer section without mentioning the apple bird which took a long time to master and meant a lot of applesauce in the process. But once mastered, it made a logical addition to buffet tables at The Flying N.

There's a picture on page 35, but I'll briefly describe the process as well. Use a fairly large apple and cut about ⅓ off on the most unattractive side. That will form the base. Keep the cut piece in lemon or pineapple juice to prevent browning. To begin the carving proper, cut a small wedge out of either side.

Next, cut thin slices from either side of the opening left by the wedge cut. Try to keep them joined at the bottom of the V, but it isn't a complete wreck if the slices come apart. These triangular pieces are cut out, becoming larger as the cuts get deeper.

For the bird, there are properly three such cuts—2 wings and one for the tail—but I'd stay with wings to begin with. Depending on the size of the apple and your ability to make thin slices, there should be 6 - 9 pieces lined up in order of size ready for assembling. Fit them together, overlapping slightly, to form the wings and tail. The moisture in the apple will hold them together. Fit them back into the apple, sliding the largest slice back in the opening so that the overlapping is even throughout.

Using the piece sliced off the bottom, carve a head and neck and with toothpicks, fasten in place just above the stem. Use small whole cloves for eyes, surround the bird with grapes or lettuce. It's particularly good in combination with cheese plates.

SOUP & CHEESE

When there is unlimited time, there is something very satisfying about making a big batch of homemade soup but I don't hesitate to use commercial brands when time is curtailed. I do try, however, to turn the commercial soups into my own with the addition of various garnishes or unexpected ingredients. Sometimes an unexpected combination is enough to produce a "house specialty" like the following Red and Green Soup.

Red and Green Soup

1 can (10 oz.)	tomato soup	1 can (284 mL)
1 can (10 oz.)	asparagus soup	1 can (284 mL)
enough unsweetened whipped cream for garnish		
asparagus tips for the final touch		

Pour each of the soups into a separate saucepan and dilute each with ½ can water or milk. The milk will dull the colour somewhat, but it will add flavour. Take your pick.

When both are heated through, pour enough of the tomato into a soup bowl to half fill the bowl. Carefully pour the asparagus into the centre of the first portion so that the colours remain distinct. Garnish with whipped cream and asparagus tips. Serve hot.

The same effect can be achieved with other combinations — tomato and green pea, tomato and cheese, potato and broccoli, to name just a few. Use your imagination.

A quick and easy soup can be made with the versatile Cheddar cheese soup available in cans. At other times, it makes a good quick cheese sauce but in this combination, it's a good hearty soup.

Shrimp and Cheese Soup

1 can (10 oz.)	cheese soup	1 can (284 mL)
½ cup	milk	125 mL
1 small can	small shrimp	1 small can

A small can of shrimp is somewhere in the neighborhood of 3.75 oz. (106 g). Be sure to drain the shrimps, rinse and then drain again. Frozen shrimpmeat could also be used — you don't need a lot.

In a small saucepan, heat the cheese soup. Dilute with the milk and add the shrimps. Heat thoroughly.

Serve with a salad and something crusty in the bread line.

After a mushroom farm opened a few miles from the restaurant and we could get fresh supplies as often as required, we took to making large kettles of fresh mushroom soup. The following version is somewhat reduced, however. You won't end up with buckets. You'll just end up with compliments.

Cream of Mushroom Soup

1 lb.	mushrooms	500 g
½ cup	butter	125 mL
1 tsp.	lemon juice	5 mL
1	small onion, sliced	1
⅓ cup	flour	75 mL
3 cups	chicken broth	750 mL
1 tsp.	salt	5 mL
¼ tsp.	pepper	1 mL
1 cup	heavy cream	250 mL

The chicken broth may be part broth, part milk.

Trim any tough parts from the bottom of the mushrooms. Remove stems and set aside. Slice the caps with a sharp knife, cutting from the round tops through to the gills. Any button size mushrooms may be left whole.

Melt butter in a large heavy pot. Sprinkle mushrooms with lemon juice and add to the butter. Saute briefly, stirring constantly. Remove with a slotted spoon and keep in reserve.

Add sliced onion and mushroom stems to remaining butter in the pot, cook until transparent and tender. Add flour and stir until blended, about 1 minute. Gradually add chicken broth (or combinations of broth and milk), stirring constantly until mixture is thickened.

In batches that will fit your blender or food processor, puree the hot mixture until smooth. Return to sauce pan, stir in salt, pepper, cream and sauted mushrooms. Reheat but do not boil.

My friend Ev started preparing the consommé for her dinner party two days in advance. That way, she reasoned, she'd have time for all the simmering, chilling, skimming, clarifying and reducing of the liquid and so on. An hour before the dinner party was due to begin, catastrophe struck. She dropped the whole kit and kaboodle. The usual happened—somehow that pot of consommé grew ten fold and there seemed no end to the clean up.

The clean up was not the only problem, however. There was still the question of what to serve in place of the spilled consommé.

Ev's Soup, No Disaster

1 can	tomato soup	1 can (284 mL)
1 can	ham and split pea soup	1 can (284 mL)
1 can	mushroom soup	1 can (284 mL)
1 cup	milk	250 mL
1 small can	shrimp	1 can (113 g)
1 small can	flaked crabmeat	1 can (142 g)
¼ tsp.	curry powder	1 mL
½ cup	dry sherry	125 mL
chopped fresh parsley		

In a large saucepan, mix together the soups and heat thoroughly. Add the milk.

Drain, rinse and drain the shrimp. Drain the crabmeat. Add both to the soups. Add curry. Just before serving, add sherry to the mixture. Sprinkle each bowlful with chopped parsley.

Naturally, being the Tomato Queen and all, I'll have to include a recipe for Gazpacho, the Spanish "liquid tomato salad".

Gazpacho with Gusto

1 cup	white bread cubes	250 mL
2-3 tbsp.	red wine vinegar	25-50 mL
2	cucumbers	2
1	onion, diced	1
2 cloves	garlic	2 cloves
1	green pepper	1
½ cup	olive or salad oil	125 mL
6	ripe tomatoes	6
salt and freshly ground black pepper to taste		
1-2 cups	ice water	250 - 500 mL
3 slices	white bread	3 slices
3 tbsp.	butter	50 mL
1 clove	garlic	1 clove
2	hardboiled eggs	2

Once the vegetables are prepared for this soup, it's a snap. But the preparation must be faced.

Prepare the bread cubes by cutting off the crusts and cubing enough of the remainder to make 1 cup. Put into a blender or food processor, add 2 tbsp. of vinegar and leave to soak.

Peel, slice and dice the cucumbers, putting one into the blender and keeping the other for garnish. Also add the diced onion, the 2 cloves of garlic and ½ the green pepper. Process or blend until smooth. Add the oil, a bit at a time, and blend until smooth.

Scald, peel and chop the ripe tomatoes. Add to the puree in the blender or food processor. (If the container is getting full, empty the first batch into another bowl while you finish the process.) Puree the tomatoes and add to the first mixture. Season to taste, adding more vinegar as necessary. Chill thoroughly. Incidentally, the soup won't be bright red—the other vegetables dilute the colour but add to the flavour, never fear.

Just before serving, stir well and thin with ice water. The amount will vary according to the juiciness of the tomatoes. Very juicy fresh tomatoes—not too much water. Not so juicy—more ice water. Overall, this soup should be fairly thin but not watered down in flavour.

Remove the crusts from the bread slices, and dice what's left. Melt butter in a heavy pan, mince the garlic and add to the butter. Saute briefly, then add the bread cubes and toss until lightly browned.

Peel and dice the eggs. Dice the remaining green pepper. Put in a small bowl. Do the same with the croutons, the remaining diced cucumber and extra icecubes. Serve the soup over ice, and invite guests to dress it up as they will.

Soup

If I'm going to be very busy with a project that won't allow time out to prepare meals, I am likely to start what I call Fabulous Four Day Soup.

Fabulous Four Day Soup

1 lb.	ground beef	500 g
2	medium onions	2
4 cups	canned tomatoes	1 L
4 cans	consommé	4 cans (284 mL each)
4 or 5	carrots	4 or 5
1	small celery heart	1
1/2-1 cup	fresh parsley	125-250 mL
1	bay leaf	1
1/2 tsp.	sweet basil	2 mL
1/2 tsp.	oregano	2 mL
1/4 tsp.	rosemary	1 mL
1/4 tsp.	tarragon	1 mL
10	whole peppercorns	10

To prepare the ingredients, dice the onions, clean and dice the carrots, chop the celery—including any leaves, chop up the parsley—including any stems since they hold most of the flavour. Parsley can be chopped by putting it in a cup and snipping it with kitchen shears.

On day #1, brown the ground beef in a heavy pot. Push to one side and brown the onions in the same way. Drain off excess fat. Add tomatoes, consommé, carrots, celery and parsley. Add bay leaf and other herbs.

Cover and simmer at least 3 hours or as long as all day. Serve with dumplings as they can float on top of the soup and be lifted out, leaving it ready for another variety the next day.

Quick & Easy Dumplings for Day 1

1 cup	instant biscuit mix	250 mL
1	egg, beaten	1
1/4 cup	milk	50 mL

Mix the biscuit mix, egg and milk to form a soft dough. Drop by teaspoonfuls into the hot broth. Increase the heat a bit, cover tightly and cook 10-15 minutes.

Serve in large bowls with dumplings floating on top. Cool the remaining soup and freeze whatever is not needed in the next few days.

Thicker Soup for Day #2

Early in the day, reheat as much of the soup as needed. Add 2 tbsp. (30 mL) pot barley for each serving. Simmer slowly 2 - 3 hours. If soup seems too thick, add water, tomato juice or consommé.

Pasta for Day #3

For the next day, or whenever, simmer the mixture and allow it to stay thick. Watch that it does not stick to the bottom of the pan. When almost ready to serve, cook enough macaroni, noodles or spaghetti to serve the numbers waiting to eat. Drain the pasta and spoon the thick soup over top as a sauce. Top with grated parmesan cheese.

Mexican Meal for Day #4

For its last appearance, heat up remaining soup. Add a small can of kidney beans, a dash or two of chili powder and some cubes of sharp cheese. Serve over tortillas or toasted bread or cornmeal muffins.

Since I can't resist the idea of using a food as its own container, I was immediately hooked by Pumpkin Soup.

Peter, Peter, Pumpkin Soup

1   large pumpkin   1
salt, pepper and butter to enhance the baking
enough good rich chicken stock to fill the pumpkin
toasted shelled pumpkin seeds or sunflower seeds

Find a large pumpkin, wider than it is deep, and cut a fairly wide lid from the top. With a spoon, scrape out all the seeds and strings from the inside. Put the now empty pumpkin into a shallow casserole dish—just in case it springs a leak in the baking process. Season with salt and pepper, add a good chunk of butter and bake for about 20 minutes in a 350°F (180°C) oven. Don't put the lid on during the baking—tuck it in beside the pumpkin.

During the baking, check for liquids which may accumulate in the bottom of the shell. If there is any buildup, remove them with a ladle so that the bottom doesn't cook too fast and collapse.

When the pumpkin meat shows signs of tenderness, fill the shell with the chicken stock. Cover with the lid this time and continue baking for another 20 minutes or so, until the pumpkin meat is soft and easily pierced with a fork.

Serve the soup in the shell, spooning out cooked pumpkin meat along with the broth. Top with toasted pumpkin seeds or sunflower seeds.

If a heartier soup is in order, add chopped chicken to the broth or fill the shell with a thick vegetable soup. Always remember to spoon out some of the pumpkin meat with the soup—that's the object of this lesson!

Notes and Variations

Soup

When I first planned my menus, I knew I'd have to figure out a way to keep the guests nibbling and happy while the main course was being prepared. Luckily, I had picked up an antique cheese cutter some years earlier, so I put that out onto a table in the restaurant—complete with a whole round of cheese—so that customers could snack on cheese while they waited for the main course.

Some helped themselves so liberally that we eventually put up a discreet sign that showed a little mouse pulling a wagonload of cheese and saying, "Please, just take what you can eat on the premises!"

The antique cutter had belonged to one of the early grocery stores in town. The son of the first grocer once told me that his first job every morning had been to turn the big cheese to keep it from drying out on one side.

Also, he remembered that the cutter had been used so much in those early days, when cheese came in a round or didn't come at all, that the blade had to be replated regularly. The cheese literally ate the finish off. There was nothing namby pamby about cheese in those days!

Back in our time, the antique cutter and huge cheese rounds proved a great attraction for our customers as well. If they weren't visible, customers quickly asked, "Where's the big cheese?" Staff delighted in telling me on those occasions that someone was asking for me.

For years, we brought in cheddar from cheese factories in Southern Alberta—Glenwood near Fort Macleod, in particular—but progress eventually took its toll. The big rounds of cheese weighing 25 pounds each, packed with 4 altogether in the traditional round cheese boxes, were discontinued because of problems with packaging and handling. We had to resort to big blocks of cheese in the cutter then, but something was lost in the process.

Notes and Variations

Cheese

I am very fond of cheese of all kinds. It's a staple item on my shelves and turns up in almost every section of this book in recipes from appetizers to main course meals, salads and desserts. (Check the index.)

I recently added quark to my inventory of cheeses. It's a soft creamy cheese, somewhere between cottage cheese and cream cheese in both texture and taste. Available now in most stores in the dairy section, it's ideal for cheesecake, especially the cooked kind which is the best kind in my opinion anyway!

Alberta Quark Cheesecake

1½ cups	graham wafer crumbs	375 mL
2 tbsp.	sugar	30 mL
1 tsp.	cinnamon	5 mL
¼ cup	butter, melted	50 mL
4	eggs, separated	4
½ cup	sugar	125 mL
1 lb.	quark cheese	454 g
¼ tsp.	salt	1 mL
½ cup	heavy cream	125 mL
1 tbsp.	lemon juice	15 mL
1 tsp.	grated lemon rind	5 mL
1 tbsp.	cornstarch	15 mL
1 tsp.	vanilla	5 mL
¼ cup	walnuts or almonds	50 mL

Note: You may also use zwieback crumbs instead of graham wafer crumbs.

Mix crumbs with sugar and cinnamon. Add melted butter and stir until crumbs are moistened. Pat evenly and firmly into bottom and sides of a buttered 9″ (23 cm) springform pan or 9″ (2 L) square cake pan. Bake in 350°F (180°C) oven for 10 - 12 minutes. Cool.

Beat egg yolks, add the ½ cup sugar gradually and continue beating until light and fluffy. Stir in the cheese and salt. Do not whip the cream. Add it as it is along with the lemon juice, lemon rind, cornstarch and vanilla. Beat egg whites until stiff and fold evenly into the cheese mixture. Spoon into the crumb crust, sprinkle with chopped nuts and bake in 325°F (160°C) oven for about 50 minutes or until set around the edges. Cover with a piece of foil to prevent further browning and bake for another 10 minutes or so. Turn off the heat and let the cake cool in the oven with the door open. Don't be alarmed if the cake falls a bit during this cooling period—most good cheesecakes do.

Remove from the open oven after an hour and cool completely on a wire rack. Refrigerate until ready to serve. Serve plain or garnished with fresh fruit.

Cheese

Welsh Rarebit—or Rabbit, if you prefer—always reminds me of a late night snack I enjoyed at the famous Fortnum and Mason store in London. I had just seen Jimmy Stewart in his famous role as Harvey and on the way home discovered late night snacks at the world famous food store. Picadilly had no happier tourist that evening!

You Say Rarebit and I'll Say Rabbit

8 oz.	Cheddar cheese	250 g
2 tbsp.	butter	25 mL
1 tsp.	prepared mustard	5 mL
1 small bottle	dark beer	1 small bottle

salt and pepper to suit individual tastes
buttered toast, enough for four servings

Use a chafing dish if you have one, and prepare Welsh Rarebit/Rabbit at the table for extra flair.

Melt the cheese with the butter. Add the mustard and enough of the beer, at least a cupful, to make a thick creamy sauce. Season to taste. Pour over the hot buttered toast and brown quickly under a broiler. If you don't have a broiler handy, sprinkle a bit of paprika or freshly chopped chives over the top.

Devilled Rarebit/Rabbit

Use the recipe above but add ¼ tsp. (1 mL) cayenne pepper, 1 tbsp. (15 mL) chopped up hot spicy pickle, 1 tsp. dry mustard.

Rarebit With Tomatoes

It's not traditionally correct, but I sometimes add tomatoes to a rarebit mixture. Mind you, I add tomatoes to most everything. I'm not called The Tomato Queen for nothing!

Simply peel and seed several fresh tomatoes, slice and add. Or use canned tomatoes with the juice removed or a bit of tomato puree. Don't add so much that the cheese flavour will be overpowered but just enough to vary the colour and enhance the taste.

Rarebit in the Great Outdoors

My dad used to enjoy this combination. In a heavy skillet on a stove or campfire, slice Cheddar cheese and cook until the cheese melts and the oil runs freely. Fry thick slices of bread in the oil, reserving the melted cheese for a topping.

Pour the cheese over the fried bread and enjoy a cheese treat quite unlike anything else!

For those who love their cheese and their wine, the best solution is a fondue. Invented by the Swiss, it was originally eaten from a communal pan—in very much the same way as we do now.

Fondue Neuchateloise

10 oz.	Emmental cheese	300 g
10 oz.	Gruyere cheese	300 g
1 clove	garlic	1 clove
1 cup	dry white wine	250 mL
1 tsp.	corn starch	5 mL
3 tbsp.	dry white wine	50 mL

kirsch, nutmeg and pepper to suit individual tastes

Grate the cheeses and set aside.

Cut the garlic clove open and rub over the surface of the fondue pot.

Now, prepare the cheese mixture in the fondue pot with the heat unit turned on, or prepare it separately and pour into the fondue container when completed.

Either way, mix together the white wine and grated cheeses. Stir over heat until the cheeses have melted and the sauce is smooth. Mix the cornstarch with the 3 tbsp. (50 mL) white wine and add to the mixture as soon as it starts to boil. Add kirsch, nutmeg and pepper to taste. Keep the heat low so that the fondue simmers gently.

Provide guests with long fondue forks, lots of French bread chunks and lots of white wine.

Cheese teams up well with rice. The following recipe is good at any time but particularly good if you've got left-over rice to use up!

Golden Cheese and Rice

2 cups	cooked rice	500 mL
3 cups	shredded carrots	750 mL
2	eggs, beaten	2
½ cup	milk	125 mL
2 tbsp.	minced onion	25 mL
salt and pepper to taste		
2 cups	grated cheddar cheese	500 mL

Grease a 2 qt. (2 L) baking dish.

Mix together the rice, carrots, eggs, milk and onion. Season to taste. Reserve ½ cup (125 mL) grated cheese. Mix remaining cheese with the first mixture. Put into prepared baking dish. Top with the reserved cheese.

Bake in 350°F (180°C) oven for 30 minutes or until set.

Cheese

BREADS

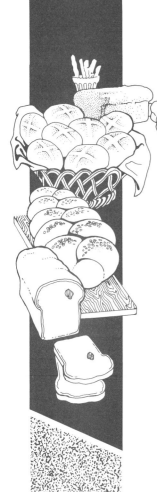

The braided loaves of bread which were one of the highlights of the Driftwillow and Flying N menus were made for us by three generations of the same local family, starting with Papa DeJong, then his son Eddie, now daughter Barbara and her family.

Before serving the whole loaves to our customers, we rebaked them so that the crust turned even crustier and the inside even lighter. Customers were then cautioned to pull the loaves apart rather than slicing them, and to use all the butter they liked. Coming at a time when many restaurants served bread by the solemn slice and butter by the careful pat, this proved a very popular part of our service.

Even though we didn't make the famous bread braids in house, we did tackle many other kinds of bread, quick and yeast, for special meals. Indian Fry Bread, for example, was made to accompany a dinner that featured foods native to North America. Proving once again that food crosses all borders, the Fry Bread turned out to be very similar to beignets or fritters.

Indian Fry Bread

3 cups	flour	750 mL
3 tbsp.	baking powder	50 mL
½ tsp.	salt	2 mL
1¼ cups	warm water	300 mL

lard or cooking oil enough to fill deep fat fryer

Combine all ingredients. Turn mixture out onto a well floured board and knead very lightly. Roll out about ½″ (1.5 cm) thick and cut into whatever shapes you like — squares, circles, long strips, whatever. Make a slit in the middle so that the dough will cook in the centre.

Deep fat fry at 375°F (190°C), turning once to brown both sides.

Eat hot, if possible. Good for dipping into stews or hot soup. Also good with jam and syrup. To serve as dessert, sprinkle with sugar and/or cinnamon.

Notes and Variations

There are numerous recipes for Bannock, all of them quite different. I became interested in what was known as "Top-of-the-sack" bannock, a version of bannock that didn't require a mixing bowl. The settler on the trail or the cook out in camp simply put a bit of water into the top of the flour sack, mixed it together into a paste and baked it over a fire. If a pan was available, a pan was used. If not, the gooey mixture could be wrapped around a green stick and held over the coals until done. If other ingredients were available, they would be added — salt, baking soda, lard.

Since mixing the batter in the top of the sack inevitably leaves behind hard little bits of dough that don't do much for the next batch, I've come up with a refined version of Top-of-the-sack bannock.

Top-of-the-Bowl Bannock or Camp Bread

3-4 cups	flour	750 mL-1 L
1 tsp.	baking soda	5 mL
1 tsp.	salt	5 mL
1 cup	liquid	250 mL

lard, as much as will fit on four fingers of mixing hand

Put the flour into a mixing bowl or dishpan or whatever is available in camp. Stir in baking soda and salt. Make a well and add the liquid — buttermilk is best or canned milk. Scoop up the lard and keep it on your fingers as you mix the liquid into the flour. Once a soft dough forms that doesn't stick to your fingers, remove the dough and pat it out into a heavy greased skillet. Any flour remaining in the bowl can be sifted and reused.

Bake over hot coals or fry as you would a Scottish scone. Watch carefully as this tends to burn easily. Just ask King Alfred.

Corn meal was also a favourite of early settlers, and is still a favourite of mine. I like the story about the origin of the name "Hush Puppies". Apparently, dogs got to be such a nuisance at fish frys in the southern states that the cooks would toss a bit of cornmeal batter to the dogs, saying "Hush, puppies; Hush puppies."

Hush Puppies, Otherwise Known as Corn Fritters

1 cup	cornmeal	250 mL
⅓ cup	flour	75 mL
1 tsp.	baking powder	5 mL
¼ tsp.	baking soda	1 mL
1 tsp.	salt	5 mL
3 tbsp.	finely minced onion	50 mL
¾ cup	buttermilk	175 mL
2 tbsp.	water	25 mL
1	large egg, beaten	1

Combine first six ingredients. Mix thoroughly. Stir in remaining ingredients. Let stand 10 minutes for batter to thicken.

Preheat lard or cooking oil in deep fat fryer or wok to 370°F (190°C). Drop cornmeal mixture by teaspoonfuls into hot oil, browning well on all sides. Drain on paper towel and keep warm in a slow oven until ready to serve.

Cornsticks are similar to Hush Puppies except that they are baked in cast iron cornstick molds and turn out looking like little cobs of corn. I can't resist a new way of presenting a tried and true old recipe!

Cornsticks

½ cup	flour	125 mL
½ cup	yellow cornmeal	125 mL
2 tsp.	baking powder	10 mL
½ tsp.	salt	2 mL
2 tbsp.	sugar	30 mL
½ tsp.	freshly ground pepper	2 mL
2 tbsp.	cooking oil	25 mL
1	egg	1
½ cup	buttermilk	125 mL

optional ... chopped red pepper, canned or fresh

Liberally grease a cornstick mold and set it in a 425°F (215°C) oven to preheat. A good flavour is added if unsalted butter is used to grease the mold instead of oil.

In a large bowl, combine the flour, cornmeal, baking powder, salt, sugar and pepper.

In a smaller bowl, beat together the cooking oil, egg and buttermilk. Add the liquid ingredients to the dry, stirring in the red pepper, if used.

Fill the cornstick molds about ⅔ full. Bake for 15 minutes or so, until a toothpick inserted in the centre comes out clean. Transfer the cooked cornsticks to a rack, regrease the mold and preheat for another 5 minutes. Repeat the filling and baking until all the batter has been used.

Notes and Variations

Breads

Before I opened my ranchhouse restaurant, I had tried to get Calgary Power to enlarge the transformer that supplied us with electrical power. Somehow, the crews were always busy, and never too worried about my 2 KVA.

As it happened, the first large group to book a banquet at the Driftwillow Room was — you guessed it — Calgary Power. They were putting on a retirement party for one of their colleagues.

Right in the middle of this gala affair, the transformer kicked out and the banquet was left in darkness. Who could ask for anything more?

The Calgary Power repair crew was johnny-on-the-spot the next day to install a bigger transformer. Fortunately, Calgary Power has remained a good friend and customer of mine.

Recipes illustrated overleaf

Red and Green Soup, page 23
Betty's Can't Miss Bread or Buns, page 45
Apple Bird, page 22

Cheese Wheel supplied by Glenwood Cheese Factory, Glenwood, Alberta.

Another oldtimer is Irish Soda Bread, delicious fresh and even better toasted.

Millie's Irish Soda Bread

4 cups	flour	1 L
3 tbsp.	sugar	50 mL
1 tbsp.	baking powder	15 mL
¾ tsp.	baking soda	4 mL
1 tsp.	salt	5 mL
⅓ cup	butter	75 mL
1½ cups	raisins	375 mL
1 tbsp.	caraway seed	15 mL
2	eggs	2
1½ cups	buttermilk	375 mL

Grease a 2 quart (2 L) round casserole dish.

In a large bowl, mix the flour, sugar, baking powder, baking soda and salt. With fingers or pastry blender, cut in the butter until the mixture resembles coarse crumbs. Stir in raisins and caraway seeds.

In a small bowl, beat the eggs. Remove 1 tbsp. (15 mL) of egg mixture for later. Stir buttermilk into remaining egg and stir both into the dry mixture, mixing just until flour is all moistened. The dough will be sticky.

Turn out onto well floured surface and knead lightly, just enough to mix thoroughly. Shape into a ball and place in prepared casserole dish. In the centre of the ball, cut a 4″ (10 cm) cross, about ¼″ (1 cm) deep. Brush the dough with reserved egg.

Bake in 350°F (180°C) oven for about 1½ hours, until top is golden brown and crusty. Cool in the pan for about 10 minutes, then remove and cool on a rack.

Notes and Variations

A jug of sourdough starter was a prized possession of many of the homesteaders in the days before supermarkets and instant yeast granules. Many recipes can be found for making your own starter, and many different methods are used. One oldtimer told me once, "Don't worry about her. She'll let you know when she's ready."

Sourdough Starter

4 cups	lukewarm water	1 L
½ cup	sugar	125 mL
4 cups	flour	1 L

Use a glass or stone crock to hold the sourdough. Metal does not work too well.

Mix water, sugar and flour together. The batter should be fairly thin. Put into suitable container, cover and place in a warm spot. When it begins to work — bubble, in other words — stir it daily.

1 cup (250 mL) of this starter is equivalent to approximately 1 pkg. dry yeast.

As it is used, replace with equal amounts of water and flour. Nothing else should be added.

Temperature is important. To get it started, the sourdough should be in a warm spot, but once it's underway, it can be kept in the frig and taken out only when needed. Warm it up before using. Keep it warm whenever additions are made. Don't let it freeze.

The sourdough starter was so important to early cooks that there are all kinds of stories about sourdough being taken to bed in the really cold nights. After all, a cook who made good bread was often forgiven other sins!

Rye Sourdough Starter

2 cups	rye flour	500 mL
1 tsp.	honey or brown sugar	5 mL
1 cup	warm water	250 mL

Mix together and put into a glass container or stone crock. Cover and let work, in room temperature, for about a week.

Notes and Variations

Breads

Use the rye sourdough starter as outlined above to make this old country style rye bread. It's heavy, like European rye breads should be, but it's lightened somewhat by the use of both sourdough starter and yeast.

Old Country Style Rye Bread

3 pkgs. (3 tbsp.)	yeast	3 pkgs. (8 g each)
2 tsp.	honey or sugar	10 mL
6 cups	warm water	1.5 L
12 cups	rye flour	3 L
2 cups	sourdough starter	500 mL
caraway seeds, if desired, on top of loaf		

In a small bowl, mix the yeast, honey or sugar and 1 cup (250 mL) warm water. Let it work for 5 minutes.

In a large mixing bowl, put the flour and sourdough starter. Add 4 cups (1 L) of warm water, reserving the other cup to add as the need arises. Add the yeast mixture which should be foamy by this time. Mix together well. Add more water if the dough gets too stiff — it should be fairly soft and sticky. Knead for about 5 minutes.

Let rise in a warm place for about 2 hours. Knead again for several minutes. Divide into loaves and place into well greased bread pans or loaf cake pans. Brush the top of the loaf with wet hands to smooth out the surface. Sprinkle with caraway seeds, if desired.

Let rise again for about an hour.

Bake in 400°F (200°C) oven for about 40 minutes or until the loaves sound hollow when tapped.

Notes and Variations

Breads

No self respecting raost of beef should appear without Yorkshire Puddings, those light crunchy hollow puffs just made for holding lots of rich brown gravy. Originally they were made in one large pan, the one that had been sitting under the roast catching the drips as the meat turned on the spit. Nowadays, they are most often made in individual pans, but there's no rule saying you can't use a flat pan as in days of yore.

Yorkshire Puddings

2 or 3	eggs	2 or 3
1 cup	flour	250 mL
1 cup	milk	250 mL
1/2 tsp.	salt	2 mL
2 tbsp.	hot roast drippings	25 mL

Have both the eggs and milk at room temperature. Use 2 eggs if they're large, 3 if small.

Beat eggs with an egg whip until they're light and frothy. Add flour and milk. Don't add the salt just yet – check the drippings first. If they have lots of salt, then cut down on the quantity used in the Yorkshire Puddings. Beat eggs, flour and milk until the batter resembles thick cream. Let stand for several hours, if possible, but the world won't fall apart if you let it stand a few minutes only. Just before pouring into the pans, add the 2 tbsp. (25 mL) hot roast drippings and give the mixture another good beating.

Pour some more of the drippings and brown juice from the roast into muffin tins or a large 9″ x 13″ (3.5 L) pan. Either way, there should be about 1/4″ (1 cm) drippings in the bottom of the container. Put the pan into the hot oven to get both pan and drippings as hot as possible.

Carefully pour the batter into the smoking hot fat, and return to 450°F (230°C) oven for 20 to 30 minutes. Yorkshire Puddings made in a flat pan will puff up in strange peaks like mountain ranges. Those in the muffin tins will form hollow cups, rising above the pans to about double their original size.

Serve immediately, but if that's not possible, leave the puddings in a 350°F (180°C) oven until needed, no more than 10 minutes.

For years, my friend Sally was in charge of a large ranch kitchen and somehow managed to turn out three meals a day plus lunches for never less than 20 people. She often relied on good old muffins.

Sally's Mincemeat Muffins

2	eggs, beaten	2
1 cup	sugar	250 mL
3/4 cup	vegetable oil	175 mL
2 cups	sweet or sour milk	500 mL
1 cup	all bran	250 mL
2 1/4 cups	flour	550 mL
2 tsp.	baking powder	10 mL
2 tsp.	baking soda	10 mL
1 tsp.	salt	5 mL
1 cup	mincemeat	250 mL
3/4 cup	raisins	175 mL

In a large bowl, mix together eggs, sugar, vegetable oil and milk. In another bowl, mix together the dry ingredients and add to the first mixture. Add mincemeat and raisins.

Leave batter in the frig overnight. Bake in greased muffin tins or paper lined muffin tins at 325°F (160°C) for 20 to 25 minutes.

The batter may be kept in the frig for up to a week, using just as much as you want fresh each day. Also, the baked muffins freeze well, so this is a good keeper in more ways than one!

If you want another way to use up those bananas that are ripening too quickly, here's the muffin version of Banana Loaf.

Banana Pineapple Muffins

3 cups	flour	750 mL
2 cups	sugar	500 mL
1 tsp.	baking soda	5 mL
1 tsp.	salt	5 mL
1 tsp.	cinnamon	5 mL
1 cup	nuts or raisins	250 mL
3	eggs	3
2 cups	mashed banana	500 mL
1 cup	vegetable oil	250 mL
1¼ cups	crushed pineapple	300 mL

Note: Use unsweetened pineapple in its own juice.

Do not drain the pineapple. Just take it as it comes!

In a large mixing bowl, stir together the flour, sugar, baking soda, salt, cinnamon and nuts or raisins.

In a smaller bowl, beat the eggs and add the mashed banana, vegetable oil and crushed pineapple. Add all at once to the dry ingredients, stirring just until everything is moistened.

Fill greased muffin tins ⅔ full, or line muffin tins with paper cups and fill to the same degree. Bake in 350°F (180°C) oven for 20 to 30 minutes or until toothpick inserted into the centre comes out clean.

Makes 30 large muffins.

This takes a little time, but it's certainly worth it!

Cottage Cheese Crescents

1 cup	butter	250 mL
2 cups	cottage cheese	500 mL
dash	salt	dash
2 cups	flour	500 mL
1½ tbsp.	light cream	20 mL
1 cup	icing sugar	250 mL

Have both butter and cottage cheese at room temperature. Use small curd creamed cottage cheese.

In a large bowl, combine the butter and cottage cheese. Add salt and flour and beat until smooth and elastic. Cover and chill overnight or for several hours at least.

Divide chilled dough into four equal parts. Roll each part into a circle about ½″ (15 mm) thick, 6″ (15 cm) in diameter. Cut each circle into 8 wedges. Roll up each wedge, starting at the larger rounded edge. Place pointy side down on ungreased baking sheet and curve slightly. Repeat with remaining portions of dough.

Bake in a 350°F (180°C) oven about 20 minutes or until nicely browned. Cool on racks.

Combine cream and icing sugar. Spread over cooled crescents.

As a variation, spread the crescents with melted butter and sugar/cinnamon mixture before baking. They will taste like very rich cinnamon buns.

A Crumb Kuchen by any other name could be called Dessert. However, we'll present it here as a rich bread for a fancy afternoon tea or a nice finish to a lingering midday brunch.

Crumb Kuchen, a Fruit Filled Bread

1 cup	lard, softened	250 mL
½ cup	sugar	125 mL
2	eggs	2
½ tsp.	salt	2 mL
1 tsp.	vanilla	5 mL
3 cups	flour	750 mL
2 tsp.	baking powder	10 mL
1 cup	milk	250 mL
fruit or jam to cover the kuchen		
1 cup	butter	250 mL
2 cups	sugar	500 mL
2 cups	flour	500 mL
a sprinkle of cinnamon over crumb topping, if desired		

Cream lard and sugar. Add eggs, salt and vanilla and beat well. In another bowl, mix together the flour and baking powder. Add to the creamed mixture alternately with the milk.

Roll out and fit into a 9″ x 13″ (3.5 L) pan. For a thinner kuchen, roll to ½″ (1.5 cm) thickness and put on a cookie sheet.

Spread with the fruit which can be fresh (apple slices, raspberries, blueberries) or canned (applesauce, pie filling) or jams. If using fresh, sprinkle with a little sugar.

Cut the butter into the sugar and flour until the mixture resembles coarse crumbs. Spread over the fruit layer and sprinkle with a bit of cinnamon, if desired.

Bake at 375°F (190°C) for 40 to 50 minutes or until done.

Another good idea for a late morning brunch or afternoon tea, maybe even a late evening snack, is a tea bread.

Orange Tea Braids

2 cups	flour	500 mL
3 tsp.	baking powder	15 mL
¾ tsp.	salt	4 mL
2 tbsp.	sugar	30 mL
⅓ cup	butter	75 mL
1 tbsp.	grated orange rind	15 mL
¾ cup	milk	175 mL
1½ cups	icing sugar	375 mL
1 tbsp.	melted butter	15 mL
3 tbsp.	orange juice	50 mL

In a large mixing bowl, stir together the flour, baking powder, salt and sugar. Using a pastry blender or your fingers, cut in the butter until the mixture resembles coarse crumbs. Blend in orange rind and milk, stirring only until the dry ingredients are dampened.

Turn dough out onto a lightly floured board, knead lightly for half a minute or so — just until the dough is elastic. Roll dough into a rectangle measuring 9″ x 14″ (23 x 35 cm) and then cut into ½″ (1.5 cm) strips.

Using three strips at a time, braid together and then cut each braided strip into 3″ (7.5 cm) lengths. Place braids about 1″ (2.5 cm) apart on ungreased baking sheet and bake in 450°F (230°C) oven for about 10 minutes or until lightly browned.

Stir the icing sugar, butter and orange juice together. Spoon over the hot braids.

Even though I don't do a lot of yeast bread baking, there is one recipe in my little black book that is thoroughly splattered … a coffee ring that my Aunt Agnes passed on to me years ago.

Aunt Agnes' Vienna Coffee Ring

1 tsp.	sugar	5 mL
½ cup	lukewarm water	125 mL
1 pkg. (1 tbsp.)	dry yeast	1 pkg. (8 g)
¾ cup	milk	175 mL
½ cup	sugar	125 mL
1 tsp.	salt	5 mL
¼ cup	shortening	50 mL
3¼ cups	flour	800 mL
1	egg, beaten	1
⅓ cup	sugar	75 mL
½ tsp.	cinnamon	2 mL
¼ cup	chopped nuts	50 mL

Dissolve the 1 tsp. (5 mL) sugar in lukewarm water. Sprinkle yeast on top to soften.

Scald the milk; remove from heat and add sugar, salt and shortening. Transfer to a larger bowl, if necessary, and cool to lukewarm. Add 1 cup (250 mL) of the flour, the beaten egg and the softened yeast. Beat thoroughly. Add remaining flour to make a stiff batter, beating for at least 3 minutes.

Pour into greased spring form pan or angel food pan. Mix sugar, cinnamon and nuts. Sprinkle over the top of the batter. Let rise until doubled in bulk, about an hour.

Bake in 375°F (190°C) oven for 35 to 40 minutes or until lightly browned and hollow sounding.

Edna takes the cake for making bread, if you'll pardon the pun. Here is her basic sweet bread or bun dough from which you can make any number of bread varieties and buns.

Edna's Sweet Bread or Bun Dough

2 cups	milk	500 mL
1 cup	butter	250 mL
¼ cup	honey	50 mL
1 tsp.	salt	5 mL
½ cup	warm water	125 mL
2 pkg. (2 tbsp.)	dry yeast	2 pkg. (8 g each)
1 tbsp.	sugar	15 mL
5½ cups	flour	1.4 L
1	egg, beaten	1
additional sugar, cinnamon, nuts and melted butter		

In a small saucepan, bring milk, butter and honey to a boil. Let stand until lukewarm and then add salt.

In a small bowl, mix together the warm water, yeast and 1 tbsp. (15 mL) sugar.

Put flour into a large mixing bowl. Make a well in the centre and add the beaten egg, the yeast mixture and the milk mixture. Beat like a cake for 2 minutes.

Put into a greased bowl and let rise until doubled in size. Punch down and let rise again.

Grease pans to be used. If cinnamon buns are the object, sprinkle some extra sugar and cinnamon in the bottom of the pan. If butterhorns are planned, add extra butter and chopped nuts.

Divide dough in half. Roll out to a rectangular shape. Brush with melted butter, sugar, cinnamon, nuts — whatever you fancy. Roll up as for jelly roll, starting with the long side. Cut in 1″ (2.5 cm) widths and place in pans, leaving some room for expansion. Let rise in a warm place until doubled.

Bake at 350°F (180°C) for about 30 minutes or until buns are nicely browned and firm to the touch. Repeat for the rest of the dough. Makes 4 cake pans full.

This is the recipe for the buns that my daughter-in-law seems able to pull out of the air like magic. She says they are best eaten hot, straight from the oven, since they are made quickly and do not keep like richer bread and roll mixtures.

Betty's Can't Miss Bread or Buns

3 cups	lukewarm water	750 mL
½ cup	sugar	125 mL
3 tsp.	salt	15 mL
2 pkg. (2 tbsp.)	dry yeast	2 pkg. (8 g each)
½ cup	vegetable oil	125 mL
2	eggs, beaten	2
7 - 8 cups	flour	1.75 L - 2 L

Put the lukewarm water into a bowl, and be sure it's still warm enough. Stir in the sugar and salt. Sprinkle the yeast on top, leaving it to stand for 10 minutes.

In another bowl, add the oil to the beaten eggs and add to the yeast mixture. Gradually add the flour. Knead well.

Place in a greased bowl, cover, and let rise in a warm place not more than an hour. Punch down and shape into 4 loaves or as many buns as you want. Cover and let rise again in the pans, not more than an hour.

Bake at 400°F (200°C) for 10 to 15 minutes; then reduce the heat to 350°F (180°C) for another 15 to 20 minutes.

Breads

With my great fondness for tomatoes, it was no surprise that I fell hook, line and sinker for Tomato Bread. The flavour reminds some people of pizza and indeed, it would make a good pizza crust if rolled out thin. If you have a good food processor, this bread is simplicity itself to make—just dump everything into the bowl and process it. However, it's not that much harder by hand and just as worthwhile!

My Favourite Tomato Bread

1 pkg. (1 tbsp.)	dry yeast	1 pkg. (8 g)
½ cup	very warm water	125 mL
1½ cups	tomatoes	375 mL
2 tbsp.	sugar	30 mL
2 tbsp.	vegetable oil	25 mL
2 tsp.	coarse salt	10 mL
1 - 2 tbsp.	fresh herbs	15 - 30 mL
3½ - 4 cups	flour	875 mL - 1 L

Note: Fresh tomatoes must be scalded, skinned and chopped before using in the recipe. Canned tomatoes are OK too, if they are blended until pureed. You'll likely have to add more flour if canned tomatoes are used. Ordinary salt may be used in place of the coarse. The fresh herbs might include parsley, dill and oregano. If using dry herbs, reduce the quantity by half.

In a large bowl or the top of a food processor, dissolve the yeast in very warm water. Add prepared tomatoes, sugar, vegetable oil, salt and herbs. In the food processor, add flour and process until the dough forms a mass and leaves the side of the bowl clean.

If working by hand, mix in as much flour as needed, remove from bowl and knead for about 5 minutes, adding more flour if necessary to have a smooth dough. Return dough to a greased bowl, cover and let rise until double in volume. Punch down, turn out on floured surface and shape as desired.

This quantity will make 1 small loaf plus 1 doz. small buns, 2 small loaves or 1 large braided roll.

Place on greased baking sheets or cake pans, and let rise again until double in volume — a process that should take about 30 minutes in a warm kitchen. (And if it's not warm, find a warm spot for the rising dough!)

Bake the buns in a 400°F (200°C) oven for 15 to 20 minutes. Bake the bread in a 400°F (200°C) oven for 15 minutes, then reduce the heat to 350°F (180°C) and bake another 35 minutes or so.

Notes and Variations

Fruit or nut breads are nice to serve with afternoon coffee or tea. You can butter them or spread them with the new soft flavoured cream cheeses. This recipe for pumpkin bread has taken top honours in baking contests.

Pumpkin Bread

3⅓ cups	flour	825 mL
1 tsp.	cinnamon	5 mL
1 tsp	nutmeg	5 mL
1 tsp.	allspice	5 mL
½ tsp.	cloves	2 mL
2 tsp.	baking soda	10 mL
1 tsp.	baking powder	5 mL
1½ tsp.	salt	7 mL
⅔ cup	cooking oil	150 mL
3 cups	sugar	750 mL
4	eggs	4
2 cups	mashed pumpkin	500 mL
⅔ cup	water	150 mL
⅔ cup	chopped dates	150 mL

Note: If you have pumpkin pie spice, use 4 tsp. of it instead of the cinnamon, nutmeg, allspice and cloves listed above.

Grease two 9x5x3″ (2 L) pans.

Mix dry ingredients together.

Beat together oil and sugar. Add eggs, one at a time, beating well after each addition. Fold in cooked pumpkin. Add dry ingredients alternately with the water, beating well after each addition. Stir in dates.

Pour batter into greased pans. Bake at 325°F (160°C) for 55 minutes or until bread tests done. Cool 10 minutes and then remove from pans. Cool completely on racks.

Notes and Variations

BREAKFAST & BRUNCH

Breakfast is not my favourite meal; I am one of those people who gathers speed as the day goes on ... which is probably why I established a restaurant that specialized in evening meals!

Every now and then, I'd give in and agree to handle a breakfast, even though I knew better. One such occasion could very well be called My Unforgettable Breakfast.

A horse show was being held at our local Agriplex and I had agreed to provide an early morning breakfast for competitors. My friend Edna came along to help me, and by opening time, we felt quite pleased with ourselves. All was ready—the counter was set with all the necessary accoutrements, iced juices were ready to pour and the hot cake batter—enough to feed all of southern Alberta—stood on a TV tray right next to the hot grill.

Who could ask for anything more?

The Agriplex building is located on the northwest edge of town with nothing but countryside beyond it as far as the eye can see. As well, it holds grain and hay for the various agricultural events. Thus, for several reasons, it is ripe territory for mice.

Every precaution had been taken to keep them out of the kitchen—traps, bait, even a cat or two. But one little old field mouse had eluded all the traps set for him, and he appeared at the very moment of opening on a ledge behind the big stove. My first thought was to head him off at the pass. After all, that big bowl of pancake batter sat just a few feet from his inquiring nose.

As things worked out, it would have been better to let him fall into the batter. We would just have had to make new batter. But no, I took a mighty swing at him with a broom and hit the TV table which promptly collapsed. My pride and joy white crockery bowl hit the stove and broke into dozens of pieces which meant that a sea of pancake batter began spreading, slowly but surely, into every crack and corner of the big stove. Some disappeared under the stove and the rest spread like glue across the floor, all over the area where we should have been standing, that very minute, flipping pancakes and cooking eggs.

We have had many hearty laughs about it since but at the time, it was very hard to find anything humorous in the situation. Several days later, I found one more piece of the bowl that had been missed in the initial cleaning. I had it mounted on a wooden stand, painted with the date and the word Agriplex, and presented it to Edna on her next birthday.

The mouse got away.

Hotcakes entered my life as soon as I moved to Alberta. We lived for awhile with Jake, an older man who had been batching for years and who could turn out mounds of light, tangy hotcakes. It took me awhile to figure out how he did it — what with my tendency to slow starts in the morning — but it turned out he left a bit of the batter in the bowl every day. It was then stored in a cool place and brought out the next morning to have its daily dose of flour, baking powder, eggs, salt and milk. He also added a splash of corn syrup, to make it brown nicely, he said, and it worked.

It wasn't exactly a sourdough starter, but it had the same effect. Anybody who makes hot cakes every morning, day in and day out, could do the same thing.

If you'd like to try for a slightly sour tangy effect without keeping the dough forever, try Yukon Hot Cakes.

Yukon Hot Cakes

⅔ cup	warm water	150 mL
2 tbsp.	dry yeast	2 pkgs. (8 g each)
2½ cups	biscuit mix	625 mL
1 cup	milk	250 mL
1	egg	1

Measure warm water into a bowl, sprinkle dry yeast over the water and stir until dissolved. Add the biscuit mix, milk and egg. Beat with beater until smooth.

Bake on hot, lightly greased griddle. Serve with lots of butter and syrup. Makes about 24 small pancakes, 12 enormous.

Jake would have a fit, but pancakes can be varied from time to time. Try adding chopped bacon, sliced cooked sausages, blueberries or apple slices, chopped nuts.

Wild Rose Pancakes

Pick wild roses (or garden roses) early in the day. Remove the petals and check for bugs. Pat dry.

When the pancake is ready to be turned, sprinkle petals on the uncooked side. Then flip and cook briefly so that the petals don't get lost in the brown of the pancake. Serve with rose hip jelly or syrup.

French Toast Tricks

4 thick slices	bread	4 thick slices
2	eggs	2
½ cup	orange juice	125 mL
1 tsp.	grated orange rind	5 mL

Cut bread (preferably homemade) into thick slices. Mix the eggs, orange juice and grated orange rind. Dip the bread into the egg mixture, brown on both sides on a well buttered griddle or pan.

Serve hot with orange marmalade.

OR; Add some brown sugar and a little cinnamon to the basic egg/milk mixture, dip bread and bake in a heated waffle iron. The little indentations will hold lots of butter and syrup.

French toast has a long and mostly noble history. After all, as long as there has been bread, there has been stale bread and the need to use it in appetizing ways. However, not many recipes have gone as far in the reclamation of stale bread as the German one called "Drunken Maidens". That particular combination requires that the stale bread be soaked in wine.

The following recipe calls for a bit of dry sherry but not enough to lead any maidens into delinquency.

Sherried French Toast

4	eggs	4
1 cup	milk	250 mL
1 tbsp.	dry sherry	15 mL
1 tbsp.	sugar	15 mL
dash of salt to taste		
1 loaf	French bread	1 loaf
½ cup	butter	125 mL
icing sugar and/or honey		

Beat eggs, milk, sherry, sugar and salt until just nicely mixed. Pour into a large shallow pan.

Slice the loaf of bread into 1" (2.5 cm) thick slices. If need be, cut on the diagonal to get good sized pieces. Discard the ends. Soak the bread slices in the egg mixture for 15 minutes on each side.

Heat butter in a heavy frypan and fry bread slices until golden on both sides, adding more butter as needed.

Serve hot, sprinkled with icing sugar. Serve with more butter and honey.

While visiting friends, I was treated one morning to what looked like a cross between a pancake and a dumpling. Thus did I meet my first Aebleskiver—but not my last!

Aebleskivers by Rhea

2 cups	flour	500 mL
2 tsp.	baking powder	10 mL
½ tsp.	baking soda	2 mL
2 tbsp.	sugar	30 mL
2 cups	buttermilk	500 mL
2	eggs, beaten	2
4 tbsp.	melted butter	50 mL
thin slices of apple or jam or jelly		

Note: You must have a proper aebleskiver pan to produce aebleskivers. The butter may be melted in the aebleskiver pan as it preheats. That way, the aebleskiver cups will be well buttered for their first round.

In a large bowl, mix together the dry ingredients. In another bowl, mix the buttermilk and eggs and add to the dry ingredients all at once. Stir briefly. Add the melted butter.

Spoon about 2 tbsp. (25 mL) of the batter into each cup, filling it just to the lip of the cup. As they start to cook, insert a slice of raw apple into each one. Jam or jelly may also be used in which case it should be inserted after the first spoonful of batter is put into the cup, and covered with the second.

The batter will rise as it cooks. Using a metal knitting needle, check the underside of the cake for doneness. If it's a nice brown and holds its shape, turn it quickly with the needle. Check for doneness with the needle as well, using it like a toothpick. When it comes out clean, the aebleskiver is done, a process that takes some 5-7 minutes.

Turn the first batch out onto a warm plate, sprinkle with icing sugar. Complete the rest of the cakes, buttering the pans each time.

Serve with more butter and jams or jelly.

"Way back when", crepes meant only one thing to me ... that delicious dessert called Crepes Suzette that involved flames and brandy and all sorts of exotic things. Now, there are restaurants that serve nothing but crepes in every combination you can think of.

As usual, there are many recipes but the one I use more often makes a very thin, almost lacy, crepe. Made with sugar, they're ideal dessert crepes; made without, they're just right for appetizers or main courses.

Lacy Crepes

½ cup	cornstarch	125 mL
½ cup	flour	125 mL
½ tsp.	salt	2 mL
1-2 tbsp.	sugar (optional)	15-30 mL
4	eggs, beaten	4
2 cups	water	500 mL
¼ cup	melted butter	50 mL

Note: It helps to have a special crepe pan kept solely for this purpose, but heavy frypans will work with some patience. Also, this is a fiddly business since you can only make one at a time, but they can be made up in advance and kept in the frig or frozen until needed. Use sugar if a dessert crepe is being made. Otherwise, leave it out.

Mix dry ingredients together, add eggs and water and beat well. Melt butter in the crepe pan and add to the batter.

For an 8″ (20 cm) pan, use about ¼ cup (50 mL) of batter each time, swirling it around to cover the bottom of the pan. Pour out any extra batter. Bake on medium high heat until crepe is set and lightly browned on the bottom. Flip over and cook for seconds only on the other side, just enough to make sure batter is cooked through. Stack on wax paper.

To use in Crepes Suzette, see page 230.

Pancakes

Once you have your crepes made, the sky is the limit as far as fillings and sauces are concerned. You can combine the filling with the sauce and put them both inside the crepe, or you can fill the crepe and pour the sauce over all. You can roll the crepes, half them or quarter them. You could probably tie them in a bow as well!

Fillings for Main Course or Appetizer Crepes

Try seafood—shrimp, crab, lobster, sole, salmon or a combination thereof. A dandy way to use up small portions left from previous meals. Make up a quick sauce by using a canned cream soup, undiluted. Could be celery, mushroom, golden mushroom (especially good with a touch of curry.)

Try adding grated Gruyere or parmesan to the sauce.

Try chopped fresh herbs—parsley, dill or chives—as a garnish.

Try making a quick sauce from packets of mix for Hollandaise and Bearnaise.

Try vegetables inside the crepes—long slivers of green beans, asparagus. A lemon based sauce is best with these.

Try using whatever has lingered longest in the frig. Who knows—you may discover a new dish just like the lowly French assistant waiter did when he put together the now classic Crepes Suzette. That's the beauty of crepes—they invite originality.

Notes and Variations

Pancakes

When I opened my out-of-the-way, out-of-the-ordinary country restaurant, my neighbours were astounded. Where is that crazy lady going to get customers, they asked one another?

The answer was hung on the walls of Driftwillow and later at The Flying N. We hung maps of the world on the walls and customers were invited to put their home town on the map with a pin.

The idea caught on. Customers would return with out-ot-town guests and say, "We've brought you another pin for your map." One such guest from Australia felt that his continent was slighted in scale on the map we had, so he hand drew another one with the comment, "This now compares with the map of California."

We left his drawing right there so that other Aussies could pinpoint their homes, down under.

Recipes illustrated overleaf

Yukon Hotcakes, page 49
Aebleskivers by Rhea, page 50
Millie's Irish Soda Bread, page 37
Rosehip Jelly, page 60

When I think of country cooking, I think of thick cream, freshly churned butter, the smell of fresh bread baking and eggs ... always a basket of eggs sits front and centre in my daydreams.

In real life, they turn up fairly frequently as well, being one of the most economical and nutritious packages around!

Eggs can be prepared for every meal of the day but they're mostly associated with breakfast. Sunday mornings, I make a Super Scramble — scrambled eggs to which I add a great mixture of goodies.

Super Scramble

2 large	eggs	2 large
1 tbsp.	heavy cream	15 mL
pinch of salt, freshly ground pepper		
2 tbsp.	butter	25 mL
fresh parsley, dill weed or chives		

Note: This is enough for one serving. Adjust your quantities according to your guest list.

Lightly stir the eggs, add the cream, salt and pepper. Melt butter in heavy skillet over medium heat, pour in egg mixture and as it begins to set around the edges, gently lift and let the runny part flow under. Don't stir vigorously.

Add the fillings at this point. Don't cook much longer — you want the eggs to be creamy and a bit shiny, not dry and crumbly. Finish with freshly cut chives, dill weed or parsley.

Serve Super Scramble with toast or toasted English muffins on the side.

Fillings for Super Scramble

Pick two or three of the following to add to your super scrambled eggs just before they're done:

— fresh mushrooms, sliced and lightly sauteed in butter
— chicken livers, trimmed, sliced, cooked in butter
— cheese cubes — Cheddar, Swiss, Mozzarella
— fresh tomato wedges, whole cherry tomatoes
— red sauce, page 130
— red or green peppers cut in fine strips
— onions, diced and cooked briefly in butter
— sliced green olives or ripe olives, pitted and sliced
— cooked shrimps or flaked fish like salmon or tuna
— crumbled or diced crisp bacon
— sausages, cooked and sliced
— a spoonful of caviar or roe (in which case, you've built a
   Super Super Scramble!)

Egg Cups for Kids

4 strips	bacon	4 strips	
4 slices	bread	4 slices	
butter enough to cover bread			
4	eggs	4	
salt and pepper to taste			

Precook the bacon until it's cooked but not crisp.

Cut the crusts off the bread slices, butter each slice and press them, butter side down, into muffin tins so that they form a little cup. If they won't go willingly, roll with a rolling pin first. Curl the bacon strip around inside each cup and break an egg into the centre. Sprinkle lightly with salt and pepper; watch the salt since the bacon may have enough.

Bake in 325°F (160°C) oven until done as much as you like — about 15 minutes.

Eggs combine well with tomatoes and since I am such an addict of anything made with tomatoes, I sometimes open a jar of home canned tomatoes (store bought will do!) or the red sauce, page 130, and make a quick version of Spanish Eggs.

Spanish Eggs

1	chopped onion	1
2 tbsp.	butter	25 mL
1 large can	tomatoes	1 large can (795 mL)
1 clove	garlic, minced	1 clove
1	diced green pepper	1
¼ tsp.	dried red pepper	1 mL
½ tsp.	oregano	2 mL
½ tsp.	sweet basil	2 mL
1 tbsp.	brown sugar	15 mL
2 eggs for every person being served		

Note: Don't handle dried red peppers; use a spoon.

In a heavy deep skillet, saute onions in butter. Add tomatoes or red sauce, page 130. Stir in garlic, green pepper, red pepper, oregano, basil and brown sugar. When sauce is hot, slide in enough eggs for present company. Try not to break them in the process but if you do, change plans and make a Spanish egg scramble.

Cook at low heat just until set.

Serve eggs and sauce over tortillas or toast or English muffins. For something completely new, try Spanish Eggs over shredded wheat biscuits. Simply dip the large size biscuits in hot water, drain well and then top with egg and tomato mixture.

Quick and Easy Poached Eggs

If you're making a breakfast or brunch dish that requires poached eggs, you can cut down on last minute work by preparing the eggs in advance, perhaps the night before. After poaching the eggs for no more than 3 minutes in lightly simmering water, carefully lift them out with a slotted spoon and slide into a pan of cold water. This stops any further cooking.

When needed, remove from the cold water and drain well. Proceed with your recipe, making sure that somewhere along the line, the eggs are quickly reheated. For instance, in the case of the Eggs Benedict below, you'd assemble the makings, then put everything under the broiler until the sauce bubbled and browned.

Eggs

Believe it or not, there is a quick and easy method of making Eggs Benedict.

Quick and Easy Eggs Benedict

4	eggs	4
4	English muffins	4
4 slices	back baon	4
	ready mix package of Hollandaise or Bearnaise sauce	

Note: Back bacon is sometimes called Canadian bacon. If it's not available, ordinary bacon strips will do, cut to fit the muffins, or ham.

Poach the eggs to the degree you prefer. In the meantime, toast the English muffins, fry the bacon and prepare the sauce according to the instructions on the package.   To assemble, simply put the bacon on the muffin, slide a poached egg on top and cover everything with sauce.

A true souffle, not the kind held up by gelatine, is often avoided by cooks for fear it's too difficult. However, once you have a proper straight sided dish that can go from oven to table and a fairly basic recipe, you need have no fears.

Classic Cheese Souffle

¼ cup	butter	50 mL
¼ cup	flour	50 mL
1 tsp.	salt	5 mL
¼ tsp.	cayenne	1 mL
1½ cups	milk	375 mL
2 cups	Cheddar cheese, grated	500 mL
6	eggs, separated	6

Prepare 2 qt. (2 L) straight sided souffle dish by buttering the bottom only. The sides must be ungreased to hold the sides of the souffle as it climbs.

In a large saucepan over medium heat, melt butter. Add flour, salt and cayenne and stir until smooth. Slowly add milk and cook, stirring constantly until sauce is thick and smooth. Add cheese, stirring until it all melts. Remove from heat.

In a small bowl, beat egg yolks slightly with a fork. Add a small amount of the hot sauce to the yolks to warm them up and prevent lumping. Slowly, pour the egg yolk mixture into the hot sauce, stirring constantly to keep it smooth.

In a large bowl, not plastic, beat egg whites until stiff but not dry. Gently fold cheese sauce into the whites, mixing carefully with a spatula. Gently pour mixture into prepared dish. If you want to put a top hat on your souffle, make a circle cut about 1″ (2.5 cm) deep and 1″ (2.5 cm) in from the edge. Use a spoon.

Bake in 325°F (160°C) oven for 1 hour or until puffy and golden brown. Do not open oven door until the full hour has passed. To test for doneness, insert a thin knife into centre and if it comes out clean, the souffle is done.

Serve at once. Make sure each person at table gets some of the top crust along with the puffy and creamy centre.

If you must hold it, leave in the oven with the heat off for up to 10 minutes. After that, it's collapse city.

Eggs

Chokecherries grow in great abundance along the bank of Willow Creek across the valley from my house and, together with the saskatoon bushes, are lovely in the spring. Late frosts often hit them in the blossom stage and the picking may be curtailed as a result, but some berries are always available in protected spots.

One year, we had a bumper crop—no frosts—and everyone was busy making chokecherry jelly, syrup and homemade wine. One particular recipe called for the berries to be put through a meat grinder before being boiled, so I followed instructions and then heaved all the pits out into the field near the house.

That spot now has a towering patch of chokecherry trees that sprang from the ground-up pits. Other people had attempted to transplant chokecherries by various delicate or scientific methods—but nothing worked like my casual pitch.

I don't get a lot of berries from my yard trees because the birds get up much earlier than I do. But I enjoy seeing the trees and pointing them out to visitors who can't believe my good luck.

Wouldn't you know it? My mother being a no-nonsense woman named her favourite jam PAPP. Just that. The initials stood for the fruits used in it—peaches, apples, pears and plums. I'm stuck with the title.

Mom's P.A.P.P. Conserve

4 cups	diced fruit	1 L
3½ cups	sugar	875 mL
¼ cup	lemon juice	50 mL
1 tsp.	grated lemon rind	5 mL

Note: The fruit should consist of 1 cup (250 mL) each of peaches, apples, pears and plums, thus making a total of 4 cups.

Wash the fruit, pare, peel and pit. (This could also be called the three P's.) Mix fruit, sugar, lemon juice and rind in a heavy saucepan. Bring to a boil and simmer until mixture is thick and clear, about 25 minutes.

Pour into sterilized jars and cover with a thin layer of melted paraffin. When first layer hardens, cover with another thin layer.

Conserves are like jams except they include raisins and nuts. Jams are generally just fruit and sugar. This conserve is fiddly, I admit, but well worth it if you like the taste of blue grapes.

Concord Grape Conserve

4 lbs.	concord grapes	2 kg
2	oranges	2
2 cups	raisins	500 mL
6 cups	sugar	1.5 mL

Wash grapes. Squeeze each one until the skin pops off. Keep the skins in a separate pot.

Cook the grape pulp until juicy. Then press through a colander or food mill to remove seeds.

Jams

In another pot, cook the grape skins in their own juice for about 5 minutes. Then add the seedless pulp.

Blanch the oranges for 2 minutes (just put into boiling water), then chop or use a food processor to grind both skins and fruit of the oranges. Add to grape mixture. Add washed raisins and sugar.

Cook for about 30 minutes over medium heat, stirring frequently until thick.

Pour into hot sterilized jars and cover with several layers of paraffin wax.

Conserves with their additions of raisins and nuts are nice to have with afternoon tea and crumpets. Mind you, they're good at breakfast too. In fact, this one is plum wonderful at any time.

Plum Wonderful Conserve

3 lbs.	purple plums	1.5 kg
2	lemons	2
2	oranges	2
4½ cups	sugar	1.12 L
3 cups	raisins	750 mL
1 cup	chopped walnuts	250 mL

Wash plums, remove pits and cut into small pieces. Grate rind from lemons and oranges, then squeeze the juice from both. In a large heavy pot, combine the plum pieces, lemon and orange rind, juices, sugar and raisins. Bring to a boil and simmer slowly until thick, stirring occasionally. This will take about an hour. Watch that the mixture doesn't scorch.

At the end of the cooking time, add walnuts. Pour into hot sterilized jars. Makes about 3 pints.

Cranberry is a wonderful accompaniment to so many dishes and although I prefer it raw, this recipe has a lot going for it too!

Scratch a Cranberry, Find a Pecan

3	oranges	3
3	lemons	3
4 cups	raw cranberries	1 L
1½ cups	sugar	375 mL
1 cup	chopped pecans	250 mL

Cut oranges and lemons in quarters and try to remove seeds. Then grind up rind and flesh in a food grinder or processor. Put into a heavy saucepan, stir in whole cranberries, sugar and pecans. Cook very slowly, stirring to prevent burning, until the cranberries pop — about 30-40 minutes.

Remove from heat, allow to cool and then seal in sterilized jars.

Alberta's provincial flower is the wild rose, a flower so beautiful in late June, early July, that we would ask no more of it than that. However, it also produces rosehips which can be used to make an attractive, nutritious jam or jelly.

P.S. If jelly doesn't jell for some mysterious reason (jelly is like that—it has its own reasons), remember that you wanted rose hip syrup all along—so there!

Rose Hip Jelly

On a nice fall day, soon after the first frost, put on your walking shoes and head out for roadsides or fields where roses bloomed earlier in the year. Seek out places that have not been sprayed. Collect several pounds—but don't try to be too exact. A nice fall day is gift enough.

Back home on the range, weigh the results of your walk. Then wash them.

In a large heavy pot, simmer 2 cups (500 mL) water to 4 cups (1 L) rosehips until fruit is tender. Place in jelly bag and let drip to get the syrup. Don't squeeze the jelly bag, no matter how tempting, or the lovely pink colour will be muddied.

When all juice has dripped out on its own, measure the collected juice. For every 2 cups (500 mL) juice, use 3¾ cups sugar and ½ bottle liquid pectin.

Mix fruit pectin with the juice and place in a large heavy pot. Place over high heat and stir until mixture comes to a hard boil. At once, stir in the sugar. Bring to a full rolling boil again and boil hard 1 minute, stirring like crazy.

Remove jelly from heat and pour at once into sterilized glasses. Cover with paraffin.

PASTA & RICE

When I was a youngster, I thought pasta was one of three things: the macaroni that we ate just before payday, the spaghetti that was apparently eaten by Italians only and the noodles that floated around in some watery soups.

Thank goodness I eventually discovered the wide and wonderful world of pasta.

There are hundreds of different dried varieties available, all of them easy to store and cook, but for a new taste treat, try homemade pasta. Or buy some from the various outlets offering freshly made pasta.

Cooking time can be substantially reduced for freshly made pasta, with the homemade kind taking the least time of all. Preservatives and the partial or complete drying make the difference.

Whether freshly made by a commercial outlet or homemade or bought off supermarket shelves, pasta should be added slowly to a very large pot of boiling salted water— you don't want to cool the water down below the boil by adding the pasta all at once. A bit of oil or butter can be added to the water, the theory being that oil or butter prevents the water from boiling over and making a huge mess. I find it's also a good idea to have as big a pot as possible.

Cook only until the pasta is al dente; that is, until it resists the teeth and isn't completely limp and soggy. Experts disagree on whether or not to rinse at this point. My opinion is that you should not rinse ... unless you're trying to rescue a gluey mess, the result of too little water or water that drops below the boil when the pasta is added. That generally produces a pasty result.

If the pasta must be kept hot after draining, return it to the pot from whence it came, add some butter and stir gently. If a sauce is to be added, or cheese, add it now to keep the pasta from sticking.

Basic Egg Dough for Homemade Pasta

3½ cups	flour	875mL
5	eggs	5
1 tbsp.	olive oil	15 mL
1 tsp.	salt	5 mL

Mound the flour on a big wooden board and make a well in the middle. Beat the eggs in a small bowl and add olive oil and salt, mixing thoroughly. Pour into the flour well.

Mix the flour with the eggs, a little at a time until the flour is absorbed. Knead the dough with both hands until it is firm and smooth. Moisten a cloth, wring it out and cover the dough with the damp cloth. Let rest for 30 minutes.

Roll out dough to desired thickness and allow to dry for 30 minutes before cooking.

For green pasta, puree spinach enough to make 1 cup (250 mL). Use only 3 eggs.

For red pasta, use 1 cup beet juice and pulp (250 mL). Use only 3 eggs.

For pink pasta, skin and seed enough tomatoes to make 1 cup (250 mL) of tomato puree. As above, use only 3 eggs in this case.

It is right and proper that an Italian should have created one of the world's most popular pasta dishes — Fettucini al'Alfredo of Rome.

Fred's Fettucine

Basic pasta recipe, see above		
boiling salted water in a big pot		
1 cup	butter	250 mL
½ cup	grated parmesan	125 mL

Make basic pasta according to recipe above. Roll into sheets about ¼" (1 cm) thick and 14" (35 cm) long. Let dry at least 20 minutes after rolling out. Then loosely roll the sheet of pasta into a scroll, place on a board and cut into strips about ⅛" (3 mm) wide. Toss the strips lightly with both hands, to spread them out, and leave on wax paper.

Bring salted water to a full boil and cook pasta to the stage preferred. Drain well and return to the pot in which it was cooked. Add half the butter and half the parmesan cheese, mixing well after each addition.

Have a warm oven-proof serving bowl ready. Put the pasta into the bowl and add the rest of the butter and parmesan, mixing gently. Bake in a 400°F (200°C) oven briefly, about 2 minutes.

Serve in hot bowl. Serves 4 people.

Try cooking up a mixture of both plain egg noodles and spinach noodles. Then add butter and cheese, as above, and call it "Hay and Straw".

I was twice lucky this past spring. First of all, a friendly waitress in a Calgary restaurant recommended a pasta dish that included noodles and smoked salmon in a creamy wine sauce. It was delicious and I tucked the combination of flavours away in the back of my mind, intending to duplicate it as soon as I could.

Then I visited friends in British Columbia and, lo and behold, they served me the same combination.

Fettucine with Smoked Salmon

3 tbsp.	unsalted butter	50 mL
2	chopped shallots	2
½ lb.	smoked salmon	250 g
1 cup	heavy cream	250 mL
½ cup	unsalted butter	125 mL
1½ lbs.	fettucine	750 g
¾ cup	parmesan cheese	175 mL
4	green onions	4

salt and freshly ground pepper to taste

Notes: If you can't find shallots, substitute 1 onion plus ½ clove of garlic, minced. Also, you can use chopped smokies in place of smoked salmon.

Melt the 3 tbsp. (50 mL) unsalted butter in a skillet and cook the shallots until fragrant and tender but not brown. Cube the smoked salmon and add to the skillet, cooking briefly for about 2 minutes. Add cream and heat thoroughly. Set aside until pasta is ready, at which time you should reheat the sauce just briefly, maybe a minute.

Before cooking the pasta, find a large flat serving dish to hold the fettucine. Cube the ½ cup (125 mL) unsalted butter and place on the platter. Slice the greeen onions and have them handy, along with the parmesan cheese. The dish must go together quickly at the end.

Now cook the fettucine until it is "al dente" or slightly resistant to the bite. If it's freshly made pasta, see recipe on page 63, it will require only 2 minutes of cooking. If it's fresh pasta from a specialty shop, it will need 4-5 minutes. If it's the dried variety sold in supermarkets, it will need 10-12 minutes. Drain well.

Working quickly to keep the pasta hot, ladle it over the butter cubes on the waiting platter. Pour hot sauce over all. Sprinkle with cheese and onion. Toss well until sauce begins to thicken and the noodles are well coated. This tossing process is important; do it gently but do it. Season to taste with salt and pepper.

Notes and Variations

Pasta & Rice

We made a lot of lasagne at the restaurants; it was a good luncheon dish and it used up the ground beef that always came along with the larger cuts of beef. But we often misjudged how many lasagne strips it would take to fill the pan, or we'd lose the slippery things or break them.

It was a happy day, believe me, when we finally discovered we could make lasagne without precooking the lasagna strips.

Happy Ever After Lasagne

1 pkg. (10 oz.)	frozen spinach	1 pkg. (300 g)
1 tbsp.	vegetable oil	15 mL
1	medium onion	1
1 clove	garlic, minced	1 clove
1 lb.	ground beef	500 g
2 cans	tomato sauce	2 cans (398 mL each)
1 can (10 oz.)	sliced mushrooms	1 can (284 mL)
½ cup	water	125 mL
1 tsp.	oregano	5 mL
1 tsp.	sweet basil	5 mL
salt and pepper to taste		
1 cup	cottage cheese	250 mL
⅓ cup	parmesan cheese	75 mL
2 tsp.	vegetable oil	10 mL
1 tsp.	salt	5 mL
1	egg, beaten	1
1 pkg.	lasagne noodles	1 pkg. (500 g)
6 oz.	Mozzarella cheese	175 g

Find a 9x13" (3.5 L) pan that's at least 2" (5 cm) deep.

Prepare spinach by thawing, then draining off as much liquid as possible. Chop and set aside.

Heat vegetable oil in large skillet. Chop onion, mince garlic and add to the hot oil, stirring until onion begins to turn transparent. Add ground beef and cook until brown throughout.

Pour off excess fat. Add tomato sauce, mushrooms plus the liquid from the can, water, oregano, sweet basil and salt and pepper to taste. Bring to a boil and remove from heat.

In another bowl, cream the cottage chese with the parmesan. Add the chopped spinach, salt and egg.

Assemble the lasagne by spooning ⅓ of the meat and sauce mixture into the bottom of the pan. Cover with a layer of the uncooked lasagne noodles, just as they come from the package. Repeat with another ⅓ of the meat and sauce, then another layer of the uncooked lasagna. Spread this with the cheese and spinach mixture, cover with more lasagna and the remaining sauce. Top with Mozzarella slices cut diagonally and arranged attractively on top.

Cover tightly with foil and bake at 375°F (190°C) for 45 minutes. Uncover and bake 15 minutes more or until the cheese starts to brown.

Serves 8.

Rice is one of the oldest cultivated crops in the world and supplies half the world with its daily bread, or starch equivalent! The western world was a bit slow in catching on to the possibilities of rice but, as with pasta, we are beginning to catch up.

Usually long grain rice is served with meats and fish while short grain is used for desserts. Mind you, that rule is not carved in stone.

Wild rice, not a true rice but a grain, is native to North America. Served by itself or in concert with long grain white rice or brown rice, it is the perfect accompaniment to game birds or Cornish game hens and quail.

Then, there's Betty's Boxing Day Fried Rice. She brought it to a Boxing Day party and it was such a hit that I knew I had to include it in the "must have ever after" list.

Betty's Boxing Day Fried Rice

1½ cups	converted white rice	375 mL
3½ cups	water	875 mL
1 tbsp.	vegetable oil	15 mL
3	eggs	3
½ tsp.	salt	2 mL
¼ cup	chopped onion	50 mL
2 tbsp.	vegetable oil	25 mL
1 cup	cooked chicken	250 mL
½ cup	diced onion	125 mL
½ cup	diced celery	125 mL
1 can (8 oz.)	bamboo shoots	1 can (227 mL)
½ cup	peas	125 mL
½ cup	mushrooms	125 mL
¼ tsp.	sugar	1 mL
½ tsp.	salt	2 mL
¼ tsp.	MSG (Accent)	1 mL
2 tbsp.	soy sauce	25 mL

Notes: There are as many variations of this recipe as there are meals out there! This particular combination uses cooked chicken and corresponding vegetables. You could also use cooked beef, pork, ham, bacon, lamb, shrimp or crabmeat, with appropriate vegetables and additions. For instance, fried rice made with cooked lamb is good with snow peas, 1 cup (250 mL) raisins, a bit of crystallized ginger and curry powder to taste. Use your imagination in varying the meats and vegetables. Otherwise, the recipe remains about the same.

Cook rice according to package directions. This amount should yield 4 cups (1 L). Set aside.

Prepare the topping. Put oil in a flat frypan, beat eggs with salt and pour into the frypan. Cook on low heat until just set. Do not stir. Remove from heat, cool and cut into long thin strips or small cubes. Sprinkle with the chopped onion. Set aside.

In a wok or heavy skillet, heat the 2 tbsp. vegetable oil and stir fry the chicken pieces, chopped onion, diced celery, diced bamboo shoots, peas, and mushrooms. Cook for 2 minutes. Add cooked rice, sugar, salt, MSG and soy sauce. Stir fry until everything is thoroughly mixed and heated.

Garnish top with prepared egg and chopped green onions. Serve piping hot. Serves 8-10.

Pasta & Rice

As a change from potatoes or rice with a hot meal, two other grains can be served. To be more precise, two wheats can be served—bulgur and/or kasha. Most larger supermarkets stock them now but if you're stuck, try a health food specialty shop.

Bulgur Casserole

1 cup	bulgur	250 mL
2 tbsp.	butter	25 mL
2	grated carrots	2
1 can (10 oz.)	consomme	1 can (284 mL)
½ cup	water	125 mL

Notes: Bulgur is also known as cracked wheat.

Brown the bulgur lightly in butter and place in a casserole large enough to allow it to double in size when cooked. Add grated carrots. Pour consomme and water over everything, mix well. Cover and bake at 350°F (180°C) for about 30 minutes.

Kasha is also known as cracked buckwheat. I know it all sounds like breakfast cereal, but it's a far cry. People from the Middle East have known about wheat as main meals for centuries.

Kasha

1 cup	kasha	250 mL
1	egg, beaten	1
2 cups	stock or water	500 mL
salt and pepper to taste		

Notes: If you don't have stock, use canned consomme or water.

In a flameproof casserole dish, combine kasha with egg and cook over medium heat, stirring constantly until the grain is dry and separate. This will take about 15 minutes. Add the stock and/or water, season to taste. Cover and bake in 350°F (180°C) oven for 20 minutes or longer—until all the liquid is absorbed and the grains are tender.

Allow to stand in a warm place for about 15 minutes before serving, a waiting period that will prevent the kasha from getting mushy.

When you get the hang of this, try it with 1 tsp. each of cumin and coriander, adding it to the stock before baking.

SALADS & VEGETABLES

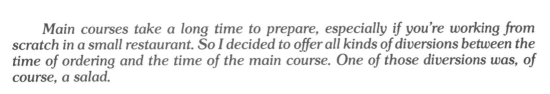

Main courses take a long time to prepare, especially if you're working from scratch in a small restaurant. So I decided to offer all kinds of diversions between the time of ordering and the time of the main course. One of those diversions was, of course, a salad.

At first, we offered fairly standard green salads filled with as many fresh salad vegetables as we could get. Eventually, we moved into the big time and offered Caesar salads.

The Flying N Caesar Salad

romaine lettuce, washed, torn into large pieces		
1-2 cloves of garlic—check with your guests		
4 fillets of anchovy—again check with guests		
1 tsp.	salt	5 mL
½ tsp.	fresh black pepper	2 mL
¼ tsp.	dry mustard	1 mL
few shakes of worcestershire sauce		
few drops of red pepper sauce		
⅓ cup	olive or salad oil	75 mL
3 tbsp.	red wine vinegar	50 mL
1	lemon	1
1	raw or coddled egg	1
1 cup	garlic croutons	250 mL
2-3 tbsp.	parmesan cheese	30-50 mL

Prepare all ingredients in advance and put the final product together at the very last minute. Thus, wash, dry and tear romaine lettuce. Have 3-4 cups for each serving. Cut the lemon in half. If using a coddled egg, poach for no longer than 1 minute. Saute cubes of bread in butter and minced garlic. Grate parmesan.

Check with guests as to strength of Caesar preferred. Then, in a large bowl, mash garlic cloves, anchovies, salt, pepper, mustard and sauces with a bit of the oil until a smooth paste forms. Add the vinegar and lemon juice. Watch for lemon seeds— they don't belong. Cover the lemon with a small piece of cheesecloth, if need be.

Keep beating vigorously with a fork as each addition is made. Add the egg, either raw or lightly coddled. Slowly add the remaining oil, beating vigorously. At this stage, the dressing should begin to thicken and turn creamy. Dip a piece of lettuce into the dressing and make a taste test. Adjust seasonings, if necessary.

Add romaine pieces to the dressing and toss well so that all lettuce pieces are coated and shining. Top with croutons and grated parmesan. Toss once more briefly and serve at once. Serves 2.

While Caesar salads had to be made on the spot, our favourite cabbage slaw was one that was made well in advance — 14 days in advance, to be exact!

Make-Ahead Cabbage Slaw

1	large green cabbage	1
3	carrots	3
1	onion	1
1 cup	sugar	250 mL
1 cup	salad oil	250 mL
1 cup	vinegar	250 mL
1 tsp.	prepared mustard	5 mL
1 tsp.	celery seed	5 mL

If by hand, grate the cabbage. If by machine, shred in a food processor and be glad you have one! Likewise, grate the carrots and slice the onion.

In a large pot, mix sugar, salad oil, vinegar, mustard and celery seed. Bring to a boil and simmer for about 5 minutes. Then pour the hot brine over the vegetables, stirring to get brine throughout.

Store in a large covered jar or crock, preferably in the frig where the slaw will keep for up to 4 weeks.

Note: Do not use red cabbage for this recipe. It turns the colour of mud.

Note #2: Do use a red and green pepper if you like the flavour. They add a nice flash of colour.

In spite of being fond of tomatoes in every way, shape and form, I had never fallen in love with an aspic recipe ... until I met Marg's Tomato Aspic! Simplicity itself, light and sweet.

Marg's Tomato Aspic

2 cups	tomato juice	500 mL
1 pkg. (3 oz.)	lemon jelly powder	1 pkg. (85 g)

chopped celery, chopped green onion, hardboiled eggs

Heat 1 cup of the tomato juice and dissolve the jelly powder in it. Add the other cup of tomato juice and let set. That's all there is to it, but add celery, onions, hardboiled eggs as the mood hits you.

If you set the aspic in a ring mold, you can fill the centre with cottage cheese, egg salad or chicken salad. Or you could insert a small bowl in the ring centre and fill it with mayonnaise made with fresh lemon juice.

Salads

Edna's Salad has so many good things in it that it can easily serve as the main course of a luncheon. It's also a make-ahead product so there's no last minute fussing— altogether a useful and delicious choice!

Edna's Jubilee Salad

2 small pkgs. or 1 large pkg. lemon jelly powder		
2 cups	boiling water	500 mL
1 tsp.	salt	5 mL
1 tbsp.	grated onion	15 mL
½ cup	salad dressing	125 mL
1 cup	heavy cream	250 mL
3 cups	diced celery	750 mL
3	hardboiled eggs	3
¼ lb.	cheddar cheese	125 g
1 cup	chopped walnuts	250 mL
1 cup	cooked chicken	250 mL
¼ cup	chopped pimiento	50 mL

Note: You can also use cooked turkey or canned tuna in place of cooked chicken.

Dissolve the jelly powder in the boiling water. Add salt and grated onion.

As the jelly mixture sets, prepare the rest of the ingredients. Whip the cream. Dice the celery. Slice the hardboiled eggs. Grate the cheese. Chop the cooked chicken. Chop the pimiento.

As soon as the jelly mixture begins to thicken, add the remaining prepared ingredients. Chill until set. If set in a ring mold, garnish with lettuce or parsley when unmolded.

Chief among the salad dressings at The Flying N was the Minted Cream dressing used on the fruit boats. The recipe for that is included on page 8. We also used to make Papaya Seed dressing which made a nice change for fruit salads with its almost peppery taste.

Papaya Seed Dressing

1 cup	sugar	250 mL
1 tsp.	salt	5 mL
1 tsp.	dry mustard	5 mL
1 cup	tarragon vinegar	250 mL
1 cup	salad oil	250 mL
1	small onion	1
3 tbsp.	fresh papaya seeds	50 mL

Note: White wine vinegar may be used in place of tarragon vinegar. Also note that to make this dressing you must buy a fresh papaya. Plan to use the papaya fruit in a salad or dessert so that nothing is wasted.

Place sugar, salt, dry mustard and vinegar in blender. Start motor and gradually add salad oil and chopped onion. When thoroughly blended, add papaya seeds. At this stage, blend only until seeds are the size of coarse ground pepper.

Excellent with either fruit salads or tossed green salads. Makes about 3 cups.

Salads

I often wonder what we did before we had blenders or food processors. Probably developed wire whisk elbows or beater bursitis. I depend on this basic blender mayonnaise made with lots of fresh lemon juice. It also forms the basis for any number of variations.

Blender Mayonnaise

1	egg	1
1 tsp.	dry mustard	5 mL
½ tsp.	salt	2 mL
dash	cayenne powder	dash
1 tsp.	sugar	5 mL
¼ cup	salad oil	50 mL
½ cup	salad oil	125 mL
2 tbsp.	fresh lemon juice	25 mL
1 tbsp.	vinegar	15 mL
½ cup	salad oil	125 mL

Put the egg, dry mustard, salt, cayenne powder, sugar and ¼ cup (50 mL) salad oil in blender; cover and blend until completely combined. With motor still going, remove centre of lid (or whole lid) and slowly pour in the ½ cup (125 mL) salad oil, lemon juice and vinegar. When that begins to thicken, add remaining ½ cup (125 mL) salad oil. Blend a few seconds longer until thick. You may have to stop occasionally to scrape the sides of the blender but that should be your only problem.

Store in frig. Use as a base for the following variations.

Thousand Island Dressing

1 cup	blender mayonnaise	250 mL
2 tbsp.	thick chili sauce	25 mL
2 tbsp.	minced green pepper	25 mL
2 tbsp.	stuffed green olives	25 mL
1 tbsp.	chopped parsley	15 mL
1 tsp.	grated onion	5 mL
1	hardboiled egg	1

Mince the green pepper, green olives and parsley. Grate onion and chop hard-boiled egg.

Add all ingredients to the basic blender mayonnaise. Store in the frig.

Russian Dressing

1 cup	blender mayonnaise	250 mL
¼ cup	thick chili sauce	50 mL
1 tbsp.	grated horseradish	15 mL
1 tsp.	grated onion	5 mL
1 tsp.	worcestershire sauce	5 mL

Note: 3 tbsp. (50 mL) caviar may also be added to this dressing.

Combine all ingredients. Use on arranged salads that include meat or fish.

What's in a name you ask?

A lot, I answer.

When we opened the restaurant in our own home, we simply named the living room The Driftwood Room. So far, so good.

Then people found out about us and wanted to find us. We could only tell them to turn west at the Pulteney Siding, go four miles on the gravel, over a Texas gate, through a couleee and up a hill. Needless to say, some people missed us.

We needed a sign.

But the Alberta government did not allow directional signs outside city or town limits. The only way I could put up a sign pointing to our location was to register myself as a ranch, which would then entitle me to one directional sign off the nearest highway.

After many name submissions and many rejections—you can't use anybody else's name—the Driftwillow was accepted. We proudly put up an arrow shaped sign that pointed the way to Driftwillow Ranch—4 miles.

You had to know in advance that the Driftwillow Ranch was the location of a restaurant called the Driftwillow Room and that both were located on Willow Creek.

Recipes illustrated overleaf

Fettucine with Smoked Salmon, page 63
Tomato Bread, page 46
The Flying N Caesar Salad, page 67

Green Goddess Dressing

1 cup	blender mayonnaise	250 mL
½ cup	sour cream	125 mL
¼ cup	chopped chives	50 mL
¼ cup	chopped parsley	50 mL
1 clove	garlic, minced	1 clove
3 fillets	anchovy, minced	3 fillets
1 tbsp.	lemon juice	15 mL
1 tbsp.	tarragon vinegar	15 mL
½ tsp.	salt	2 mL

freshly ground black pepper to taste

Combine all ingredients and store in the frig. Good for green salads and cold meat.

When I was growing up, we only had one kind of salad dressing in our house ... and that was because this particular dressing didn't require any "fussing" and my father liked it enormously.

Magic Mayonnaise, Now You See It/Now You Don't

⅔ cup	sweetened condensed milk	150 mL
¼ cup	lemon juice or vinegar	50 mL
¼ cup	salad oil or butter	50 mL
1	egg yolk	1
1 tsp.	dry mustard	5 mL
½ tsp.	salt	2 mL

dash of cayenne pepper

Place all ingredients in a small jar, screw top on tightly and shake vigorously for 2 minutes. Chill at least half an hour before using because it thickens up as it cools.

Let the special flavour of chutney turn up in an unexpected place — in the salad dressing used for a spinach or lettuce salad.

Chutney Dressing

1½ cups	chutney	375 mL
2 tsp.	minced garlic	10 mL
1½ tbsp.	dry mustard	20 mL
1 cup	red wine vinegar	250 mL
1 cup	vegetable oil	250 mL

Notes: Peach or pear chutney would work well in this recipe. See pages 134 , 135 .

In a food processor or blender, mix all ingredients except the oil. With motor running, add the oil in a thin stream until all ingredients are thick and smooth.

Pour into serving dish and chill for at least an hour. Especially good with spinach salad.

Salads

Tomatoes are appetizing in so many ways—their colour, perfect shape, taste. No wonder they make such good beginnings to our meals!

Patsy's Tomato Appetizer

2 lbs.	tomatoes	1 kg
2 tbsp.	parsley stalks	30 mL
¾ cup	olive or salad oil	175 mL
1 cup	tarragon vinegar	250 mL
1 clove	garlic, minced	1 clove
1	medium onion	1
¼ tsp.	dry mustard	1 mL
½ tsp.	cayenne pepper	2 mL
2 tbsp.	sugar	30 ml

Blanch and peel tomatoes. If they're small, leave them whole. Otherwise, slice into thick slices. Place in a serving bowl and sprinkle with parsley stalks.

To make the dressing, get a jar with screw top. Measure in the oil and vinegar. Add the minced garlic, chopped onion, mustard, cayenne pepper and sugar. Shake like crazy.

Pour dressing over the tomatoes and chill overnight. Serves 4-6.

A marinated vegetable salad is a great help during busy times. Make it up in advance and then use it for up to 3 weeks.

Doesn't lose its snap or colour ... or nutritional value!

Marinated Vegetable Salad

broccoli, cauliflower, cherry tomatoes, mushrooms, zucchini slices, black olives, cucumbers, carrots

1½ cups	red wine vinegar	375 mL
1½ cups	water	375 mL
½ cup	vegetable oil	125 mL
2 tbsp.	sugar	30 mL
2 tsp.	salt	10 mL
¼ tsp.	pepper	1 mL
3 cloves	garlic	3 cloves
2 tsp.	dried oregano	10 ml
1 tsp.	dried basil	5 mL
½ cup	chopped parsley	125 mL

Prepare vegetables. Break broccoli and cauliflower into flowerettes and blanch about 2 minutes—just enough to take the edge off and enhance the colour. Clean and slice carrots, using a corrugated knife to give slices a frilly edge. Blanch the carrots about 10 minutes. Simply wash and slice remaining vegetables. You can use whatever your garden is producing, incidentally. Slices of small fresh turnips would be good, so would radishes.

To make the marinade, combine the remaining ingredients and stir or blend well to dissolve sugar and salt. Pour over vegetables, cover and marinate at least overnight.

Keep refrigerated. Use for up to 3 weeks.

I have a dreadful time keeping track of this recipe which uses rice in a salad form. Every time I serve it, someone asks for the recipe, and the hunt is on. Fortunately, most of my friends have recorded the ingredients by now and I call on them whenever I'm stuck.

Chinese Mandarin Rice Salad

1 cup	converted rice	250 mL
2 cups	boiling water	500 mL
1 tsp.	salt	5 mL
½ cup	salad oil	125 mL
¼ cup	cider vinegar	50 mL
2 tbsp.	soy sauce	25 mL
1 can	button mushrooms	1 can
1 cup	chopped celery	250 mL
2 tbsp.	green onions	30 mL
½ cup	slivered almonds	125 mL
1 small can	mandarin oranges	1 small can (284 mL)

Cook rice in 2 cups boiling salted water.

In a small bowl, mix together the oil, vinegar and soy sauce.

Drain the mushrooms. Slice big ones and leave tiny button mushrooms whole.

As soon as the rice is cooked, add the mushrooms and the oil, vinegar and soy sauce mixture. Stir well and chill overnight.

When ready to serve, mix with celery (cut on the diagonal), chopped green onions, almonds and drained orange sections. Garnish with some of the orange pieces.

Notes and Variations

Salads

Our potatoes were great favourites at the restaurant and time and time again, we were asked what we did to make them taste so good.

The answer was simple. From the earliest possible date in the spring until late summer, we served new potatoes — white or red skinned, as small as possible. We scrubbed them clean, removed a narrow strip of skin around the middle, and then boiled them in lightly salted water until just barely tender.

Then we served them up in big bowls, added lots of butter and freshly chopped chives and/or fresh dill weed. And that was it — our big secret!

The Secret Flying N Potatoes

new potatoes no bigger than a plum
boiling salted water
lots of butter
fresh chives or dill weed, chopped fine

Clean the potatoes. Do not peel. Just cut a strip from around the middle.

Boil in salted water until just barely tender. Drain.

Put in a serving bowl, add lots of butter, chives or dill weed.

We also found we could reheat potatoes cooked this way by adding the potatoes, butter and herbs to fresh water and cooking just until piping hot. The waxy texture of real new potatoes will take two or three such reappearances without disintegrating into soup.

The Secret Flying N Potatoes Revisited

— Slice cooked potatoes, still with the thin skin on them. Quickly fry in lots of butter until golden brown and crispy. Sprinkle with chopped chives and/or dill weed.

— Slice cooked potatoes into a greased casserole dish. Cube about ¼ cup (50 mL) hard butter and sprinkle on potatoes. Then cover with thick cream. Bake until cream has thickened. In the last 10 minutes, cover with grated cheddar cheese and allow to melt and bubble up.

— Remove skins and use the potatoes in salad. Dice, then add first dose of salad dressing. Because new potatoes don't absorb dressing as well as older ones, you should let new potatoes sit in dressing longer before adding onions, hardboiled eggs, cut up celery, mustard, salt and pepper, and whatever else you like in potato salad.

Vegetables

When we couldn't possibly find another potato with the thin skin and flavour of the early crop, we would resign ourselves to other ways with potatoes—all kinds of other ways . . . except baked in foil! I prefer honest baked potatoes—the kind baked in their own skins.

A perfect baked potato needs about an hour at 400°F (200°C). Clean the skins carefully, rub with butter or oil to get a crisp outside skin and then bake until soft when pinched. A skewer or potato nail inserted through the centre of the potato will speed up the cooking time.

Double Baked Potatoes

4	large potatoes	4
salt and freshly ground pepper to taste		
½ cup	butter	125 mL
¼ cup	chopped chives	50 mL
½ cup	grated cheddar	125 mL

Clean potatoes, rub with oil or butter and bake at 400°F (200°C) for about an hour or until soft when pinched. As soon as they have cooled enough to handle, remove a thick slice from the top and scoop out the potato, leaving the skin intact. This is best done when the potato is still warm; otherwise the potato gets hard.

Whip or mash the potato, adding salt, pepper, butter, chives and cheese. If the mixture seems too thick, add a bit of cream. Refill the potato skins. If you have a pastry bag with a star tip, apply some decorative touches. Otherwise, use a fork to finish with some scoops and swirls.

At this point, the potatoes can be refrigerated and reheated when needed. Otherwise, they can be reheated immediately. Be sure to heat thoroughly—the butter and cheese should be bubbling hot.

Serves 4.

Stovies made with Tatties

6	potatoes	6
2	medium onions	2
¼ cup	bacon fat	50 mL
salt and pepper to taste		
1 cup	stock or water	250 mL

Notes: In place of bacon fat, you can use chicken fat or butter or margarine. These potatoes were originally made by thrifty Scots so they would naturally have used whatever they had on hand—most likely leftover bacon fat which gave the potatoes a very nice flavour anyway.

Grease a large flameproof casserole dish or Dutch oven.

Peel and slice potatoes and onions. Layer into casserole or Dutch oven with bacon fat dotting the layers. Salt and pepper to taste. Pour stock or water over all, cover and simmer over very low heat until the potatoes are quite soft.

Vegetables

Now that I often cook for just one person, I've developed some tricks by which to have my potatoes and eat them too! The following is a quick and easy taste of potato for one.

Better Than Hash Browns

1 large or 2 small potatoes		
2 tbsp.	butter	25 mL

Wash but do not peel the potatoes. Grate on a medium size grater.

Heat the butter in a medium size iron skillet and slide the grated potatoes carefully into the centre of the pan. Cover with a lid that fits right down inside the skillet, resting on the bottom of the pan and enclosing the potatoes. Lower the heat and cook, without lifting the lid, for 5 minutes.

With a wide spatula, check under the mound of potatoes. If they're nice and brown, turn over the whole mound. Cover again and let cook another 5 minutes. The finished product should be crisp and light brown on the outside, semi-transparent and creamy in the middle.

Eat at once and enjoy. Serves 1.

I can't resist a recipe with an unusual name, and the Scots gave two of their potato dishes particularly interesting names. Clapshot and Stovies

Clapshot

Potatoes, half as many as you'll need
Turnips, half as much as you'll need
Butter, as much as your conscience will allow
salt, pepper and fresh chives

Peel, cut up and boil both potatoes and turnips. When thoroughly tender, drain and mash.

Combine equal amounts of mashed potatoes and mashed turnips, to be served as one dish — which is why you only needed half as many as usual. Whip together with lots of butter, salt and pepper. Sprinkle final serving with chopped chives.

Sweet potatoes and yams are interchangeable in recipes although they are two different vegetables. Yams are the round, sometimes huge, tubers with moist yellow to deep orange flesh. Sweet potatoes are long and slender with a darker skin and pale flesh.

Rum Runner Sweet Potatoes

4	large cooked yams	4
5	good sized oranges	5
¼ cup	brown sugar	50 mL
2 tbsp.	dark rum	25 mL
1 tsp.	salt	5 mL
¼ tsp.	cinnamon	1 mL
dash of	nutmeg and ginger	dash
1	egg, beaten	1

Vegetables

Clean yams and bake in 400°F (200°C) oven for at least an hour or until soft to the pinch. Set aside.

Cut the oranges in half, using a zigzag cut if you can do it. Remove the orange flesh—work carefully because the shells are to hold the sweet potatoes eventually. Chop the edible flesh into little bits and discard the seeds and white membranes.

Mash the cooked yams, add the chopped orange, brown sugar, rum, salt, spices and egg. Beat well. Pile this mixture into the orange shells and keep refrigerated until half an hour before serving.

When ready to bake, put the orange shells into muffin tins, bake at 350°F (180°C) until thoroughly warmed through and the top begins to brown.

This is another of my recipes using edible containers. I can't resist them—they both look and taste good.

Squashen Husken Pie

1	butternut squash	1
¼ lb.	mushrooms	125 g
1	corn-on-the-cob	1
1 cup	pearl onions	250 mL

green beans, sugar snap peas, snow peas
salt, pepper and butter as needed

Cut the squash in half. Fill bottom half with a mixture of mushrooms, slices of corn-on-the-cob, pearl onions, beans and peas. Top with salt, pepper and lots of butter. Cover with top half of squash and bake at 350°F (180°C) for 20-25 minutes or until squash is tender.

Bring the squash to table and serve some of the baked squash along with the vegetable filling.

Variations: Try a less elaborate combination of vegetables—perhaps a creamed mixture of onion and peas baked in an acorn squash. Or go even more elaborate and stuff a pumpkin with beef or chicken stew. Bake the pumpkin first as in Peter, Peter Pumpkin Soup, page 27. Food baked in squash containers fits in very well with native Indian or Mexican theme meals.

It almost seems sacrilegious to suggest improved ways of serving up fresh peas. However, there are several tricks that can accentuate the positive.

Fresh Peas Plus

If the new peas are past their finest, add a few pods to the water in which they're cooked to help pick up the flavour. Or try the French touch and cook fresh peas with some lettuce leaves. That too adds to the flavour. A mint leaf or two also enhances.

To get little kids to eat peas, tell them not to—especially not straight out of the garden. The same with carrots.

Vegetables

I thought everyone would appreciate the first fresh asparagus of spring, but I thought wrong. After hearing enough remarks like, "I'll skip the grass, thanks", I stopped serving it except for special occasions and special guests!

Asparagus As It Should Be

**fresh asparagus, enough for the company at hand
butter or a butter sauce such as Hollandaise** (below)

Wash asparagus well, break the stalks off and discard the tough ends. (They will break naturally at the right spot.) Stand upright in a deep pot, something like a glass coffee percolator with the insides removed. Fill the pot half full of water which will have the effect of cooking the tougher bottom parts and steaming the tender tops.

For easy handling, tie the stalks together with a string and then lift them out of the pot when ready. Cook for 10-15 minutes, depending upon the age of the asparagus.

Serve with butter or Hollandaise sauce.

Hollandaise sauce resembles mayonnaise in that it's made from egg yolks, butter and lemon juice. The difference is that the egg yolks have to be heated to thicken the butter and the trick is to get the heating done without scrambling the eggs.

Blender Hollandaise

1 cup	clarified butter	250 mL
3	egg yolks	3
salt and white pepper to taste		
1 tbsp.	fresh lemon juice	15 mL

Notes: To clarify butter, melt the butter over low heat. Remove from heat and let stand a few minutes, allowing the milk solids to settle to the bottom. Skim the butter fat from the top and discard the solid leavings. The pure butter fat is known as clarified butter.

For the hollandaise recipe, heat clarified butter over low heat and keep warm. Put remaining ingredients into blender and mix at high speed until blended thoroughly. With motor running at high speed, add the hot butter in a thin stream. As soon as the sauce thickens, adjust the seasonings and enjoy.

If there's any sign the eggs are going to turn into scrambled eggs because of the heat of the butter, add a few drops of cold water or a sliver of ice to the mixture.

Notes and Variations

Vegetables

Hollandaise can also be made from ready mix packages available at most delicatessans or supermarkets. They truly are never fail, but many people prefer to be purist about Hollandaise and make their own.

If you'd like to gild the lily, or add insult to injury as far as your figure is concerned, make Sauce Mousseline. It's essentially Hollandaise and absolutely irresistible.

Sauce Mousseline

1 recipe Hollandaise sauce, see page 80		
⅓ cup	heavy cream	75 mL

Make up recipe of blender Hollandaise and keep warm. Whip heavy cream until stiff peaks form. Just before serving, fold into warm Hollandaise. Serve with steamed vegetables — any that take well to butter will take equally well or better to this sauce.

I can't imagine cooking without using onions. One of my friends claimed that I put onions in everything except maybe desserts and she even wondered about them!

Onions to Stay Home For

whole onions, enough to serve company at hand
buttered bread crumbs, don't spare the butter
or … undiluted cream soups

Do not peel the onions. It's easier to remove the outer skins after cooking.

To prevent a family exodus, cook onions in a steamer so that they are over water, not in water. That way, they don't smell up the house. Steam for about 30 minutes or until done — depends on the size of the onions. Slip the tender centres out and serve with buttered bread crumbs (don't go light on the butter!) or a cream sauce made with a soup such as cheddar cheese soup, mushroom soup or cream of celery.

For variety, whole onions can also be baked — in a 375°F (190°C) oven for about 1½ hours. When baked through, discard the outer layers and serve with butter, salt and pepper. Good with barbecued beef. In fact, onions can be baked in hot coals, as above, and served with outdoor meals.

Onion Rings Without Fuss

1 cup	pancake mix	250 mL
enough milk to make a firm but not thick batter		
onion rings cut from large red or yellow onions		
vegetable oil for deep fat fryer or skillet		

Measure out the pancake mix and add enough milk to make a firm batter, not too thick. Cut the onion into thin slices and separate into whole rings. Put vegetable oil into deep fat fryer or skillet, enough to cover the rings as they fry. Heat oil to medium high temperature.

Dip an onion ring into the batter and fry it in the hot oil. If the batter is too thick, add a bit more milk. If too runny, add a bit more pancake mix. Turn each ring as it browns, giving each side 3-4 minutes. Drain on paper towelling. Serve as soon as possible or keep warm in oven.

Vegetables

I had a lot of fun doing the cooking for the Wild Game Dinner in Claresholm in spring, 1983. But even as I hunted up recipes and ideas for such far out things as caribou and bear, I also had to find more mundane things—like the proper accompaniments for all the wild game. One of the side dishes I finally decided upon was Baked Onion with Apples which can also serve as a main dish if it just so happens you're not serving caribou or bear that day!

Baked Onion with Apples

8 slices	bacon	8 slices
½ cup	soft bread crumbs	125 mL
6	medium sized onions	6
4	medium sized apples	4
¾ cup	hot stock or water	175 mL
½ tsp.	salt	2 mL

Note: If you don't have any meat stock on hand, use hot water or hot canned consomme.

Grease a large casserole dish or baking dish.

Fry the bacon, then remove from the fat and cut into chunks. In the remaining bacon fat, toss the bread crumbs until they're coated and browned.

Peel onions, cut crosswise into thin slices. Peel apples, core and cut crosswise into thin slices. Arrange onion and apple slices along with the bacon in alternate layers in the greased casserole. Pour the hot stock and/or water and/or canned consommé over everything. Sprinkle with salt and cover with browned bread crumbs.

Cover casserole and bake at 350°F (180°C) for 30 minutes. Uncover and cook about 15 minutes longer.

Cabbage doesn't often make the hit parade as a cooked vegetable anymore—a fact that's probably due in part to its overpowering smell as it cooks. Still and all, it has a lot going for it as some of these old fashioned combinations prove. This version of cabbage was featured at a St. Patrick's Day dinner.

Colcannon

1	small head cabbage	1
4	medium potatoes	4
2	carrots	2
1	small turnip	1
2 tbsp.	butter	25 mL
1 tbsp.	soy sauce	15 mL
salt and pepper to taste		

Shred the cabbage and simmer in lightly salted water until tender.
Peel potatoes, carrots and turnip. Dice and cook together in another pot until tender. Don't use too much water—you don't want to boil all the goodness out of them.

Drain both pots. Put vegetables together in one pot and mash with butter, soy sauce, salt and pepper.

Cabbage Stuffed in a Bag

1	large cabbage	1
1 pkg. (10 oz.)	frozen mixed vegetables	1 pkg. (300 g)
¼ cup	water	50 mL
¼ tsp.	salt	1 mL
½ cup	cheddar cheese	125 mL
¼ tsp.	onion salt	1 mL
heavy plastic bag that can stand up to boiling		
2 tbsp.	melted butter	25 mL

Remove several outer leaves from a large head of cabbage and set aside. Scoop out the centre of the cabbage to form a bowl about 1″ (2.5 cm) thick. Chop the cabbage that's been removed. Cut off the stem so that cabbage stands easily.

Cover and simmer the chopped cabbage, frozen mixed vegetables, water and salt for 8 minutes. Drain.

Grate the cheese and add with the onion salt to the mixed vegetables.

Pour into the cabbage bowl. Cover the top of the mixture with one of the reserved outer leaves and put everything into a heavy plastic bag. Freezer bags work well. Squeeze out the air and close the top.

Lower into a deep kettle of boiling water and steam for 20-30 minutes.

Remove from hot water and cut the bag away. Blanch the remaining outer cabbage leaves briefly — 2-3 minutes — in the water that the bag just came out of. Now, make the final arrangement.

Put the cabbage and contents into a big bowl. Arrange the cabbage leaves around it as garnish. (Or use other greens from the garden, if the cabbage leaves were just too tight.) Pour melted butter over the cooked vegetables.

Serves 6.

Parsnips didn't impress me until I had them cooked by our neighbor, Herb's mother.

Perfect Parsnips

parsnips fresh from the garden, if possible		
a good chunk of butter		
¼-½ cup	sugar	50-125 mL

Cut cleaned parsnips into small chunks, put into a heavy skillet on medium heat and partially cover with water. Most important, add a good chunk of butter. Cover the pan and cook until parsnips are almost tender and water has boiled away. With fresh parsnips, this doesn't take too long, 10-15 minutes. With older ones, it may take longer. Make sure they don't boil dry.

Once cooked, add more butter if necessary and sprinkle lightly with sugar, stirring with a fork so that the sugar and butter join to coat the parsnips.

Keep warm until ready to serve.

Zucchini has taken the country by storm, and sometimes it takes the frig by storm as well ... generally about the end of August! Here's a recipe to help use up the beast!

Zucchini with Sour Cream

6	small zucchini	6
2 tbsp.	butter	25 mL
1 tbsp.	water	15 mL
salt and pepper to suit individual tastes		
⅓ cup	sour cream	75 mL
paprika as garnish when all is said and done		

Wash, dry and remove ends of zucchini. Do not peel. Using a fine grater or food processor, grate the zucchini.

In a heavy skillet on lowest possible heat setting, mix together the butter and water. Add the grated zucchini. Cook and stir for 5-7 minutes, until just barely heated and still crisp. Add salt and pepper. Turn off heat, add cream and mix carefully.

Transfer into a heated serving dish, sprinkle with paprika and enjoy.

Another solution for the zucchini overflow is the following recipe which was selected some years ago in a Star Weekly contest. Of course, the recipe did not call for zucchini then; it required cucumber in the original. But they work equally well.

Prize Winning Vegetable Casserole

2	medium onions	2
2	cucumbers or zucchini	2
salt and pepper to taste		
½ cup	hot water	125 mL
1½ cups	chili sauce	375 mL
1 tsp.	chili powder	5 mL
2	ripe tomatoes	2
1 cup	grated cheddar cheese	250 mL

Use medium sized cucumbers or zucchini. If using cucumbers, peel them but don't bother peeling zucchini unless the skin is particularly tough. Cut vegetables into thin slices.

Grease a large casserole dish and arrange in several alternate layers the onions and cucumber or zucchini. Season with salt and pepper.

Combine hot water with chili sauce and chili powder. Pour over the vegetables.

Slice tomatoes into thick slices. Grate the cheese. Arrange both over the vegetables. Bake at 350°F (180°C) for 1½ hours or until vegetables are fork tender.

Good served with cold meat and hot biscuits. Serves up to 6.

Vegetables

In keeping with my fascination for unusual names, I knew I had to try Imam Bayildi when I first found out about it. The name means either the Priest Has Fainted or the Sultan Has Swooned. Stories vary as to the cause of all this fainting. Some say the wonderful taste of the dish brought on the faint spell. Others say it was the cost of the ingredients.

Whatever, it's very good and provides a change of scenery on the dinner table!

Imam Bayildi

2	eggplants	2
1 tsp.	salt	5 mL
3 tbsp.	olive oil	50 mL
3	chopped onions	3
3 cloves	garlic, minced	3 cloves
3	tomatoes	3
2 tbsp.	chopped parsley	30 mL
salt and freshly ground pepper to taste		
5 tbsp.	olive oil	60 mL
1 cup	water	250 mL
1	lemon, juice only	1
½ tsp.	sugar	2 mL

Remove stems from eggplants and cut off skin in strips about 1″ (2.5 cm) wide, leaving some skin on in between the strips. The eggplants will end up in stripes. Cut the eggplants in half, lengthwise, leaving a hinge to join the halves on one end. Sprinkle the cut surface with 1 tsp. (5 mL) salt and let it stand for 30 minutes to draw out the excess moisture and bitter taste. Rinse and pat dry.

To make the filling, heat 3 tbsp. (50 mL) oil in a heavy skillet and saute the onions until golden. Add garlic and cook another minute. Remove from heat. Peel, seed and chop the tomatoes. Add to the onion mixture along with chopped parsley and salt and pepper to taste.

Place the eggplant halves, opened up flat, in a casserole or baking dish. Pile the filling on top of the halves.

Mix together the 5 tbsp. (60 mL) olive oil, water, lemon juice and sugar. Pour over the filling in the eggplant halves. The liquid should come about ¾ the way up the sides of the eggplant.

Cover and simmer until eggplants are very tender and most of the liquid has evaporated. Remove the lid for the last 15 minutes of cooking in order to reduce the liquid to ½ cup (125 mL).

Remove from heat and cool just as is in the pan. When ready to serve, transfer the eggplants to a serving dish and pour the liquid from the pan over them. Serve at room temperature.

Vegetables

No matter what you picture of cowboy life—whether it be horses or 4 wheel drives—somewhere in the background is always a pot of beans. Naturally, Driftwillow and The Flying N served its share of this traditional food, a fact that eventually led to its being called "Jean's Beans".

I doubt if Jean's Beans were ever the same twice. We'd start with a mixture of dry beans—as many as 6 or 7 different kinds, then add ham joints, pork hocks, salt pork or bacon ends, then add the sauce makings.

Jean's Beans at Home or in Camp

1½ cups	dried beans	375 mL
water to cover, usually four times as much as beans		
1	large onion	1
8	whole cloves	8
¼ cup	molasses	50 mL
3 tbsp.	ketchup	50 mL
1 tbsp.	dry mustard	15 mL
1 tsp.	salt	5 mL
1 tbsp.	worcestershire sauce	15 mL
½ cup	boiling bean water	125 mL
bones from baked ham or salt pork or bacon ends		

Notes: Beans may include one or more of the following: small white navy beans, the larger Great Northern beans, pinto, limas, kidney, blackeye, garbanzos or chick peas.

Put bean assortment into a large heavy pot and cover with water—3 or 4 times as much water as beans. Let stand overnight. Drain and cover with fresh water. Cover, bring to a boil and then simmer slowly until tender. Test the doneness of a bean by blowing on it. If it's done, the skin will blow off. The small navy bean often takes the longest, so check it for sure. Do not add salt or salt pork or bacon at this stage.

When beans are tender, drain and reserve the liquid in which they cooked.

Stick the whole cloves into the onion and add to the cooked beans. Also add molasses, ketchup, dry mustard, salt, worcestershire sauce and the ½ cup (125 mL) bean water. Tuck in the ham bones or salt pork pieces or bacon ends. Cover and bake at 250°F (120°C) for 6-9 hours, adding extra bean water if the mixture becomes dry. Uncover for the last half hour and adjust seasonings, if necessary.

If working in a camping situation, prepare the beans up to the final baking stage. Then dig a hole at least 4″ (10 cm) deeper than the heavy iron bean pot. Prepare enough coals to have a good layer underneath the pot and on top of it. Put the bottom layer of hot coals into the hole, then lower the pot into the hole, covering the lid with foil to keep out any dirt. Cover with remaining coals and bury with at least 3″ (8 cm) dirt.

Bake in the pit for at least 4 hours, watching that the dirt stays in place, thus holding in the heat.

A final word about beans. If you want to speed up the soaking process, cover the dried beans with water, bring them to a boil and simmer for 2 minutes. Then remove from heat and let stand, tightly covered, for 1 hour. Blanching beans like this is equivalent to about 8 hours soaking.

Vegetables

I've left the best for the last. As far back as I can remember, I've always preferred tomatoes to every other choice and recipes turn up in every section of this book for their use. Here, I present an old favourite—Baked Tomato Pudding.

Baked Tomato Pudding

1 large can	tomatoes	1 large can
1 cup	brown sugar	250 mL
1 tsp.	salt	5 mL
¾ cup	boiling water	175 mL
3 cups	white bread cubes	750 mL
½ cup	melted butter	125 mL

Notes: Large cans of tomatoes should be about 28 fl. oz. (795 mL).

Strain the tomatoes through a sieve, crushing the pulp thoroughly to get all the juice. Or use a food mill. You want everything but the seeds. Put into a saucepan along with the sugar, salt and boiling water. Simmer for about 5 minutes.

While tomatoes are simmering, cut bread (fresh or stale) into ½″ (1 cm) cubes. Grease a medium size casserole and put bread cubes into the bottom. Melt the butter and pour over the bread cubes, stirring slightly to get butter to all parts. If the bread is very dry, it may need more butter.

Add the boiling tomato mixture and stir again. Bake at 375°F (190°C) for about 50 minutes. Serves up to 6.

Tomatoes also team up very obligingly with eggs for this unusual breakfast dish.

Tomato Surprise

enough fresh tomatoes to serve one to each guest
salt, pepper and basil to taste
eggs
buttery bread crumbs and/or grated parmesan

Hollow out the tomatoes. A melon ball scoop helps with this process. Drain well. Save the pulp and juice for use later in a sauce or stew. Sprinkle the inside of each tomato shell with a dash of salt, pepper and basil.

Break eggs, one at a time, into a small dish and gently slip one into each tomato shell. Bake in a 350°F (180°C) oven for about 20 minutes or until eggs are almost set to the degree of doneness you like. Sprinkle each with bread crumbs and/or parmesan cheese. Put back under the broiler until bread crumbs are browned and/or parmesan is bubbly.

Vegetables

When people ask me for recipes for stuffed tomatoes, I am absolutely flabbergasted. Whoever heard of a recipe for stuffed tomatoes? All you do is hollow out the tomatoes and fill them with whatever is overflowing your frig, your garden or your grocery bags. However, I'll try to be a bit more specific.

Stuffed Tomatoes

Round firm fully packed ripe tomatoes
eggs, chives, mayonnaise, mustard, seasonings
blackeyed peas, oil and vinegar dressing
creamed cottage cheese, fresh dill, salt and pepper

Cut the tomatoes so that they can be hollowed out and refilled. That could mean something as simple as cutting the tomato in half crosswise and going on from there. It's more fun to experiment with different cuts — a zigzag, for instance, or a flower petal cut. (See the picture on page 125 .)

Once cut, carefully hollow out the tomato meat, reserving it for some other use like tomato sauce or stew or something. Drain juice completely.

An egg filling is one of the best. Hardboil eggs, add cut up chives, mayonnaise, mustard, whatever seasonings you generally use in an egg salad combination. Pile into tomato shells, top with more chopped chives and enjoy.

I couldn't resist blackeyed peas when I found them in a supermarket one day so I cooked them up, added a bit of vinegar and oil dressing and piled them into a tomato shell.

Use ordinary creamed cottage cheese and dress it up in any way that you like. Pile into tomato shells, top with sprig of fresh dill and enjoy!

You can also stuff tomato shells with a fish salad, something like crabmeat, or chicken salad or coleslaw or avocado chunks. Tomato is very obliging that way — it enhances and encloses all sorts of other foods.

The Flying N was asked to supply lunch for a television crew who were in Claresholm shooting a commercial with Wayne and Shuster, the two most famous comedians in the country. We were glad to oblige but from the instructions we were given, it didn't look like it would be a whole lot of fun.

The instructions detailed, in no uncertain terms, how we were supposed to serve sandwiches only—no fancy stuff. Just sandwiches and coffee.

We managed to stick to the letter of their law and have some fun at the same time. I ordered 6 foot long submarine loaves from the local bakery. We split them lengthwise and filled them brimming full with cheese, meats, tomatoes, lettuce, whatever else that fit in. Then we held them together with long skewers upon which we built great towers of pickles, cherry tomatoes, olives, pearl onions and the like.

Then, just for good measure, we baked them a cake, since we knew they were coming and all!

Both Wayne and Shuster congratulated us on our architectural abilities—as demonstrated by our wild and wonderful sandwiches. They left an autographed picture that reads, "To Jean of the Flying N from Johnny Wayne, the lazy W, and Frank Shuster, the smart S."

Recipes illustrated overleaf

Chicken in the Gold, page 92
Betty's Boxing Day Fried Rice, page 65
Marigold Watermelon Rind Pickle, page 129
Peach Chutney, page 134

Dishes courtesy Bowring's, Southcentre, Calgary

POULTRY

At the restaurant, we heard a lot of chicken jokes, what with being called The Flying N and all. In fact, some customers used to call us "Flying Hens", a nickname that I never particularly appreciated. However, it was appropriate that a chicken dish eventually became our house specialty. Known as Chicken in the Gold, it was a colorful dish that appealed equally to sight, smell and taste!

It even passed the staff test. After years of serving it to customers, staff would ask to have it served to them for special occasions. That, I think, is a great tribute.

Some time after I sold The Flying N, a recipe for Chicken in the Gold appeared in a Chatelaine article about house specialties in various restaurants across Canada. I was never able to find out what happened, but the recipe printed in the magazine bore very little resemblance to the one we'd used for years ... which fact was called to the attention of the restaurant and to me at my home. One irate reader even suggested taking legal action!

Some of us take our recipes seriously!

On the menu at The Flying N, we offered chicken in three different ways: broiled with butter, barbecued or in the gold.

To prepare for any of the above, we precooked chicken halves and had them ready for any of the above finishes. To precook, wipe chicken clean, place cut side down in a flat roasting pan, and season with salt and pepper. Cover tightly with foil, don't add any water, and bake in 350 F (180 C) oven for an hour.

Save any juices that have collected in the pan. They are pure essence of chicken and can be used in soups, gravies or as stock for various other dishes. Freeze for future use in ice cube trays. When solid, remove the cubes and store in a plastic bag, retrieving as many as needed when needed.

Chicken in the Gold

2	chickens, halved	2
1 cup	honey	250 mL
1 cup	prepared mustard	250 mL
1 tbsp.	curry powder	15 mL

Note: Buy chicken in the 2½-3 lb. (1-1.3 kg) weight range.

Also note: Essentially, the Chicken in the Gold sauce requires an equal amount of honey and prepared mustard along with curry to taste. The recipe given above would serve 4 fairly conservative people. Increase the amount of curry powder for more daring types. The mustard used is the kind used in hot dogs.

Precook the chickens. Prepare the sauce by heating together the honey, prepared mustard and curry powder.

Reheat the chickens until they are hot throughout but not browned. (If being finished immediately after cooking the chickens, this preheating step will not be necessary.) Brush underside of the chicken with sauce first. Put under broiler until brown and bubbling. Turn and brush sauce on the skin side, being very generous with the sauce. Broil again until brown and bubbling. Watch very carefully at this point as the honey will brown very quickly. You want Gold, not Burnt Offerings.

Serve with sliced orange and parsley, arranged in whatever frilly way you can contrive.

Plain Broiled Chicken

See above for instructions about preliminary steps for precooking chicken halves.

When ready to use, reheat in a hot oven or under a broiler. When heated through, dot chicken pieces generously with butter and return to oven or broiler to brown up nicely.

Serve with cranberry sauce or relish.

Barbecued Chicken

See above for instructions about preliminary steps for precooking chicken halves.

When ready to use, reheat in a hot oven or under a broiler. When heated through, brush with French style catalina bottled salad dressing on the cut side first. Let it bubble up and brown. Then turn over and brush generously with more of the salad dressing. Again, return to oven or broiler and let it bubble and brown.

The salad dressing gives a lighter more attractive look to the chicken and tastes better than some of the heavier barbecue sauces. Serve with a tomato garnish.

If you've been yearning for some old fashioned fried chicken, yearn no more. Marj's Chicken is done in the traditional way that country cooks have used for years.

Marj's Fried Chicken

2	cut up fryer chickens	2
1 cup	flour	250 mL
salt and pepper to taste		
3	eggs, lightly beaten	3
2 cups	fine dry bread crumbs	500 mL
oil for deep fat frying		

Note: Try to get chickens in the 2½ lb. (1 - 1.3 kg) weight range. They're a good size for frying.

Cut up the chickens. Put flour, salt and pepper into a plastic bag and shake the chicken pieces in it so they get an even coating. Then dip chicken pieces into lightly beaten egg mixture and then into fine crumbs.

Fry a few pieces at a time in deep hot fat, 400°F (200°C), just long enough to seal the crumb coating and turn the chicken a very light brown. When all the pieces have been so done, place in a roasting pan, cover and bake at 350°F (180°C) for 45 - 60 minutes, depending on the size of the chickens. Don't crowd the pieces or the delicate crust will break off. This method produces a very moist fried chicken with all of the flavour intact.

One Easter, we tried a new way with chicken, and came up with a dish that looked like an Easter egg but tasted like Cordon Bleu.

Easter Chicken in the Cordon Bleu Way

4	chicken breasts	4
4 slices	cooked ham	4 slices
¼ lb.	Swiss cheese	100 g
1 cup	flour	250 mL
salt and pepper to taste		
2	eggs, lightly beaten	2
1 cup	fine dry bread crumbs	250 mL
oil for deep fat frying		

Note: Chicken breasts should be boneless. Use one small boneless breast or half a large boneless breast per serving.

Between wax paper, flatten the chicken with the side of a wooden cleaver or rolling pin. Remove the wax paper. On the flattened chicken, place a slice of ham slightly smaller than the chicken. Cut Swiss cheese in cubes about the size of an egg yolk and place in the middle of the ham slice. Roll the cheese up into the ham/chicken slice, folding in the sides to make a neat package.

Combine flour, salt and pepper in a small bowl and roll meat packages in it. Then dip them in the egg mixture and fine bread crumbs. If the rolls threaten to come apart, fasten them with a toothpick but these are often a nuisance to get out after cooking.

Deep fat fry in oil at 325°F (160°C) for 5 - 7 minutes until golden brown. Put into slow oven and continue cooking for 20 minutes.

When cut in half crosswise, these look like a large egg with a brown shell and melting inside yolk.

Poultry

One large roasting chicken (4 - 5 lbs.) can give a small family "Chicken All Week". I don't mean you have to use it exclusively seven days in a row but you can get the makings of seven meals from one chicken. Besides, the process provides several important basic chicken recipes.

Chicken All Week
Day #1 ... Chicken Broth

	all the bones, skin and meat not used in other ways	
12 cups	water	3 L
4 stalks	celery	4 stalks
1	onion	1
2	carrots	2
1	bay leaf	1
8	whole peppercorns	8
2 tsp.	salt	10 mL
sprigs of fresh parsley		

Cut the chicken into the usual portions. At the neck opening of the breast, slice crosswise and remove the wishbone together with the meat surrounding it. Cut along the breastbone, removing the meat from either side. Skin and bone the drumsticks. Leave the skin on the thighs but remove the bones. Cut wings into 3 pieces. Break the backs in two.

In a large heavy pot, put all the bones that have been removed, the wishbone and surrounding meat, the tips of the wings, the neck, the backs, gizzard and heart. Cover with water and bring to boiling. Skim off froth and fat, reduce heat and skim again if necessary.

Add vegetables and herbs and simmer over medium heat for about 2 hours, or until the liquid is reduced by half. Cool, then remove the bones with a slotted spoon. Don't throw them out — they have the meat on them needed for other dishes!

If not being used immediately, chill quickly and freeze until required.

Cut the meat off the wishbone and other bones. Freeze whatever is not needed immediately.

Day #2 ... Chicken Sal San

Use the cooked meat from the wishbone area. Dice it up, add mayonnaise and celery and whatever else strikes your fancy, and make a chicken salad sandwich.

Day #3 ... Chicken Casserole

Use the cooked meat from remaining bones. (It should already be cut up and waiting in frig or freezer.) Turn it into creamed chicken by making a cream sauce or using an undiluted cream soup, adding your own bits of pimiento and chives for colour. Serve on toast with a green vegetable or small salad.

Poultry

Day #4 ... Oriental Chicken Wings

2 lbs.	chicken wings	1 kg
2 tbsp.	vegetable oil	25 mL
1 clove	garlic, minced	1 clove
¼ cup	soy sauce	50 mL
⅓ cup	dry sherry	75 mL
2 tbsp.	lemon juice	25 mL
⅓ cup	light corn syrup	75 mL
¼ tsp.	ground ginger	1 mL

Note: Use the chicken wing pieces from the original chicken or buy enough wings. They are the least expensive cut of chicken.

Cut off the wing tips. Keep them for soup stock. Then cut the wings at the centre joint. In a wok or heavy skillet, brown wing pieces in hot vegetable oil. Remove with a slotted spoon and set aside.

To the hot oil, now add the remaining ingredients. Stir until well mixed and heated through. Return wings to the pan and bring to a boil. Lower heat, cover and simmer for about 20 minutes or until chicken is done. Turn wings once.

Remove the lid, increase the heat and cook 10 minutes longer until the sauce thickens and the wings are glazed.

Garnish with lemon wedges.

Day #5 ... Stir Fry Vegetables with Chicken Pieces

Use the meat from the drumsticks in a Chinese stir fry dish, perhaps with mushrooms, snow peas, zucchini and tomatoes. If cut into small bite sized pieces, the meat need cook only a few minutes in a wok.

Day #6 ... Roast Chicken with Sage Dressing

With the thighs which have been boned but not skinned, make a small scale roast with dressing.

Make up a small amount of your favourite dressing. Flatten the thighs by placing them between sheets of wax paper and then pounding with the flat side of a cleaver until they are about ¼" (1 cm) thick. Divide the stuffing in two portions, put a portion on each of the flattened thighs and wrap the meat loosely around the stuffing. Place them, wrapped side down, in a shallow baking pan, brush lightly with melted butter and bake in a 350°F (180°C) oven for about 2 hours or until done. Baste with butter and pan juices as needed.

Make up gravy from pan juices and if more is needed, add one or two of the cubes of frozen broth.

Day #7 ... Easter Chicken

For its final appearance, this patient bird has saved the best for the last ... the boneless breast pieces. Use them in the Easter Chicken recipe or any other recipe that requires boneless chicken breasts.

Thus can one large chicken make meals for a small family for one week.

Poultry

Cornish game hens or quail are also a good choice when numbers or quantities are small.

Cornish Game Hens or Quail

4 Cornish game hens or 6 quail		
½ cup	butter	125 mL
1 cup	sauterne wine	250 mL
2 tbsp.	melted butter	25 mL
2 tbsp.	lemon juice	25 mL
2 tbsp.	dried tarragon	30 mL
salt and freshly ground pepper to taste		

Note: Any white wine will do if sauterne is not available.

For either game hens or quail, begin by cutting out the backbone. Slit down either side of the backbone from top to bottom. Use these pieces for soup stock. Then turn the bird over, breast side up, and flatten with the flat side of a cleaver or a board — even pressing heavily with the heel of your hand may do the trick. The idea is to crack the bones so that the meat can be handled easier.

If the game hens are more than a pound in weight (500 g), cut them in two along the breast line.

Make a slit in the skin between thigh and breast and tuck leg ends through to hold them in place. Tuck the wings behind the breast.

In a heavy skillet, melt the ½ cup (125 mL) butter and fry the birds until brown. Remove to a rack in a roasting pan. To the butter left in the skillet, add the sauterne and mix thoroughly. Pour this mixture over the birds.

Mix together the remaining sauterne, 2 tbsp. (25 mL) melted butter, lemon juice, tarragon, salt and pepper. Use it for basting.

Roast the birds uncovered in a 350°F (180°C) oven for about 40 minutes, basting all the while with the herb mixture.

Serve on a bed of brown or wild rice or both.

Notes and Variations

Poultry

My friend Marj from Stavely had a big family who never got their fill of dressing when she stuffed a turkey in the normal way. Consequently, she came up with the idea of stuffing the bird inside and out.

Marj's Inside Out Stuffing

1	turkey	1
2 loaves	bread	2 loaves
3	large onions	3
1 cup	melted butter	250 mL
1 lb.	ground beef	500 g
18	eggs	18

salt, pepper, sage or poultry dressing to taste

Note: This amount of dressing filled an 18 lb. (8 kg) turkey.

Clean and prepare the turkey.

Dice or break up the bread, homemade if possible. Chop or grind onion and add to the bread. Add butter, ground beef and eggs. Take care with the eggs — every kind of bread is different. Some kinds require a lot of moisture; others not so much, so add 14 eggs automatically and then use your judgment from then on. The mixture should be gooey but not sloppy — if that makes sense! Add seasonings to taste.

Loosen and lift the skin on the turkey in the hip, breast and neck areas. Pack dressing into areas between skin and meat. Don't pack too tightly or the skin will burst. Fill the cavity as well, although the turkey will cook much faster if stuffed on the outside only.

The end product looks rather surprising — like a bloated turkey — but it works beautifully. Roast the turkey as long as you would normally. Usually allow about 25 minutes per pound (500 g) at 350°F (180°C).

When it comes time to serve the turkey, slice the dressing along with the meat. That's another beauty of this method — it slices beautifully and everyone gets their fair share.

Jelly Sandwich Stuffing

bread, enough to fill chicken or turkey in question
butter and cranberry jelly
chopped up onion
salt, pepper and poultry dressing
½ cup (125 mL) melted butter
milk to moisten
corn syrup and additional melted butter

Make bread slices into jelly sandwiches. In a frypan or sandwich grill, toast sandwiches on both sides. Cut into small cubes, add onion and seasonings to taste. Pour melted butter over the mixture and enough milk to moisten.

Stuff chicken or turkey. Brush corn syrup over the outside of the bird and place in roaster on its side. Keep basting with additional butter. Roast at 350°F (180°C) for about 30 minutes per pound.

Poultry

After the holidays, you sometimes have leftover ham and turkey or chicken. This recipe serves it up in a whole new interesting way ... nobody would recognize it as leftovers!

Ham And Chicken With Yam Biscuits

¼ cup	butter	50 mL
¼ cup	flour	50 mL
1 cup	chicken broth	250 mL
1 cup	light cream	250 mL
½ cup	chopped onion	125 mL
¾ cup	sliced mushrooms	175 mL
salt and pepper to taste		
2 cups	diced cooked ham	500 mL
2 cups	diced cooked chicken	500 mL

Note: In place of chicken broth, you may use canned chicken bouillon or powdered broth reconstituted.

In a heavy skillet or saucepan, melt butter. Blend in flour. Add chicken broth and cream and stir until thick and hot. Add seasonings, onion and mushrooms.

Cut up ham and chicken and place in the bottom of a large casserole dish. Pour sauce over top and put into 350°F (180°C) oven while making the Yam Biscuits.

Yam Biscuits

1 cup	mashed cooked yams	250 mL
⅓ cup	melted butter	75 mL
1	egg, beaten	1
1 cup	flour	250 mL
2 tsp.	baking powder	10 mL
½ tsp.	salt	2 mL

Combine cooked yams with melted butter and egg. Mix together the dry ingredients and add to the yam mixture. Drop by spoonsful around the edge of the hot ham and chicken mixture.

Bake in 350°F (180°C) oven for about 45 minutes.

If my dad were given a choice, he'd always ask for Chicken and Dumplings, sometimes known as Chicken Fricassee. To make the dish, my mother would simply boil up a chicken and when it was just about falling off the bones, she'd make up a batch of dumplings and drop them on top. The dumplings thickened the broth and the combination was quite wonderful.

Dumplings for Dad's Fricassee

1	egg, beaten	1
milk to add to beaten egg to make ½ cup liquid		
1 cup	flour	250 mL
2 tsp.	baking powder	10 mL
¼ tsp.	salt	1 mL

Break egg into measuring cup, beat slightly and add enough milk to make ½ cup. Mix dry ingredients in a bowl and add the egg/milk mixture slowly. Beat well. The dough should be stiff but moist enough to hold together when dropped from a spoon.

Drop onto the boiling broth by first dipping a teaspoon into the hot liquid and then scooping out a spoonful. It will slide off the moistened spoon. Dip and scoop until all dough is used. Do not crowd the pan which should be fairly wide to accommodate enough dumplings. This quantity should make about 18 dumplings, 1″ (2.5 cm) across.

Cover pan and simmer about 10 minutes or until toothpick inserted in the centre of a dumpling comes out clean. Try not to remove the lid too often — the steam is important to this process.

My mother didn't fool around with her basic recipe but I am always tempted to "gild the lily", adding different ingredients to the basic batter or using a different broth base.

Dumpling Variations:

—Parsley dumplings: Add ¼ cup (50 mL) finely chopped fresh parsley.

—Herbed dumplings: Add 1 tbsp. (15 mL) fresh or 1 tsp. (5 mL) dried tarragon, basil, rosemary, oregano.

—Cheese dumplings: Add anywhere from 2 tbsp. (25 mL) to ½ cup (125 mL) grated cheese. The dumplings will be heavier than usual but if you like cheese, you won't mind heavier dumplings.

—Tomato dumplings: Cook plain dumplings in a tomato sauce like Basic Red Sauce, page 130.

When the first peas of the season are ready, add them to this easy one dish meal.

First Peas of Summer with Chicken

¹⁄₃ cup	butter	75 mL
1	frying chicken	1
1 lb.	small new potatoes	500 g
salt and freshly ground pepper to taste		
2 tbsp.	lemon juice	25 mL
3	green onions and tops	3
1 cup	fresh peas	250 mL
¹⁄₄ cup	fresh parsley	50 mL
1 cup	sour cream	250 mL
1 tsp.	thyme	5 mL

Note: Frozen peas can be used in place of fresh.

Cut up frying chicken. Melt butter in a large skillet and slowly brown chicken pieces on all sides. Do not crowd the pan; do this in two batches, if necessary. Remove from heat and set aside.

Scrub the potatoes, remove a small strip of skin from around the centre and add them to the skillet. Brown in the same way as the chicken. Return chicken to pan (you can crowd now since the browning's finished) and season both chicken and potatoes with salt and freshly ground pepper. Sprinkle chicken with lemon juice, reduce heat, cover pan and simmer for 30-40 minutes.

Cut up green onions, tops included, and add to the chicken and potatoes, working onions down into the butter on the bottom of the skillet. Sprinkle peas and cut-up parsley over the chicken and potatoes, cover again and simmer another 10 minutes. Remove chicken and vegetables to a warm serving platter and keep warm.

Remove skillet from heat. Add sour cream and thyme to the liquids remaining in the skillet and stir until all bits have been worked into the sauce. Pour over the chicken or serve as a separate sauce.

Should serve 4.

Notes and Variations

If you are nervous about trying choux pastry (cream puff pastry), there is an excellent ready mix available at most supermarkets. However, it's not that hard. Try it at least once—as in this different recipe for an appetizer using choux pastry and chicken livers.

Gougere with Chicken Livers

²/₃ cup	water	150 mL
¹/₃ cup	butter	75 mL
²/₃ cup	flour	150 mL
3	large eggs	3
¹/₂ cup	diced cheddar cheese	125 mL
salt and pepper to taste		
¹/₄ cup	butter	50 mL
1 cup	chicken livers	250 mL
2	medium onions	2
6	large mushrooms	6
1 tbsp.	flour	15 mL
1 cup	chicken stock	250 mL
2	tomatoes	2
2 tbsp.	grated parmesan	30 mL
¹/₄ cup	bread crumbs	50 mL
1 tbsp.	butter	15 mL
2 tsp.	chopped parsley	10 mL

Note: In place of chicken livers, you may use strips of ham or small pieces of cooked game. Also, if you don't have chicken stock on hand, use a powdered chicken stock that can be reconstituted or canned chicken bouillon.

Thoroughly grease a large pie plate, baking dish or 8 individual souffle dishes.

Prepare choux pastry by putting water and butter into a heavy saucepan. As soon as the mixture boils, add the flour all at once and stir quickly with a wooden spoon. As soon as the pastry comes away from the sides of the pan, remove from heat. Add eggs one at a time, beating well after each addition. Stir in the cheese and season to taste.

In prepared dish or dishes, arrange the choux pastry, building it up around the sides and leaving an indent in the middle for the filling.

To make the filling, melt half the butter in a heavy skillet and saute the chicken livers over medium high heat for about 3 minutes until browned on all sides. Remove livers with a slotted spoon and set aside. Chop onions. Put remaining butter into skillet and cook onions slowly until soft. Slice mushrooms and add to the onions in the pan. Cook another 2 minutes.

Remove from heat and stir in the flour. Mix well and add stock. Return to heat and bring to a boil, stirring constantly. Remove from heat again. Stir in the cooked livers (or ham or other meat already cooked). Peel and slice tomatoes. Add.

Pour filling into prepared choux pastry. Sprinkle with parmesan cheese and bread crumbs which have been browned in 1 tbsp. (15 mL) butter.

In 400°F (200°C) oven, bake large gougere for 30-40 minutes; smaller ones for 15-20 minutes. The finished product should be puffy and brown, just begging to be eaten!

Garnish with parsley.

Poultry

One of the casseroles most often requested at the restaurant was Curried Chicken in Pineapple Shells, a request I was always happy to fill because I always liked the idea of serving food in its own container.

Curried Chicken in Pineapple Shells

2	large pineapples	2
3 tbsp.	butter	50 mL
1 tbsp.	curry powder	15 mL
½ cup	sliced onion	125 mL
1	green pepper	1
1 cup	sliced mushrooms	250 mL
2 cans	golden mushroom soup	2 cans (284 mL each)
pineapple cubes	cut from pineapples	
3 cups	cooked chicken	750 mL

Note: You could also use cooked shrimp or crabmeat in this recipe — in place of the cooked chicken.

Cut the pineapples in half, cutting right through the leaves so that each half has its share of leaves. Cut meat out of the pineapples, leaving 1″ (2.5 cm) shell. Discard the hard core. Chop the pineapple fruit that remains and set aside.

In a large skillet, melt butter. Stir in curry powder and let it warm slowly with the butter to bring out the flavour. Add sliced onion. Remove seeds from green pepper and cut it into strips. Add to the butter mixture. Add sliced mushrooms. Cook everything slowly until onions are transparent and other vegetables are well coated with butter and curry.

Add the cut-up pineapple, the 2 cans soup, undiluted, and the cooked chicken. Heat thoroughly. Put hot meat mixture into the pineapple shells and serve immediately.

Should be enough for 6 people but depends somewhat on the size of the pineapples. You can also find small pineapples and serve one half pineapple, filled with the chicken filling, to each individual.

Poultry

MEAT

Driftwillow Ranch and later The Flying N were primarily steak houses. Nothing else would have been suitable for a dining room located in the heart of beef ranching country.

My luck held out once more. Bud Harwood who had spent his earlier years as a butcher for clubs and restaurants in eastern Canada, learning his trade at a time when butchering was an art, was now semi-retired in Claresholm. Whenever I got into something beyond my depth — which seemed to be often in the early days, he'd come to my rescue.

From him, I learned how to make use of the larger cuts — the quarters, halves and loins of beef. From him, I learned how to cut and carve "Barons" of beef which, incidentally, are more than just a big chunk of roast. From him, I learned how to cut three sizes of steak: club, T-bone and porterhouse. And also from him, I learned how to deal with cuts of lamb … but that's getting ahead of the story. Westerners are beginning to enjoy lamb but there are still many who remember the mutton offered overseas during the war, or even more ingrained, remember the feuds between cattle ranchers and sheep farmers.

Anyway, Bud was and is still a great help.

Fashions in food come and go as with every other area of life. We did our share of adding and removing "in" things like beef fondue, steak shish kebab and even the unlikely combination of steak and seafood.

For special occasions if ordered in advance, we would prepare Beef Wellington. I don't use the liver paté layer. It seems too heavy for a delicate cut like beef tenderloin.

Beef Wellington

2 lbs.	beef tenderloin	1 kg
½ lb.	fresh mushrooms	250 g
3 tbsp.	butter	50 mL
1 tsp.	flour	5 mL
salt and freshly ground pepper to taste		
prepared puff pastry		

Notes: The easiest way to prepare puff pastry is to buy it in frozen food sections of the supermarket.

Remove any muscle tissue left on the whole tenderloin. Then place in an uncovered roasting pan and roast no more than 20 minutes at 400°F (200°C). This precooking step is important; otherwise the meat might not be cooked enough.

Chop the mushrooms up very fine. Melt butter in a frypan, add the mushrooms, flour, salt and pepper. Stir for several minutes.

Roll out the puff pastry and spread with the mushroom mixture. Place partially cooked tenderloin in the centre of the pastry, roll pastry over it and make a bottom seam. With extra puff pastry, make decorations to add to the top of the Wellington.

Bake according to the instructions on the puff pastry package.

Serves 4. Serve with tomatoes and/or mushrooms carved in interesting shapes.

For some special occasions, we'd roast a whole hip of beef. Depending on the size of the animal, these could weigh from an average of 40 pounds to as much as 80 pounds. In fact, putting one of these monsters into the oven one New Year's Eve put my back out and I spent the holiday bound up like a mummy with two positions to choose from—straight up or flat out.

Whole Hip of Beef

Buy a whole hip. Get the butcher to remove the bones but leave the meat in one big piece.

Put into a hot oven, 450°F (230°C), and sear quickly on the outside. Then turn the heat down to 200°F (95°C) and roast with the aid of a meat thermometer. If it looks as if it won't be ready by the time required, increase heat. If it's cooking too quickly, hold it.

When we needed a big roast for noon, we started the roast anywhere from 3 am-6 am.(The one pictured on page 107, a Murray Grey roast of 50 lbs., went into the oven at 8 am. and came out done just right at 3 pm. Apparently, some kinds of beef cook faster than others, the Murray Grey among them.)

When deciding whether to cover the roast or not, decide on your priorities. If left uncovered, the outside will be browner, ideal for those who like an outside cut. If covered, there will be more juices for gravy.

Beef

Speaking of gravy, the best kind is made without adding any extra liquid. Season pan juices with salt and pepper, and thicken with flour mixed into the fat floating on top. Stir well to prevent lumps although one cook used to claim that "a few lumps make it look more like home!"

If juices have cooked down too much, use water in which potatoes have been boiled but go easy on any extra salt. There's probably enough in the potato water.

The sauces generally known as "barbecue" sauces are usually made from the same basic ingredients — only the details differ. This recipe was a prize winner, chosen from hundreds of entries, so it should be one of the best. Use it for ribs, chicken, big roasts on the spit, hamburger, whatever you're doing on your barbecue.

Barbecue Sauce to Write Home About

1 cup	ketchup	250 mL
½ cup	water	125 mL
½ cup	dry sherry	125 mL
¼ cup	lemon juice	50 mL
2 tbsp.	vinegar	25 mL
¼ cup	butter	50 mL
2 tbsp.	worcestershire	25 mL
2 tbsp.	brown sugar	30 mL
½ cup	chopped celery	125 mL
1 clove	garlic, minced	1 clove
1	onion, chopped	1
1 tsp.	dry mustard	5 mL
2 drops	tabasco	2 drops
salt and pepper to taste		

Mix all ingredients together and simmer for 10 minutes. Cool and refrigerate until needed.

Use for basting meats before barbecue, or use during the barbecuing procedure.

Notes and Variations

Beef

Beef stroganoff became a great favourite at the restaurant, especially when Marj made homemade noodles! There are many versions of stroganoff — this is my favourite.

Beef Stroganoff

1 cup	flour	250 mL
1 tsp.	salt	5 mL
½ tsp.	pepper	2 mL
1½ lbs.	sirloin steak	750 g
4 tbsp.	butter	50 mL
2	medium onions	2
½ lb.	mushrooms	250 g
1 clove	garlic	1 clove
2 tbsp.	flour	30 mL
1 can (14 oz.)	consomme	1 can (284 mL)
2 cups	sour cream	500 mL
salt and pepper to suit the tastes of the household		
1 tsp.	paprika	5 mL
2 tbsp.	worcestershire sauce	25 mL
chopped parsley and more paprika for garnish		

Put the first three ingredients in a heavy plastic bag. Trim any fat or gristle off the steak and cut into pencil thin strips. (Try to use good quality steak for this recipe; there won't be as much to trim off and the flavour wil be that much better.) Toss the strips of steak in the flour mixture until lightly coated.

In a heavy skillet, melt the butter. Slice the onions and mushrooms, mince the garlic and add to the butter. Saute for about 5 minutes until the onions are just beginning to become transparent. Don't cook them completely because they will get more cooking as the meat is added.

Add the meat strips to the vegetables, adding more butter if necessary. Keep the pan fairly hot and sear the meat quickly on all sides. Keep tossing the pieces as they fry. For rare steak, fry for about 3 minutes, no more.

Remove meat and vegetables from the skillet and keep warm, not hot. You don't want them to cook anymore at this stage. About 2 tbsp. (25 mL) drippings should be left in the skillet. Pour off excess or add more butter to bring it up to that amount. Blend 2 tbsp. (30 mL) flour into the drippings, stirring well over medium heat to bring up all the brown bits left by the meat and vegetables. Add the undiluted consomme and stir until thick and smooth.

Turn heat down and add half the cream, salt and pepper to taste. Don't let the mixture get too hot or it will curdle. Add paprika and worcestershire sauce.

Just before serving, return meat and vegetables to the sauce and reheat to the point of boiling but do not boil.

To serve, spoon into a heated serving dish and garnish with remaining sour cream, paprika and chopped parsley.

When we moved the restaurant to the old airbase, we couldn't bring along the name Driftwillow which we had worked so hard to get in the first place! It was a registered ranch name and couldn't be transferred to an old supply depot. So it was back to the drawing board.

We wanted to keep our country and western atmosphere but we also wanted to recognize the fact that we were now part of an airport.

Some cattle brands have "flying" letters, especially some of the older ranches like the Flying U and the Flying E. This means that curves are added to the ends of the block letters on the brand, and it is read as "flying".

That seemed to be the solution—to take on a "flying" brand which would still sound like a western stopping place but would salute its new location as well.

Thus, we became The Flying N.

Recipes illustrated overleaf

When we first came to Alberta, a Scandinavian neighbor told me that the best meatballs had to be made with a mixture of beef, pork and, if available, a little veal. Then the meat must be put through the meat grinder several times to get just the right texture. Svea was right and we made her kind of meatballs for every smorgasbord.

Scandinavian Meatballs

2 slices	bread	2 slices
water, milk or stock to soak the bread		
½ lb.	ground beef	250 g
½ lb.	ground pork	250 g
½ lb.	ground veal	250 g
2	eggs	2
1 tbsp.	butter	15 mL
¼ cup	chopped onion	50 mL
3 tbsp.	chopped parsley	50 mL
1 tsp.	lemon juice	5 mL
1 tsp.	worcestershire sauce	5 mL
½ tsp.	grated lemon rind	2 mL
1 tsp.	salt	5 mL
¼ tsp.	paprika	1 mL
cornstarch to coat the meatballs before frying		

Soak bread in water, milk or stock to cover.

Put the three ground meats through a food grinder or food processor to produce a very fine mixture. Mix well together and add eggs.

In a small skillet, melt the butter and saute the onions until transparent. Add onions and butter to the meat mixture. Wring the liquid from the bread and add the bread to the meat.

Add remaining ingredients except the cornstarch. Mix well with your hands. Shape into 2″ (5 cm) balls which should result in about 60 small meatballs. If you have the patience, make the meatballs even smaller. Chill shaped balls.

When ready to cook, roll each ball in cornstarch. Heat oil in deep fat fryer to 370°F (190°C). Carefully drop the balls, one at a time, into the oil. Don't try to do more than 12 at a time and watch that the oil doesn't foam over the top of the pan. Fry until meatballs are golden brown and rise to the top of the oil. About 1-2 minutes should be enough but break one open to be sure they are cooked through — there shouldn't be any pink showing because of the pork in the mixture.

Drain on paper towels, Be sure to reheat oil between batches. Continue process until all are cooked. This can be done in advance and the meatballs frozen until needed. If frozen, reheat in a covered baking dish in a 400°F (200°C) oven for about 20 minutes.

Beef

Sweet and Sour Sauce for Meatballs

2 cups	pineapple juice	500 mL
1 cup	cider vinegar	250 mL
²⁄₃ cup	brown sugar	150 mL
1½ cups	beef bouillon	375 mL
¼ cup	soy sauce	50 mL
2 cloves	garlic	2 cloves
2 tbsp.	fresh ginger	30 mL
½ cup	cornstarch	125 mL
1 cup	water	250 mL
½ tsp.	salad oil	2 mL

Notes: The pineapple juice may include pineapple chunks in their own juice, unsweetened. Just be sure the total liquid measurement is 2 cups (500 mL). Ginger may be fresh, preserved or crystallized.

In a medium sized saucepan, mix together the first 7 ingredients. If you're using pineapple chunks, leave them out until the sauce is completed. Bring everything to a boil.

In a small bowl, mix the cornstarch with the water and salad oil. Using a wire whisk or wooden spoon, stir the cornstarch mixture into the boiling liquid. Cook, stirring furiously for 3 minutes. Add pineapple chunks if desired. Then place over hot water to keep hot.

To serve, place meatballs (see recipe above) in a chafing dish or electric wok and add enough sauce to coat all the meatballs.

If you like eye-watering freshly ground horseradish, serve it as is from the jar or the garden, but be sure to warn your guests! Otherwise, you can temper the flavour somewhat by mixing it with sour cream or whipped unsweetened fresh cream. Add the ground horseradish, a bit at a time, until you reach the desired strength.

There is a Danish recipe for a frozen horseradish cream that's made much the same way.

Frozen Horseradish Cream

2 cups	whipping cream	500 mL
1-2 tsp.	sugar	5-10 mL
1 tbsp.	lemon juice	15 mL
4 tbsp.	ground horseradish	50 mL
salt and white pepper to taste		

Notes: You may use freshly ground horseradish, or the kind that comes already prepared in jars. If using the prepared variety, cut down on the lemon juice. Most prepared horseradish is packed in a vinegary solution.

Whip the cream until it begins to thicken, then add sugar. Whip some more until cream is quite stiff. Fold in lemon juice, horseradish, salt and pepper to taste.

Pour into mold or small tray and freeze to sherbet consistency.

Serve with hot beef or chicken, herring, salmon or boiled codfish. Makes about 2 cups.

Whenever you have steak or roast, you always have stewing meat too. They haven't found a cow yet that produces nothing but expensive cuts. So we learned to make hamburgers, casseroles, stews and goulash (actually a high falutin' name for stew but who's checking?)

Beef Goulash with Noodles

4 lbs.	stewing beef	2 kg
salt and pepper and flour		
3 tbsp.	oil or shortening	50 mL
2 cloves	garlic, minced	2 cloves
2 cups	chopped onion	500 mL
5 tbsp.	paprika	60 mL
4 cups	water	1 L
¼ cup	tomato paste	50 mL
1 can (10 oz.)	beef broth	1 can (284 mL)
1 lb.	wide noodles	454 g

Dredge the beef cubes in a mixture of flour, salt and pepper. In a heavy skillet in hot oil or shortening, brown the beef on all sides. Add the garlic, onion and paprika (all five tablespoons which sounds like a lot but works just fine). Cook until onions are limp but not brown.

Add water and tomato paste. Cover tightly and simmer about 2 hours or until the meat is very tender. Lift out the meat and skim off the fat. Put meat back in and add beef broth. Mix well.

Cook noodles in boiling salted water until tender. Drain and rinse with boiling water. Add to the meat and gravy and mix well. Put into a casserole dish and keep warm until time to serve.

Serves 8.

Even if you're not wild about liver, reserve final judgment until you taste it cooked this way.

Golden Tower Liver

1 lb.	liver, beef or calf	500 g
⅓ cup	wine or wine vinegar	75 mL
¾ cup	fine bread crumbs	175 mL
¼ cup	parmesan cheese	50 mL
2 tbsp.	chopped parsley	30 mL
¼ cup	butter	50 mL

Trim membrane from pieces of liver. Marinate in wine or wine vinegar for several hours.

Mix together bread crumbs, parmesan cheese and chopped parsley. Roll the liver in this mixture to coat well on both sides. Melt butter in skillet and fry liver very quickly in hot butter. Do not overcook — about 2 minutes a side should do. What you want is a crisp brown outside and a faintly pink inside.

Serve at once. Serves 4.

Beef

Stew by any other name is Carbonada Criolla, an Argentinian version of stew.

Carbonada Criolla

½ cup	oil	125 mL
2 cloves	garlic, chopped	2 cloves
1	onion, chopped	1
1½ lbs.	rump beef cubed	750 g
½ cup	butter	125 mL
salt and freshly ground black pepper to taste		
1 bay leaf, a shake of oregano and parsley		
1	potato	1
1	medium winter squash	1
1	sweet potato	1
½ cup	kernel corn	125 mL
1 cup	beef broth	250 mL
1 cup	uncooked rice	250 mL
1	apple	1
3	peaches	3

Place oil in heavy large saucepan, add cut up garlic and onion and fry until golden. Add the beef, butter and spices, browning up the meat as you prepare the vegetables.

Peel both potatoes and cut into slices. Peel the squash and slice. Add potatoes and squash to the meat mixture along with the corn and beef broth. Cover the pot and let boil until vegetables are nearly cooked.

Peel the apple and slice. Scald the peaches, slip skins off and slice. Add both apple slices and peach slices to the hot mixture as well as the rice. Again cover the pot and let simmer until the rice is cooked. If more broth is needed because of evaporation, add it because the carbonada must be juicy though dense.

Serves 6. Accompany with crisp bread and a salad.

Don't let the stories of haggis put you off. Think of it as a Scottish meatloaf, nothing more. True, the original recipe called for it to be boiled in a sheep's stomach bag but very few people have access to such things anymore. Most of us make haggis in a baking dish, just like meatloaf. What did I tell you?

Haggis

½ lb.	liver	250 g
1	sheep's heart	1
1 cup	oatmeal	250 mL
½ lb.	beef suet	250 g
2	medium onions	2
1 cup	meat stock	250 mL
salt and pepper to taste		

Notes: Buy sheep or beef liver. Get your friendly neighborhood butcher to grind the suet, if possible. You can do it with a food grinder or processor but it's easier done elsewhere. As for the oatmeal, don't use the instant kind or you'll have instant mush.

In a large pot, boil the liver and heart for an hour. Remove from water and cool. Reserve the liquid that the meat was boiled in. Chop the heart fine and grate the liver, or process it in a food processor.

While the meat is boiling, toast the oatmeal in a shallow pan in the oven, shaking occasionally to get it evenly brown.

In a large bowl, mix everything together, adding the meat stock and salt and pepper to taste. Spoon into a deep baking dish (Pyrex is good) and cover with two layers of foil. Place on a rack over boiling water and steam for 2 hours, adding to the water supply as necessary. A canner works well for this step.

Serve with Clapshot, page 78, or Stovies Made With Tatties, page 77.

For the St. Patrick's Dinner (one in our series of international meals), we included Corned Beef and Cabbage. Of course.

Corned Beef and Cabbage

2 lbs.	corned beef	1 kg
1	leek	1
2 sprigs	parsley	2 sprigs
2	bay leaves	2
6	small potatoes	6
6	small carrots	6
cut up turnip, if desired		
1 head	green cabbage	1 head

Rinse the corned beef to remove any surplus brine. Place in Dutch oven and barely cover with hot water. Cut the leek partly through the green part, add it with the parsley and bay leaves to the water. Bring water to a boil, reduce heat, cover tightly and simmer the corned beef until fork tender. Generally, corned beef needs 1 hour per pound of total weight.

About 30 minutes before the meat should be ready, add the peeled potatoes and carrots and turnip, if desired. Increase heat slightly during this period to help cook the vegetables.

Meanwhile, cut the cabbage into eighths and cook in a separate pan in boiling salted water until tender.

Drain the corned beef, place it on a large platter and surround it with the drained cooked vegetables. Serve with hot mustard, fresh horseradish and/or mustard pickles.

When carving, cut on an angle across the grain. Watch the grain however; it changes! Serves 4.

My approach to cabbage rolls is a quick and easy one. Instead of making dozens of little packages of rice and meat tied up in cabbage, I make one big one. It's beautiful to look at, time saving and tasty to boot.

Super Cabbage Roll

1	cabbage	1
4 cups	canned tomatoes	1 L
1 can (6 oz.)	tomato paste	1 can (175 g)
2 tbsp.	brown sugar	30 mL
½ tsp.	worcestershire	2 mL
dash of allspice or nutmeg		
dash of salt		
1 lb.	lean ground beef	454 g
1	diced onion	1
1 clove	minced garlic	1 clove
½ tsp.	fresh ground pepper	2 mL
1 tsp.	sweet basil	5 mL
1 tsp.	dill weed	5 mL
1 cup	cooked rice	250 mL
2½ cups	water	625 mL

Pick a cabbage with bright green generous outside leaves. Don't get one that's been trimmed down to a tight centre section. Leave outside leaves on, washing off any soil and cutting a thin slice from the bottom of the core so it will stand up in a deep pot for cooking. To soften the leaves, immerse for a few minutes in boiling water, remove and carefully fold back the outer leaves. About 2 layers of leaves should be enough to wrap the filling. Remove the centre of the cabbage and set aside.

If the cabbage simply won't cooperate, remove outer leaves completely and reserve until just before serving. Blanch when ready to serve and place around cooked cabbage. If this method is used, hollow out the centre of the remaining cabbage but leave a shell of about 1″ (2.5 cm).

In either case, dice the remaining cabbage.

In a large heavy saucepan, mix tomatoes, paste, brown sugar, worcestershire, spices and salt. Over medium heat, bring to boiling; reduce heat and simmer 20 minutes, stirring occasionally. Remove from heat and set aside.

In a large deep Dutch oven, brown the ground beef, onion, garlic and pepper. Add 1 cup (250 mL) chopped cabbage. Cook over medium heat for about 15 minutes. Add cooked rice and 1 cup of the prepared tomato sauce.

Fill the cabbage shell with this meat and rice mixture and wrap securely with outer leaves. Tie, if necessary.

In the Dutch oven over medium heat, add water and stir, scraping up all the brown bits from the browning of the meat. Then add the rest of the chopped cabbage and the rest of the tomato sauce. Mix well. Put the filled cabbage, stem down, into this sauce. Simmer for 2 hours, basting occasionally.

To serve, remove string and expose the filling. Tuck the reserved outer leaves (if that's the route you went) around the cabbage and spoon a bit of the sauce on top.

Cut in wedges and serve. Serves 6-8.

Once upon a time, there was a lawyer in Calgary who raised sheep as a hobby. He asked us to prepare a special meal featuring lamb in every way, shape and form. And so we did.

We started with an appetizer of lamb kidney and liver. Then it was a Scotch broth made with ground up lamb, then a serving of moussaka made with eggplant, tomatoes and ground up lamb. And last but not least— a beautiful crown roast of lamb.

No, we didn't use lamb in the dessert.

Crown Roast of Lamb

Get a crown roast prepared by a reputable butcher. Ask for 2 chops per serving. Be sure the chine bone (part of the backbone connecting the ribs) is removed. This will allow the roast to be cut easily into manageable servings.

Crown roasts of lamb may be roasted exactly as they come from the butcher or you may wish to fill the centre with a bread or bread and ground meat stuffing. If not filling the centre, roast the crown upside down and insert a small tin can (both ends removed) to ensure the roast keeps its shape. If the crown is to be stuffed, cover the ends of the ribs with foil so that they won't burn.

Preheat oven to 450°F (230°C) but reduce to 350°F (180°C) as soon as you put the meat in the oven. Roast on a rack in a roaster, uncovered, allowing 25-35 minutes per pound, depending on whether you want rare or well done. Well done will register 180°F (85°C) on a meat thermometer; rare will be in the vicinity of 165°F (75°C).

Remove from oven, top each bone with a paper frill and listen for the accolades.

Leg of lamb isn't quite as spectacular as a crown roast but it's equally delicious and very easy.

Roast Leg of Lamb

5 lb.	leg of lamb	2 kg
salt and pepper to taste		
cloves of garlic to taste		

Remove any papery skin from the leg and rub the meat with seasonings. If you like the taste of garlic, make small slits deep into the meat and insert slivers of fresh garlic.

Preheat oven to 450°F (230°C). Place meat, fat side up, on a rack in an uncovered pan. Put into the oven and reduce the heat to 350°F (180°C). Roast 30 minutes per pound or until the internal temperature is about 175°F.

Serve with fresh mint chutney (page 136), tiny new potatoes (page 76) and new peas—if you should be so lucky!

My cousin Doris is as fond of lamb as I am and passed on this terrific recipe. Since her maiden name was Good, I'll call these Very Good Lamb Chops.

Very Good Lamb Chops

4	shoulder lamb chops	4
1 tbsp.	oil	15 mL
2	medium onions	2
4	medium potatoes	4
⅓ cup	white wine	75 mL
⅓ cup	chicken broth	75 mL
½ cup	tomato paste	125 mL
1 clove	garlic, minced	1 clove
¼ tsp.	thyme	1 mL
1 tsp.	minced parsley	5 mL
salt and pepper to taste		

Note: If you don't have any chicken broth around, you can use chicken bouillon or cubes that have to be reconstituted.

Brown the lamb chops in oil in a heavy fry pan. Transfer to a large baking dish. Chop up the onions and arrange in a layer over the lamb chops. Peel and slice the potatoes. Arrange them over the onions.

Combine wine, chicken broth, tomato paste, garlic, thyme, parsley and seasonings. Pour over the potatoes, onions and lamb chops.

Cover and cook over low heat on top of stove until vegetables and meat are done. Add more broth if necessary. Or bake in a 350°F (180°C) oven for about an hour.

And finally, a lamb stew. This one comes from South Africa and should be served with mealie pap which is just another word for cornmeal mush. If you'd rather eat this stew with crisp rolls and a salad, I won't tell.

Cape Town Bredee (Lamb Stew)

1½ cups	dried white beans	375 mL
2 tbsp.	oil or butter	25 mL
3	chopped onions	3
4 lbs.	mutton, cubed	2 kg
9	tomatoes	9
1 tsp.	salt	5 mL
¼ tsp.	dried chili pepper	1 mL
2 tbsp.	curry powder	30 mL
1 tbsp.	sugar	15 mL
¼ cup	water	50 mL
2 tbsp.	vinegar	25 mL
1 cup	chopped sour apple	250 mL
½ cup	raisins	125 mL

Place the beans in a large saucepan. Cover with water and let soak overnight. In the morning, drain, cover with water again and boil for at least an hour.

Lamb

Heat oil or butter in a heavy saucepan that has a tight fitting lid. Add onion and saute for about 5 minutes. Add meat and brown well on all sides. Peel and chop the tomatoes. Add along with the salt and chili peppers. Cover and cook over very low heat for 30 minutes.

In a small bowl, combine the curry powder, sugar, water and vinegar; stir until well blended. Add to the meat and onion mixture and stir until all ingredients are well blended. Drain the beans and add. Finally, add the apple and raisins. Stir well once again.

Cover and cook over very low heat for $2\frac{1}{2}$ hours or until meat is very tender. Small amounts of water may be added as required. The bredee should be thick, smooth and rich.

Now and then, local butchers forget the age old enmity between ranchers and sheep farmers, and they buy some local lamb and put it out for sale. There it sits unless someone like me comes along and snaps it up. I even get bargains in lamb because of the negative feelings in the west toward lamb.

The situation is changing somewhat, I think, judging by the number of restaurants which now offer rack of lamb.

Rack of Lamb Provencale

3 lbs.	rack of lamb	1.5 kg
2 cloves	garlic	2
3 tbsp.	olive oil	50 mL
1 tsp.	rosemary	5 mL
1 tsp.	thyme	5 mL
salt and pepper to taste		
$\frac{1}{2}$ cup	white wine	125 mL
$\frac{1}{2}$ cup	stock	125 mL

With a boning knife, trim rib ends of rack, removing meat and fat between the ribs down to the meaty part of the rack. Add these trimmings to $1\frac{1}{2}$ cups (375 mL) water, salt and pepper and boil for an hour. Remove from heat, chill and remove fat. This is the stock needed for the sauce.

Make incisions in the lamb with the point of a knife and insert slivers of garlic.

Heat oil in a roasting pan, put in the lamb, baste and sprinkle with the herbs and salt and pepper. Roast, basting often, in a 375°F (190°C) oven for about an hour or until meat thermometer registers 170°F for medium. It is not necessary to cook lamb until all the colour is gone as with pork.

Remove lamb to serving platter and keep it warm. Decorate with paper frills, if you want.

Remove and discard fat from the pan and add wine and stock to what's left in the pan. Mix well, scraping up all the bits that add colour and flavour. Bring to a boil and continue boiling until reduced in quantity by one half. Do not thicken in any way. Strain, adjust for seasonings and pass separately as a sauce.

Lamb

The following recipe for lamb has the best gravy, and is particularly good for dieters since most of the fat is removed before the lamb is served.

Top of the Stove Lamb

5 lbs.	lamb	2.5 kg
1 cup	water	250 mL
1 tbsp.	butter	15 mL
2	large carrots	2
4 stalks	celery	4 stalks
10 sprigs	parsley, chopped	10 sprigs
1 tsp.	dried sweet basil	5 mL
1	large onion, cloves	1
3 slices	unpeeled oranges	3 slices
3 tbsp.	lemon juice	50 mL
salt and pepper to taste		
1 cup	meat stock	250 mL
¾ cup	dry red wine	175 mL

Note: Lamb may be either a leg or shoulder cut. If you don't have beef or lamb stock on hand, used canned consomme but it will alter the flavour somewhat.

In a heavy Dutch oven with lid, place lamb and add water. Boil, covered, until water has evaporated and the fat has begun to run from the roast. At this point, add the butter to the fat in the pan and brown the meat, turning as necessary. More of the lamb fat will be released. When nicely browned, remove the roast and discard all the fat in the Dutch oven. Don't wash it just yet, however!

Clean and slice carrots and celery. Chop up the parsley. Put all three along with the basil into the bottom of the unwashed Dutch oven. Stick about 5 whole cloves into the onion and arrange it on the bed of vegetables as well, cutting it in half, if need be, to leave room for the roast. Top with the orange slices. Put the roast back in the pan, right on top of the vegetable/citrus base. Add salt and pepper to taste, and pour the meat stock (or canned consomme) over the lamb.

Cover and simmer on the stove for approximately 2 hours on the lowest heat possible. Add red wine at this point and return to simmer for another 15 minutes.

Remove meat and keep warm. Pour the sauce in the pan into a food mill, or blend in a blender, until pureed. Taste and adjust seasonings.

Serve roast with sauce separate.

Notes and Variations

Lamb

After you have enjoyed the leg of lamb as above, hope that you have enough left over to make Super Left-over Lamb with Onions.

Super Left-over Lamb with Onions

2-3 cups	cooked lamb	500-750 mL
3 tbsp.	butter	50 mL
2	medium onions	2
1 clove	garlic, minced	1 clove
¼ cup	dry white wine	50 mL
¼ tsp.	thyme	1 mL
1	bay leaf	1
1 tsp.	chopped parsley	5 mL
salt and pepper to taste		

Remove cooled cooked lamb from the bone and cut into bite sized pieces, removing excess fat. Reserve bone.

Melt butter in a heavy Dutch oven or big fry pan and add chopped onions and garlic. Saute until golden. Add cut up meat, bone, wine and seasonings. Cover and cook over very low heat for about an hour, stirring occasionally. When done, remove bone.

Serve with rice, noodles or small new potatoes. Serves 2-4.

Notes and Variations

Lamb

While western ranchers may not have liked lamb (without some persuading), they had no such problems with pork. Anything went—from whole roast suckling pigs to the lowly porkchop.

And speaking of the lowly porkchop, why not try Stuffed Double Pork Chops, a version that's not so lowly at all.

Stuffed Double Pork Chops

4	double pork chops	4
¼ cup	melted butter	50 mL
½ cup	chopped onion	125 mL
2 stalks	celery	2 stalks
2 cups	bread crumbs	500 mL
1	apple, chopped	1
salt, pepper and poultry seasoning to taste		

Note: You can't buy double wide pork chops off the counter. You'll have to special order from a friendly butcher. Ask for chops about 1½″ (3 cm) thick. Also ask that a pocket be cut in from the fat side right to the bone. This is the area that will be stuffed.

Melt butter in a skillet, add chopped onion and chopped celery and saute for a few minutes. Add bread crumbs and chopped apple and mix together. Season to taste.

Stuff bread dressing into the pockets of the pork chops. Brown chops in a heavy skillet and then finish baking in 350°F (180°C) oven for about an hour. The meat should be white when done with no sign whatsoever of pink. If using a thermometer, it should read at least 185°F (85°C).

After the holiday baked ham has been twice around—hot and cold—it's time for an entirely new idea. The following recipe uses ham in a sweet and sour sauce with a potato topping, and it's a welcome change.

Island Style Ham and Potatoes

6	sweet potatoes	6
1 tbsp.	butter	15 mL
½ tsp.	salt	2 mL
dash of black pepper and nutmeg		
enough milk to whip the potatoes		
2 cups	diced cooked ham	500 mL
2 tbsp.	butter	25 mL
½ cup	green pepper	125 mL
2½ cups	pineapple chunks	625 mL
2 tbsp.	brown sugar	30 mL
1 tbsp.	cornstarch	15 mL
¾ cup	pineapple juice	175 mL
2 tbsp.	vinegar	25 mL

Note: Sweet potatoes are traditionally associated with ham but, if you prefer, you can use white potatoes for the topping.

Boil or bake the potatoes or use canned potatoes that have been drained well. Mash with butter, salt, pepper and nutmeg. Using a portable mixer, whip the potatoes with enough milk to make them soft but not sloppy.

In an oven proof skillet or flame proof casserole, melt the 2 tbsp. (25 mL) butter and saute the ham until golden. Add diced green pepper. Drain the pineapple chunks, reserving the juice. Add drained pineapple to the ham mixture and cook for 2-3 minutes.

In a small bowl, mix together the brown sugar, cornstarch, pineapple juice and vinegar, stirring until all lumps are worked out. Add to the hot ham mixture and stir until clear and thickened.

Drop spoonfuls of potatoes on top and bake in a 400°F (200°C) oven for 30-40 minutes until potatoes are nicely browned and the ham is bubbling hot.

Every western restaurant, worth its monosodium glutamate, must have a sweet and sour recipe. So did we, minus the you-know-what.

Sweet and Sour Spareribs

2 lbs.	pork spareribs	1 kg
2 tbsp.	salad oil	25 mL
2 tbsp.	ground ginger root	30 mL
1 clove	garlic	1 clove
4 tbsp.	cornstarch	50 mL
½ tsp.	dry mustard	2 mL
1 tsp.	salt	5 mL
½ cup	sugar	125 mL
4 tbsp.	soy sauce	50 mL
⅓ cup	vinegar	75 mL
2 cups	water	500 mL

salted almonds to top the dish when finished

Note: Get the butcher to cut spareribs into 1-rib pieces.

In a large saucepan, cover the spareribs with boiling water and simmer, covered, for about 10 minutes. Drain thoroughly and dry with paper towels.

In a large skillet, heat the salad oil and brown the ribs well. Drain off all fat and leave ribs in pan.

While ribs are browning, peel and grind fresh ginger root. Chop garlic in fine pieces. Place both in a small bowl along with cornstarch, dry mustard, salt, sugar, soy sauce, vinegar and water. Mix together well and pour over browned drained ribs in skillet. Cover and simmer, stirring occasionally, for about 20 minutes.

Serve on a bed of rice and top with salted almonds.

Pork

The restaurant used to cater to regular meetings of service clubs, the members of which always requested a plain "meat and potatoes meal". The only exception they allowed was this casserole which uses both cooked chicken (or turkey) and ham.

Country Buffet Casserole

5 lb.	chicken	2 kg
1 small can	mushrooms	1 small can
1 cup	ripe olives	250 mL
¾ lb.	wide noodles	375 g
⅓ cup	chopped onions	75 mL
⅓ cup	green peppers	75 mL
1 can (10 oz.)	mushroom soup	1 can (284 mL)
1½ cups	cheddar cheese	375 mL
¼ cup	pimientos	50 mL
1 cup	green peas	250 mL
½ tsp.	salt	2 mL
½ tsp.	celery salt	2 mL
1 cup	diced cooked ham	250 mL

Note: You don't have to start from scratch on this recipe. You could also use 4-5 cups chicken or turkey already cooked.

However, if you are starting from scratch, boil the chicken first in 4 cups water, 1 tbsp. (15 mL) salt, some celery tops, 1 sliced onion, 1 bay leaf. Simmer, covered, for 1½-2 hours or until tender. Remove from broth and allow to cool. Then cut meat off for the following recipe. Skim the fat off the broth and reserve both the broth and fat.

To the broth, add the liquid from the cans of mushrooms and olives. Measure and add water, if necessary, to make 6 cups. Bring to a boil and add noodles, cooking them until just barely tender.

Meanwhile, in 2 tbsp. of the reserved chicken fat, saute chopped onion, green pepper and mushrooms for about 5 minutes. Add to the chicken pieces. If you are very fond of olives, add the entire quantity called for to the meat pieces as well, but if your family is divided, reduce the quantity by one half and use on top of the casserole — where they can be seen and avoided by those who don't like them.

Do not drain the noodles. Just leave them in the liquid they were cooked in, and add the soup, grated cheese, pimientos, green peas, salt and celery salt.

In large casserole, arrange meat and noodle mixtures in layers, ending with noodles. Top with the diced ham and olives (if you have some left). At this point, casserole can be chilled or frozen.

If baking from a chilled state, bake at 325°F (160°C) for about 2 hours until bubbling hot. If the casserole has just been assembled and is still hot, bake for about 1 hour.

Pork

When we moved to our land high on a bluff overlooking Willow Creek, I could see where the buffalo must have roamed years and years ago, before fences and roads and guns. But there were certainly none to be seen then — even back in the Porcupine Hills behind us. The few remaining specimens had been collected up by the Canadian government and given sanctuary in Wood Buffalo National Park, a huge wilderness refuge in northern Alberta and the Northwest Territories.

As the herds grew in this protected environment, a limited number were made available through sale by tender, and one or two ranchers in our area stocked the great beasts. It was fun to see them again — home on the range where they belonged!

It was even more fun to come up with ways of using the meat — on those rare occasions when a buffalo was slaughtered and used for a banquet or special party.

In fact, buffalo can be used in any way that beef is used. The bones are heavier, the meat is darker and the fat usually has a yellow tinge but other than that, it looks and behaves much like beef. However, all that aside, I think it's important to present buffalo for what it is — buffalo — with its own taste and style.

Baron of Buffalo Roasted

Roasting time can vary so greatly from one animal to another that it's safest to use a meat thermometer inserted into the thickest part of the roast. Don't let it touch the bone or the readings will be off. For rare, the thermometer should read 140°F (60°C); for medium it should read 160°F (70°C); for well done it should read 170°F (75°C).

If you don't have a thermometer, estimate that the roast should take 15-18 minutes per pound for rare, 22-25 minutes per pound for medium, and 27-31 minutes per pound for well done.

There will be less shrinkage if roasted in a slow to moderate oven.

Rub a mixture of salt and freshly ground pepper over the roast. If it's very lean, wrap with extra suet — either buffalo or beef — and that will baste the roast as it cooks.

Buffalo Steaks

Steaks cut from the loin can be broiled or grilled as you would any good beefsteak. For less tender cuts, marinate the steaks for 24 hours. Marinade, page 105.

Buffalo Stew

Buffalo meat cut into small cubes may be substituted for the deer meat in the recipe for Deer in Beer on page 127. Prepare the casserole as outlined in the deer recipe, right up to the time of baking. Then put it into a large casserole and let cool.

About an hour before serving, cover with a good rich pastry (page 181). Cut a steam hole in the middle or use an ornamental blackbird baked in a pie, little ornaments especially made for letting steam escape from pies.

Bake at 425°F (215°C) for 45 minutes or until crust is browned and the meat has reheated thoroughly.

Wild Game

Buffaloaf

Use ground buffalo as you would ground beef in meatloaf, buffalo burgers, meat sauces for pasta dishes. For meat balls, use the recipe for Scandinavian Meat Balls on page 109 . Let the buffalo meat replace the beef.

Buffalo Ribs

After several special dinners featuring buffalo meat, we ended up with a lot of rib bones. They looked like they had possibilities so I sawed them up, seared them quickly in a hot oven — 450°C (230°C) — to get them browned and then let them cook slowly at 325°F (160°C) for the next several hours.

As they cooked, I sprinkled generous handsful of the dry mix used for making onion soup over the bones and added about an inch (2.5 cm) of red wine. The ribs were turned as they got brown on top.

After 2-3 hours of roasting, the wine had cooked down into a thick glaze and the meat was beautifully tender. Finger lickin' good, if ever there was such a thing!

You could do the same with beef ribs.

Spit Roasted Buffalo

Sometimes, large roasts done on a spit are more trouble than they're worth. The barbecue has to be rigged up with special equipment to keep the spit turning, or relays of willing volunteers have to be enlisted to keep everything moving.

The best size for a spit roast is no more than 10 lbs. (4.5 kg). Get the meat boned and tied into rolls that will balance evenly on the spit or rotisserie. Rub a mixture of salt and freshly ground pepper over the roast, wrap with extra fat if possible.

With this type of cooking, expect a fair amount of shrinkage. You can cut down on that somewhat by precooking the roasts in an oven and just finishing on a spit outside, thus getting the best of both worlds.

To prevent charring from flare-up flames, keep coals to either side of the roast with a drip pan underneath the meat.

For timing, see Baron of Buffalo, page 123.

Notes and Variations

Wild Game

Getting enough water was an eternal problem at the first restaurant, the one out in the country. Many's the time that water had to be hauled from town several times in an evening just to keep the cistern full enough to supply the kitchen.

No wonder then that a sign on the bathroom door read, "Do not flush unless absolutely necessary." That bathroom sign was mentioned in almost every news story about the restaurant and was prominently featured in a television special ... once more proving that one person's news is another person's problem!

Recipes illustrated overleaf

One of the recipes I made for the Wild Game Dinner in Claresholm in 1983 was Deer in Beer, a combination that seemed to appeal to the imagination and the taste buds of the stag audience.

Willowcreek Deer in Beer

4 lbs.	deer	2 kg
½ cup	flour	125 mL
½ cup	oil	125 mL
2 lbs.	onions, chopped	1 kg
6 cloves	garlic, crushed	6 cloves
3 tbsp.	brown sugar	50 mL
¼ cup	wine vinegar	50 mL
½ cup	chopped parsley	125 mL
2	bay leaves	2
2 tsp.	thyme	10 mL
1 tbsp.	salt	15 mL
¼ tsp.	pepper	1 mL
2½ cups	beef broth	625 mL
3 cups	beer	750 mL

Cut deer meat into cubes and dredge in flour. In a large heavy skillet, heat the oil and brown the deer chunks, a few pieces at a time. Transfer browned meat to a large heavy casserole or baking dish.

Brown the chopped onions and garlic in the oil remaining in the skillet, then add to the casserole. Also, sprinkle the brown sugar, 2 tbsp. (25 mL) of the vinegar, the parsley, bay leaves, thyme, salt and pepper over the meat in the casserole.

Pour any excess oil out of the skillet; add broth and heat, stirring to deglaze and bring up all the brown bits left from the frying process. Pour over the casserole. Finally, pour the beer into the casserole mixture.

Cover and bake for 2 hours or until meat is tender. At the end of the baking period, add the remaining vinegar.

Serve with dumplings, recipe page 98. Serves 12.

Notes and Variations

Wild Game

I can't leave the subject of wild meat without telling you about Barbwire Johnny and his recipe for porcupine. At the time I had the privilege of meeting him, he was 83 years old and one of the most colourful characters in southern Alberta.

He moved to the west in 1890 when he was ten years old. At 14, he began working at various ranches, then for the CPR and finally—when he had enough money to buy two horses and a saddle—he went cowboying.

He got the name Barbwire from the owner of the ranch where he was breaking colts and night riding. He came in, night after night, so scratched up from tangles with newly strung barbwire, that he was dubbed "Barbwire".

Stories of his ranching and exploring exploits would fill a book but what I like best are his recipes. Incidentally, I have not tested any of these but they are among my favourites!

This is from a tape made when he visited Driftwillow.

Porcupine Pie and Other Ideas

"Catch the porcupine, hang him hind end up over a blazing fire. Skin him first, soak in salt and soda to get the barkey taste off. To skin him, slit him up the belly, roll the skin out so you won't get them quills. Them quills has a screw in them like an auger; they bore right into you. If you get one they go right through you; if one gets to bealing, you got to cut it out.

Parboil the porcupine three times, then throw away the water. Turn him end for end and the grease just sizzles out. They taste good, better'n a skunk.

I've et lots of muskrats too; they're good and the skin's worth money.

One time on the Livingstone, a young lad was with me. He had a .22 and he was hungry, so he shot a porcupine. We skinned him and cooked him and ate two legs for supper and two legs for breakfast. He was good. He's good with potatoes or bread too.

To can fish, catch yore trout and clean them. Pack in sealers, five or six on their end and put in a teaspoon salt. Some people put in water, not me. I just let them cook in their own juice. Put them in a boiler on the stove; don't seal them tight or they blow up. Just as good as salmon."

Wild Game

PICKLES & RELISHES

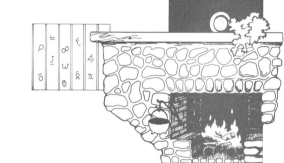

I am never happier than when I'm in the midst of making pickles and relishes. First of all, there's the smells coming from the big pots as the mixtures cook down to rich fiery sauces. Then there are the sights — whole pink crabapples with cloves, pale translucent squares of watermelon rind, blue plum catsup, chopped pepper relish. The whole experience is a pleasure from the time the fruits and vegetables come into the house until they are finally eaten or given away!

Using so many large watermelons in fruit boats for the restaurant, I had lots of material and opportunity to make watermelon rind pickles. The best watermelon for this purpose is one with a very thick shell.

Marigold Watermelon Rind Pickle

7 lbs.	watermelon rind	3 kg
Water to cover and alum		
4 lbs.	sugar, not brown	2 kg
4 cups	vinegar	1 L
4 oz.	stick cinnamon	125 g
2 oz.	whole cloves	60 g

Use watermelon for fruit boats or enjoy it out of hand. Then ... cut into 1″ (2.5 cm) strips, peel off the green, peel off all but a very thin layer of the pink. Cut into 1″ (2.5 cm) squares.

In a large crock or non-metal container, cover the rind with water, adding 1 tsp. (5 mL) powdered alum for each 4 cups (1 L) of water used. Let stand overnight. In the morning, drain, rinse and put into large heavy kettle. Cover with water again, bring to a boil and cook until tender. Check by piercing with a toothpick. Drain well, and dry on cloth towels. Weigh the rind at this point — this is when you should have 7 lbs. (3 kg).

In the same large heavy pot, combine the sugar, vinegar, cinnamon and cloves. Cook for 20 minutes. Add dried melon and cook slowly another half hour until melon is very tender and almost clear.

Pour into sterilized jars, tucking a piece of cinnamon into each jar, and seal.

Notes and Variations

When I fell heir to several bushels of small tomatoes, thanks to a local gardener who began a hydroponic experiment, I discovered this basic red tomato sauce which has since become a staple in my household. I use it as a base in all kinds of ways.

Basic Red Tomato Sauce

9 lbs.	raw tomatoes	4 kg
1½ cups	vinegar	375 mL
1½ cups	sugar	375 mL
⅔ cup	ground onions	150 mL
½ cup	green pepper	125 mL
1 tbsp.	pickling salt	15 mL

Note: You may use white or cider vinegar, brown or white sugar. You may also use ordinary salt, but the coarser pickling salt is better.

Wash tomatoes and remove any leaves, stems or bad spots. Put into large heavy pot and cook, without adding any water, until juices form and tomatoes are soft. Turn into a colander and drain, reserving the juice.

At this point, you can either reduce the juice by boiling it on high heat until only ¼ of the original is left — a process that takes about 30 minutes. Or you can simply freeze it in plastic containers to be used later for soups or pot roasts or beverages.

In the meantime, press the drained tomatoes through a food mill or colander to remove the skins and most of the seeds. Heat the remaining tomato mixture to boiling, add the reduced juice if you've gone that route. Stir in the vinegar and sugar. Grind up the onion and green pepper and add. Finally, add the pickling salt.

Simmer until thick, about an hour. Stir occasionally.

Seal in hot sterilized jars.

The sauce is very mild in this form but with the addition of suitable seasonings, it can become a barbecue sauce, a paste for pizza or other pasta dishes, a quick addition to baked beans, a base for stews. It's one of the most versatile things in my bag of tricks!

When tomatoes are plentiful and you have company or family who will eat everything promptly, make this uncooked Tomato Chutney.

Uncooked Tomato Chutney

4 lbs.	tomatoes	2 kg
2 tbsp.	minced onion	25 mL
2 tbsp.	fresh ginger root	25 mL
1½ tsp.	grated lemon rind	7 mL
¼ tsp.	turmeric	1 mL
salt and pepper to taste		

Note: There's really no good substitute for fresh ginger root. The best idea is to get a good sized chunk and keep it in the freezer. Whenever you need some, just remove the brown peel and grate what you need or chop it up fine.

Blanch and skin tomatoes. Chop and allow to drain in a colander, pressing out the colorless liquid. Discard the liquid. Put the pulp into a food processor or blender.

Mince the onion, grate the ginger root and lemon. Add to the tomato pulp along with the spices. Blend briefly—you don't want mush.

Serve with beef or fish, and use up within a few days or the flavours will flounder.

At Driftwillow, we have a problem keeping deer out of our vegetable garden. Some years they eat more than we do. In fact, last year, the only things they did not eat were potatoes and zucchini, the potatoes which we had plenty of and the zucchini which reproduce faster than any kitchen can ever keep up with!

Miss a day's picking and little green zucchini that look just right for salads have exploded into monsters that are good only for stuffing and baking, or pickles. This is when Pearl's recipe for zucchini relish comes in handy, and even zucchini haters love it. It's an excellent relish for hot dogs and hamburgers and disappears quickly at cookouts.

Pearl's Zucchini Relish

10 cups	grated zucchini	2.5 L
4 cups	chopped onions	1 L
2	green peppers	2
2	red peppers	2
5 tbsp.	pickling salt	60 mL
4 cups	sugar	1 L
2¼ cups	vinegar	550 mL
1 tsp.	celery seed	5 mL
1 tsp.	turmeric	5 mL
1 tsp.	dry mustard	5 mL
1 tbsp.	cornstarch	15 mL

Wash at least 2 large zucchini, 5 or 6 medium sized. Remove the seeds but leave the peel on. Grate with the medium sized blade on a food processor to make a total of 10 cups. Also chop up enough onion, the red and green peppers.

Put into a large crock or bowl (not metal) and sprinkle with the coarse salt. Mix well and let stand overnight. Next morning, rinse well and drain.

In a large kettle, mix the sugar, vinegar, celery seed, turmeric, dry mustard and cornstarch. Make sure all lumps are worked out. Cook, stirring occasionally, until clear. Add the prepared vegetables and cook another 15 minutes.

Pour into hot sterilized jars and seal.

Pickles

When the red and green peppers are in good supply and a good price, buy in quantity and toss them into your deep freeze. They can be used in any cooked recipe that calls for peppers—just cut off as much as you need and toss the remaining piece back into the freezer. They're really very obliging that way!

Thus, you can make this relish when the peppers are at their fresh best, or later in the winter when you have more time.

Pepper Relish

12	red and green peppers	12
1	hot red pepper (optional)	1
7 cups	sugar	1.8 L
1½ cups	cider vinegar	375 mL
1 bottle	liquid pectin	1 bottle (170 mL)

Note: The color of this relish is prettiest if both red and green peppers are used, but if red are not available, the flavour will be the same with all green.

Cut open peppers and remove the seeds. If you're including a hot red pepper, take care not to touch it directly. Use a fork. Put all the peppers through a food chopper or food processor, using the finest blade possible. If necessary, put through grinder twice. Drain in a colander and you should end up with about 2 cups (500 mL) pepper mush.

Put ground-up peppers into a large heavy saucepan. Add sugar and cider vinegar. Place over high heat and bring to a full rolling boil. Boil hard for 1 minute, stirring constantly. Remove from heat and add the liquid pectin. Stir and skim, if necessary, for 5 minutes to allow the mixture to cool a bit and to prevent the peppers from floating to the top.

Spoon into sterilized jars and cover at once with melted paraffin.

Makes about 10 jelly jars (10 oz. each). Delicious with hot or cold meats.

I couldn't count the gallons of raw cranberry relish I have ground up over the years. It's quick and easy, keeps well, and is extremely versatile in that it can serve as a layer in a jellied salad (combined with a red jelly powder in a layered salad, for instance) or serve as salad on its own.

Raw Cranberry Relish

4 cups	raw cranberries	1 L
2	large oranges	2
2	large apples, cored	2
2 cups	sugar	500 mL

Note: Frozen cranberries can be used but it will change the nature of the relish. Do not thaw but put into grinder along with other fruits just before serving. The product will be a semi-frozen slush which is very refreshing and different. If it has to hold for any length of time, pop it back into the freezer but do not let it freeze hard.

If using fresh cranberries, wash first. Put cranberries, whole oranges and cored whole apples through grinder or medium blade of food processor. Stir in sugar.

Pickles

This basic formula can be changed in many ways — use more or less apples and oranges, for example, or add lemons and cut down on the other fruits. (In which case, you'd better increase the sugar … use your judgment.) Also, try 1½ cups (375 mL) honey in place of the sugar.

If the relish isn't eaten within a week, you can turn it into cooked relish simply by adding up to 1 cup (250 mL) extra sugar, boiling it all together for about 30 minutes and sealing in sterilized jars.

Pickled or spiced fruit is another standby to have on hand for company and family. Small firm peaches, pears or crabapples are all processed with the same syrup.

Mom's Pickled Fruit

30-35	small peaches	30-35
4 cups	water	1 L
4 cups	sugar	1 L
2 cups	vinegar	500 mL
2	cinnamon sticks	2
2 tsp.	whole cloves	10 mL
½ tsp.	ground ginger root	2 mL

Note: Pears, crabapples or apricots may be used in this recipe as well.

Prepare the fruit. For peaches, scald in boiling water for 2 minutes, remove skins and cut in half, removing the pit. If using apricots, there's no need to peel. Just make a slit in one side and slip out the pit, leaving the fruit more or less whole. Pears should be peeled, their cores removed. A melon ball cutter will help in the core removal and with luck and some skill, will leave pears whole. Crabapples are simply washed and left whole with stems still attached.

In a large heavy saucepan, mix together the water, sugar and vinegar. Put spices into a cheesecloth bag or metal tea ball and add to the syrup. Heat and stir until sugar is dissolved.

Add the fruit to the syrup and boil gently for about 10 minutes or until the fruit in question is tender but not soft. Remove from heat, take out the spice bag, and let the fruit stand in the syrup for several hours, stirring occasionally.

Sterilize pint jars and carefully place fruit in jars — about 7 peaches per jar, equivalent amounts of other fruits. Reheat the syrup and pour over fruit in the jars, filling each jar to a point about ¼″ (1 cm) below the lip of the jar. Seal.

This amount of syrup should fill about 5 pint jars.

Prune plums, I discovered, can be the base of very tasty chutneys as well as the power behind some powerful catsups (ketchups?) that can rival any of the store bought numbers.

Plum Catsup

4 lbs.	plums	2 kg
4 whole bulbs	garlic	4 whole bulbs
2 cups	vinegar	500 mL
4 cups	sugar	1 L
1 tbsp.	cinnamon	15 mL
½ tbsp.	cloves	7 mL
1 tsp.	pepper	5 mL
1 tsp.	salt	5 mL

Note: There is no need to spend time and tears trying to wrestle the skins off garlic cloves. Simply lay the cloves on a good solid board, one that you won't be using for cakes, and cover them with the flat side of a cleaver, small axe or broad kitchen knife. Then bring your clenched fist down on the cleaver or whatever, watching for sharp edges, and that's all there is to it. The garlic cloves will have shrunk away from their skins and will be ready to be plucked out in one piece.

Wash plums and remove pits. Peel garlic. Put both into a large heavy saucepan, add the vinegar and cook until tender. Cool and then press through a food mill or colander, thus removing plum skins.

Put the pulp back into the pot, add sugar and spices, salt and pepper. Boil until thick and seal in sterilized jars.

The word "chutney" comes from an Indian word meaning "to lick", which is only just and right. Once you discover chutneys, you can't stop licking!

Peach Chutney

3 lbs.	fresh peaches	1.5 kg
4	big apples	4
4 cups	brown sugar	1L
2 cups	raisins	500 mL
½ tsp.	preserved ginger	2 mL
½ tsp.	cayenne	2 mL
3 cups	white vinegar	750 mL
4 cloves	garlic, chopped	4 cloves

Note: There is a difference between preserved ginger and crystallized ginger. The crystallized is in candy form, covered with bits of sugar. The preserved comes in little jars. It is this kind we want.

Blanch peaches in boiling water for about 2 minutes and remove skins. Also remove pits and cut pulp into fairly small pieces.

Peel, core and chop up apples.

Put both into a large heavy saucepan. Add remaining ingredients and boil together until thick, about an hour.

Pour into hot sterilized jars and seal.

Besides being credited with aphrodisiac powers, chutney is supposed to work wonders for relationships between mothers-in-law and daughters or, as the case may be, mothers and daughters-in-law. Just make the chutney before the first monsoon and your troubles will vanish.

Pear Chutney

3 lbs.	pears	1.5 kg
10	green chili peppers	10
3 cups	raisins	750 mL
1¼ cups	sugar	300 mL
2	oranges	2
12	peeled cardamom seeds	12
¼ cup	poppy seeds	50 mL
10	whole cloves	10
1 stick	cinnamon (3″ long)	1 stick
1 tsp.	paprika	5 mL
¼ tsp.	nutmeg	1 mL
1 cup	white vinegar	250 mL
1 cup	chopped cashews	250 mL

Note: Whole cardamom seeds are cheaper to buy than the ground cardamom. Just peel something like garlic. Also note: Canned green chili peppers are available in ethnic sections of supermarkets. You can seldom find them fresh.

Prepare the ingredients: Peel, core and dice pears. Chop up chili peppers. Wash raisins and chop, if they're big. Grate oranges and squeeze juice, reserving both. Break up the cinnamon and put with the cloves into a cheesecloth bag or metal tea ball.

Combine all ingredients except for the vinegar and cashews. Add only ¾ cup of the vinegar at this point. Bring to a boil and simmer for at least 2 hours. Add remaining vinegar and cashews and simmer again until quite thick, perhaps another hour.

Pour into hot sterilized jars and seal. Store for at least a month before using.

Makes about 5 pints. Exceptionally good with ham.

Notes and Variations

Pickles

Most chutneys keep indefinitely but this one made with fresh mint has to be eaten up within 2-3 days. So far, this hasn't been a problem ... especially if fresh lamb is part of the menu!

Fresh Mint Chutney

½ cup	fresh mint leaves	125 mL
3 tbsp.	onion	50 mL
1 tbsp.	canned green chilies	15 mL
1 tsp.	fresh ginger root	5 mL
1 tsp.	sugar	5 mL
dash of salt		
1 tbsp.	cider vinegar	15 mL

Put mint, onion and chilies into blender. Chop up ginger root and add. Add remaining ingredients and blend until mixed. This will be a more solid form of mint sauce than the usual.

Chill for several hours before serving. Excellent with curries or lamb.

FISH

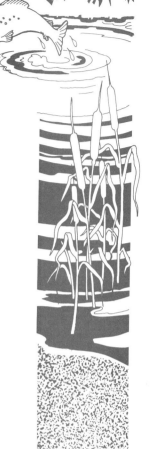

With the restaurant located on the western edge of the prairies, in the shadow of the magnificent Porcupine Hills, it goes without saying that we weren't able to get fresh salt water fish or shellfish. We couldn't even use our local fresh water trout because of government regulations. So we learned to do the best we could with frozen, smoked and canned fish and shellfish.

Some commercial establishments have set up fish farms recently and will someday be able to provide restaurant needs. But in the meantime, there's nothing like a Dolly Varden or rainbow trout caught in a pool fed by an icy cold mountain stream, cleaned and then cooked at the earliest possible moment over an open fire.

If you should be so lucky, dip the trout first in seasoned flour or cornmeal. Fry in lots of butter or bacon drippings and enjoy a rare treat.

Percy who brought us the trees that now tower over the highest part of the roof at Driftwillow could catch his limit of trout no matter how poor the luck of his fellow fishermen. He once told me that the only way to eat trout, after catching and cooking immediately, was like a cob of corn.

With the luck of Percy, a person might actually be able to duplicate the world famous Blue Trout of Switzerland, otherwise known as "truite au bleu". This recipe has always fascinated me, probably because it's nigh on impossible. You have to catch a trout, kill and clean it with the barest possible handling of the outside and get it into a vinegar water solution within seconds.

If you've been fast enough, the waterproof film on the outside of the fish will turn blue, proof positive that your fish is as fresh as it's possible to be. Other cooking steps follow, but this split second timing is the essence of truite au bleu.

Writers have waxed downright poetic over fish prepared this way. Hemingway and others called it "ambrosial nectar" and "pure unadulterated essence of trout".

Percy didn't have the high falutin' words or the complicated cooking procedures, but he would have approved.

I was once given a trophy that featured a mounted pike's head. It was an impressive sight, I must admit — this fish with its mouth gaping wide open, showing row upon row of needle sharp teeth. The local newspaper took a picture of the presentation and showed me holding up this prized memento. Under the picture ran the caption, "Old Fish Head".

I have endured many nicknames in my time but I was glad when this particular one faded from the scene.

A much happier memory is that of our trip across Canada by train, and of sitting in the dining car and ordering Lake Superior Whitefish, of course. I could almost see the chef throwing out a line and hauling in my fish right there and then.

In my food related collection of books, I have a 1920 manual of instructions to the dining car staff which sets out very precisely the size of the portions, the prices and exact instructions on how to make every item on the menu.

Nowhere does it mention catching a fish right out of the train window. So much for that fantasy!

The secret to successful fish cookery is DO NOT OVERCOOK. Cooking does not tenderize the flesh as is the case with meat. It toughens it instead.

Magic 10 Minute Rule for Fish

Measure fish at its thickest part, including stuffing if used. For *each* inch of thickness (2.5 cm), cook at high heat:
— 10 minutes if fresh or fully thawed
— 12-15 minutes if partially thawed
— 20 minutes if solidly frozen.
— If fish is cooked in foil, cooking time will be longer.
— Microwave cooking times will differ from the above. Consult the microwave manual.

When fish is cooked just right, it will separate into solid moist flakes when firmly prodded with a fork.

If fish is frozen, don't bother thawing unless you want to cut it into smaller pieces or marinate it, in which case thaw in the frig in the original wrappings, or if speed is of the essence, put the frozen fish into cold running water.

There are many ways to handle salmon ranging all the way from delicious to delicious. For many of the recipes, you'll need· this basic marinade.

Salmon Marinade

½ cup	salad oil	125 mL
¼ cup	lemon juice	50 mL
¼ cup	fresh parsley	50 mL
2 tbsp.	grated onion	25 mL
½ tsp.	dry mustard	2 mL
salt and freshly ground pepper		

Mix ingredients together.

Notes and Variations

Fish

The easiest version of baked salmon isn't really baked at all; it's steamed in a foil wrapping but produces a fine dish without too much trouble. Good for the novice.

Easy Baked Salmon

Clean a whole salmon. Place on foil and brush inside and out with basic marinade (above). Add about 2 tbsp. (25 mL) extra of the marinade to the package. Secure the foil around the salmon and bake over campfire or barbecue. Turn occasionally. Use the Magic 10 Minute Rule, page 138, but add about 1/3 more time because of the foil wrappings.

If barbecuing salmon fillets, get proper wire baskets to hold the fish. Otherwise, you're in constant danger of losing your dinner to the coals. It also helps to marinate the fillets for several hours in the marinade outlined above. That has the effect of tightening up the flesh. Also, brush the steaks with melted butter or the marinade as they cook on the barbecue.

If you're attempting to cook and decorate a large salmon for a buffet or special occasion, I recommend you cut it into sections first, then poach it in court bouillon and coat with Sauce Chaud-Froid.

Pacific Rim Salmon in Total

Clean and scale the fish. Then remove head and tail and poach them separately to be attached back onto the fish when the time comes. Bone the remaining centre section and cut in half lengthwise. Slice each half into 1/2″ (1 cm) pieces, arranging them on the pan in the proper order so you can reassemble the fish properly.

Poach head and tail for about 10 minutes in court bouillon; poach the centre slices about 5-8 minutes.

Cool, reassemble and glaze.

Court Bouillon

8 cups	water	2 L
1	small onion	1
1/4 cup	chopped carrot	50 mL
1/2 cup	chopped celery	125 mL
1/4 cup	fresh parsley	50 mL
1/2	bay leaf	1/2
1/2 cup	vinegar	125 mL
1 tsp.	salt	5 mL

Note: In place of the vinegar, you could use 1 cup (250 mL) dry white wine.

In a large heavy pan, bring water to a boil and add the remaining ingredients. Boil for 30 minutes and then strain.

Use for poaching salmon, or if you're planning on catching some very fresh fish, use as the base for truite au bleu, page 137.

Once the fish is cooked let it cool and cover with Chaud Froid. This Chaud Froid recipe works equally well as a covering for baked ham.

Fish

Quick and Easy Chaud Froid

2 pkgs.	unflavoured gelatine	2 pkgs. (7 g each)
¼ cup	cold water	50 mL
2 tbsp.	vinegar	25 mL
⅔ cup	cold water	150 mL
2 cups	mayonnaise	500 mL

Open one of the gelatine packages and measure out ½ tsp. (2 mL) gelatine. Place ¼ cup (50 mL) cold water in a small saucepan and sprinkle gelatine over it. Stir over low heat until dissolved. Set aside to cool. This will be the clear gelatine used as final decoration for the fish.

To make the chaud froid (or mayonnaise topping), combine vinegar and ⅔ cup (150 mL) water in another saucepan. Sprinkle on remaining gelatine and stir over low heat until it's dissolved. Cool.

Beat cooled vinegar mixture into mayonnaise until smooth; strain, if necessary.

Spoon over the fish and let it set 5 minutes. Coat again. If it isn't as smooth as you'd like, put it into a 375°F (190°C) oven for barely a minute. then chill. Keep spooning it on until you have a smooth even coat of chaud froid all over the fish.

Keep approximately ⅓ of the mixture for special touches — like ocean waves made by tinting some of the extra chaud froid and applying it through a pastry bag.

Green onion stems are often split and curled to make special garnishes for whole salmon. To attach onion pieces, dip them briefly into hot water to set the color and then into the clear aspic. Dip other decorative touches into the clear aspic as well. It will hold them in place as well as make them look shiny and attractive.

Further garnish with egg frogs and/or penguins, page 21. Serve with lemon slices or lemons cut in fancy patterns.

Tartar sauce also enhances salmon. This recipe comes from Rhea and Kirk, who serve me salmon every chance they get!

Tacoma Tartar

1 cup	mayonnaise	250 mL
1 tbsp.	chopped parsley	15 mL
1 tbsp.	sweet pickle	15 mL
1 tbsp.	green olives	15 mL
1 tbsp.	chopped capers	15 mL
1 tbsp.	chopped pimiento	15 mL
1 tsp.	minced shallots	5 mL
1 tsp.	prepared mustard	5 mL
1	hardboiled egg	1

Note: For recipes like this, buy the broken or salad olives. No need to pay for big perfect round ones. Also, you may find pieces of pimiento included in the jar which saves buying that item. If fresh shallots are not available, try to get a small package of the freeze dried variety. They reconstitute very easily. Or you can substitute a mixture of garlic and onion for the shallots.

Also note: The blender mayonnaise is outlined on page 70. Use lemon juice when making it for tartar sauce. Ordinary mayonnaise will work also.

Chop all ingredients that need chopping. Then mix everything together and taste. Adjust seasoning, and thin out with lemon juice, if need be.

Gravlax, otherwise known as Gravad Lox, otherwise known as a favourite Swedish treat, is another way to use fresh salmon.

Gravlax Instead of Smoked Salmon

2-3 lbs.	centre cut salmon	1 kg
²/₃ cup	sugar	150 mL
¹/₃ cup	pickling salt	75 mL
2 tsp.	ground pepper	10 mL
2 tbsp.	dried dill seed	30 mL
fresh dill weed, chopped		

Note: Get a centre cut of salmon. Pickling salt is best but ordinary salt may be substituted. If fresh dill is out of season, use dried dill weed.

Wash and scale the fish, pat dry. Cut the salmon piece in half along the line of the backbone. Remove any bones.

Mix sugar, salt and pepper. Rub this into the flesh side (the inside) of the fish halves. Place one piece, skin side down, in a glass or ceramic casserole. Sprinkle with half the dill seed, a layer of the fresh or dried dill weed and the remaining dill seed. Cover with the second piece of fish, flesh side down, reversing the slice so that the thick edge of one piece is on the thin side of the other. Sprinkle top with any remaining sugar/salt mixture and tuck extra dill weed around the edges.

Cover with wax paper and a plate that will fit down into the casserole. Weigh this down with a large can or rock. Place in refrigerator for 48 hours, turning the fish every 12 hours and carefully replacing the plate and weight. Liquid will start accumulating around the fish and this is where recipes differ. Some say this leached fluid should be poured off; other equally reliable sources say the liquid should remain until ready to serve. If you're faithful about turning the fish, I think you can safely drain off most of the liquid.

To serve, drain and open up the salmon halves. Scrape off the dill and spices from the inside. With skin sides down, slice diagonally through the fish to get very thin slices. Don't slice through the skin—leave that behind.

Serve on very thin wafers as an appetizer and garnish with lemon wedges, cucumber slices, chopped green onion and more fresh dill. It's particularly good on thin slices of rye bread which have been buttered with cream cheese. Top with chopped green onion and a squirt of lemon.

Very much like salmon lox, but much less expensive.

Fish

Many years ago, I found a recipe for a seafood casserole that was large enough to serve at least 10 people, delicious enough for special dinners and clever enough to allow most of the work to be done ahead of time.

My Favourite Devilled Seafood Casserole

2 lbs.	white fish fillets	1 kg
1 lb.	lobster meat	500 g
2 tbsp.	oil	25 mL
4 tbsp.	flour	50 mL
2½ cups	milk	625 mL
2 tbsp.	cornstarch	30 mL
¼ cup	dry sherry	50 mL
1 tbsp.	lemon juice	15 mL
1 tbsp.	grated horseradish	15 mL
1	minced clove garlic	1
1 tsp.	prepared mustard	5 mL
½ tsp.	salt	2 mL
1 tsp.	soy sauce	5 mL
1 tbsp.	worcestershire sauce	15 mL
4 tbsp.	ketchup	50 mL
4 tbsp.	chopped parsley	50 mL
1 tbsp.	butter, melted	15 mL

bread crumbs enough to cover top of casserole

Note: If using canned lobster meat, save out one or two of the red claw pieces to be used for garnish later.

Grease a large casserole dish and set aside, or grease large scallop shells.

In the top part of a double boiler over medium heat, cook the white fish fillets. Do not add any liquid. After about 20 minutes, the fish should flake easily. Set aside.

If the lobster is frozen, cook it in a similar manner for about 20 minutes. Don't break the fish into small pieces — it's better to be chunky. Canned lobster may be used as is.

In a large heavy saucepan, heat up the oil and add the flour, stirring well. Slowly add the milk, again stirring well until bubbly and thickened. Mix cornstarch with sherry and add to the creamed mixture, cooking for another 10 minutes.

Add the remaining ingredients except for the butter and crumbs. Also, add the fish and lobster to the creamed mixture and heat through.

Melt the butter in a small frypan and brown the crumbs in it.

Pour the creamed mixture into the casserole and top with buttery crumbs. If not required until later in the day, stop here and refrigerate until needed. If refrigerated, bring back to room temperature before final baking.

Bake in 400°F (200°C) oven for 30 minutes or until heated through and beginning to bubble around the edges.

Garnish with lemon wedges, parsley sprigs, and one or two of the red claw meat parts of lobster.

Fish

When we first opened the doors of the ranchhouse restaurant, people predicted no one would find us since we were "in the middle of nowhere".

Some years later, after we had moved to the old airport, I looked out the window. Several planes were parked on a nearby runway, now part of a private airstrip. Innumerable cars were parked in the parking lot and alongside the road. And to top it off, three horses were tied to the hitching rail. The various owners and drivers were in the restaurant having dinner.

We even had people literally "dropping in" to eat with us, dropping out of the sky in parachutes, since Claresholm quite regularly hosts sky diving competitions.

Who says we were in the middle of nowhere? I prefer a later description by a newspaper reporter who said we were "halfway to everywhere".

Recipes illustrated overleaf

My Favourite Devilled Seafood Casserole, page 142
Marinated Vegetable Salad, page 74
Cornsticks, page 34

Salad bowl courtesy Culinary Arts, Calgary

The Active 20/30 Club in Claresholm tried a first this year—a wild game dinner. I couldn't resist the challenge. They were to find the wild game, and I was to find a way to cook it. Thus did I spend a good part of the early spring looking for recipes for cougar, antelope, beaver, elk, moose nose, caribou and brown bear. We started the meal with poached rainbow trout.

Poached Rainbow Trout

4	rainbow trout	4
½ cup	dry white wine	125 mL
1 tsp.	seasoning salt	5 mL
¼ tsp.	dill seed	1 mL
¼ tsp.	rosemary	1 mL
romaine lettuce		

Note: Trout should be 6-8 oz. (200-250 g) each. At that size, this recipe will serve 4 main course meals or 8 appetizers.

Clean trout; remove head, tail and fins. Add seasonings to wine and poach the fish in the wine mixture for 15-20 minutes or until done. Allow fish to cool in poaching liquid.

When cool, remove skin and lift meat from bones in one solid piece.

Serve on bed of romaine lettuce with mayonnaise or tartar sauce. Mayonnaise recipe—page 70. Tartar sauce—page 140.

Recipes with imaginative names have always caught my fancy, but I prefer oysters in a recipe with a rather mundane name—Scalloped Oysters and Corn.

Scalloped Oysters and Corn

3 cups	cracker crumbs	750 mL
½ cup	butter	125 mL
16	canned oysters	16
4 cups	creamed corn	1 L
½ cup	cream	125 mL
1 tsp.	salt	5 mL
½ tsp.	pepper	2 mL

Butter a deep large casserole dish and set aside.

Crumble crackers into fairly large crumbs. Melt butter in a large skillet over low heat, add the cracker crumbs and toss together.

Open oysters and drain, reserving 1 cup (250 mL) of the liquor.

Mix together the corn, cream, salt and pepper.

Now, start layering the casserole. Put 1 cup (250 mL) of the crumbs in the bottom of the casserole dish. Cover with half the corn mixture. Cover with half the oysters and ½ cup (125 mL) oyster water. Add another layer of crumbs, the rest of the corn and oysters and the final layer of crumbs.

Bake in a 375°F (190°C) oven about 40 minutes.   Serves 8.

Fish

This molded crabmeat combination is the best I've ever found, made even more special by the unusual accompaniment of cranberries. It can be made in a ring mold and served with the cranberries in the centre. I generally make it in a fish shaped mold and pass the cranberries separately—in Grandma's cut glass bowl.

One of my guests at the first restaurant was horrified to discover me using the beautiful old bowl for customers. He explained how a chip or a bad scratch would destroy both the beauty and the value, but it added so much to the appearance of the table and the food that I just couldn't put it away. My worried customer came back a few years later, bringing his parents from Vienna for a genuine western experience. I brought out the cut glass bowl and they treated us in turn with the sight of them circling the floor in a graceful waltz.

Hazel's Crabmeat Mousse

1 pkg.	unflavoured gelatine	1 pkg. (7 g)
½ cup	cold water	125 mL
1 cup	salad dressing	250 mL
1 small pkg.	cream cheese	1 small pkg. (125 g)
1 can (10 oz.)	mushroom soup	1 can (284 mL)
1 cup	shredded crabmeat	250 mL
1	small onion, minced	1
1 cup	diced celery	250 mL
1 tsp.	worcestershire sauce	5 mL

In top of double boiler, melt gelatine with water, salad dressing and cream cheese. Add remaining ingredients, mixing well.

Pour into mold and chill. Turn out onto chilled platter, garnish and serve with jellied cranberry sauce.

I once served this as a stop gap; the really big meal would come the next night, I assured my guests. They liked it so well they asked for it the next night as well which has to be some kind of record! It also has the added advantage of being a good way to use up—you guessed it—zucchini.

Crab and Zucchini Casserole

1¼ lbs.	small zucchini	625 g
1	medium sized onion	1
½ cup	butter	125 mL
salt and freshly ground pepper to taste		
2 cloves	garlic	2 cloves
1½ cups	cooked crabmeat	375 mL
1⅓ cups	Swiss cheese	325 mL
1 tsp.	sweet basil	5 mL
1 cup	fresh bread crumbs	250 mL
3	fresh tomatoes	3

Grease a large casserole dish and set aside.

Wash but do not peel zucchini. Cut into ½" (1 cm) slices. Chop the onion. Melt half the butter in a heavy skillet and saute zucchini and onion until limp but not brown. Season to taste. Remove with a slotted spoon and set aside.

Cut garlic cloves in half. Add remaining butter to the skillet and briefly saute garlic and crabmeat. Discard garlic.

Cut cheese into small sticks. Cube the fresh bread. Scald, peel and chop the tomato. Add all three to the crabmeat in the skillet. Also return the zucchini and onions to the skillet. Mix lightly.

Pour into prepared casserole and bake, uncovered, in 350°F (180°C) oven for 30 minutes.

Serves 6-8. Can also be baked in large scallop shells.

I didn't use a lot of jellied salads in my cooking, but this one always brought them back for more. I got so used to making it that I lost the orginal recipe and had to make one all over again just to rewrite the recipe.

Jellied Shrimp and Cucumber Salad

1 large pkg.	lime jelly powder	1 large pkg. (170 g)
2 cups	boiling water	500 mL
¼ cup	lemon juice	50 mL
½ tsp.	salt	2 mL
1 small can	shrimp	1 small can (113 g)
cucumber slices, celery flowers as garnish		
¾ cup	diced celery	175 mL
¾ cup	diced cucumber	175 mL
3	green onions	3
1 small can	flaked tuna	1 small can
1 cup	mayonnaise	250 mL

Note: You can also use lemon jelly powder. Also, if you like your salad to bite back, use a combination of vinegar and lemon juice rather than lemon juice alone.

Dissolve the jelly powder in the boiling water. Add lemon juice (or combination of lemon juice and vinegar) and salt. Pour ½ cup (125 mL) into the bottom of a jelly mold, preferably a fish shaped mold but any shape will do in a pinch.

Rinse and drain the canned shrimp. Try to keep them whole. Place, one by one, into the jelly mixture in the bottom of the mold, making a pattern of some sort. Add cucumber slices and celery flowers to complete the pattern. Spoon more of the jelly mixture over the shrimps and let set.

Dice the celery, cucumber and green onion—tops and all. Mix with the flaked tuna and any shrimp left from first layer. Spoon into the mold.

To what's left of the jelly mixture, add the mayonnaise and beat until smooth. Spoon into the mold as the final layer. Let set.

DESSERTS

By now, readers of this book will be fully aware of my fondness for desserts. In fact, dinner or even a light lunch just does not seem compelte without something to finish off the meal. Obviously, my favourite time of the year is Christmas.

Long before the shortbread or cookies get under way, I set aside a day to make the Christmas pudding, a carrot pudding that has been in my mother's family for many generations. There are many similar pudding recipes but this one does not call for either spices or nuts, using instead lots of raisins, candied fruit and whole cherries. There's nothing to stop you from making your own additions — spices, nuts, dates, figs, whatever. You can also substitute butter for the suet. The pudding will still be good but it won't be Grandma's Carrot Pudding.

Grandma's Carrot Pudding

1 cup	raw potato	250 mL
1 cup	raw carrot	250 mL
1 tsp.	baking soda	5 mL
1 cup	raisins	250 mL
1 cup	glaceed fruit mix	250 mL
1 cup	whole cherries	250 mL
1 cup	flour	250 mL
1 cup	chopped suet	250 mL
1 cup	dry bread crumbs	250 mL
1 cup	brown sugar	250 mL
2	eggs	2
½ tsp.	salt	2 mL
1	lemon, juice and rind	1

Grate the potato and carrot. Add the baking soda and let stand.

Wash the raisins and mix together with fruit mix and cherries. Sift the flour over the fruit mixture and toss well.

Grind the dry bread crumbs until very fine.

Now, in a large bowl, beat the eggs, add the sugar, salt, lemon juice and rind. Fold in the bread crumbs, suet, fruit mixture and raw vegetables. Mix well.

If you want a large pudding to be turned out and brought flaming to the table, pack the batter into a large pyrex or glazed pottery bowl. Cover firmly with foil. If you prefer smaller containers, pack the batter into pint or quart sealers, filling them about ⅔ full with the tops on but not tightened. Steam for 2½ to 3 hours, depending on the size of containers used. If you used sealers, tighten them when the steaming is through and store in a cool place. For longer storage, freeze and bring to room temperature before resteaming.

To serve, reheat over hot water. Unmold the larger puddings whole and decorate as desired. For the pudding in the jars, spoon out the hot or reheated pudding and serve with suitable sauce such as the one that follows.

Tony's Favourite Hard Sauce

1 cup	icing sugar	250 mL
²⁄₃ cup	butter	150 mL
dash	salt	dash
2 tbsp.	rum or brandy	25 mL

Be sure butter is room temperature or softened by some means.

Add the sugar gradually to the butter, beating until smooth. Add the salt and rum or brandy. Continue beating until creamy. Chill in a bowl and let guests help themselves if you're serving the pudding or cake hot.

If you're serving the pudding cold, pipe the sauce onto the serving, using a rosette tube, and allow to harden.

As a variation, brown sugar can be used in place of icing sugar. The texture will be slightly grainy but the flavour is excellent.

When the restaurant was located in the old house at Driftwillow, customers found their way by turning at the Pulteney Siding, which in those days consisted of three grain elevators and two houses. The story is often told how Pulteney was the first place in Canada to have 100% volunteer enlistment at the beginning of World War II. Both men joined up!

One of my staff often made a dessert she called Pulteney Pudding, another version of Half Hour Pudding or the self-saucing puddings that are available in packages. This version is easy and very tasty.

Pulteney Pudding

1³⁄₄ cups	brown sugar	425 mL
3 cups	boiling water	750 mL
1 tbsp.	butter	15 mL
1 tsp.	vanilla	5 mL
2 tbsp.	butter	25 mL
¹⁄₃ cup	brown sugar	75 mL
1 cup	flour	250 mL
2 tsp.	baking powder	10 mL
¹⁄₂ tsp.	salt	2 mL
¹⁄₂ cup	milk	125 mL
¹⁄₂ cup	raisins	125 mL

Grease an 8x12″ (3 L) pan.

In a small saucepan, mix together the brown sugar, boiling water, butter and vanilla. Boil gently for 5 minutes.

In a medium sized bowl, cream the 2 tbsp. butter and the ¹⁄₃ cup (75 mL) brown sugar. Mix the dry ingredients together and add to the creamed mixture alternately with the milk. Fold in the raisins. Spread the raisin mixture over the bottom of the prepared pan. Pour the hot sauce over top and bake in 325°F (160°C) oven for about half an hour.

Serves 6-8. Serve warm or cold.

Aunt Dorothy's Coffee Marshmallow Pudding is quick and easy, and tastes like a terribly sophisticated mousse besides! If you find a bag of rock hard marshmallows in the back of your cupboard, don't despair. They'll work beautifully in this recipe.

Aunt Dorothy's Coffee Marshmallow Pudding

16	large marshmallows	16
½ cup	boiling hot coffee	125 mL
½ cup	whipping cream	125 mL

In a small bowl, stir the marshmallows into the hot coffee. Don't worry if they don't dissolve completely. Cool.

Whip the cream and fold into the cooled coffee mixture. Chill in serving dishes, topping with more whipped cream, if desired.

Serves 4-6.

My mother was a good cook but she stayed away from anything that she thought was "fussy". Thus, whenever she made Lemon Fluff Pudding, we knew that company must be coming for that pudding was as "fussy" as she'd ever get!

Mom's Lemon Fluff Pudding

4	eggs, separated	4
2	lemons	2
½ cup	sugar	125 mL
3 oz.	lemon jelly powder	85 g
½ cup	boiling water	125 mL
½ cup	sugar	125 mL
1 cup	whipping cream	250 mL
16	vanilla wafers	16

In the top of a double boiler, beat the egg yolks until creamy. Grate the lemon and squeeze the juice, adding both the rind and the juice to the egg yolks. Beat well. Add the sugar. Cook over hot water until thick.

In a small bowl, dissolve the jelly powder in the boiling water and add to the egg yolk mixture while still hot. Remove from heat and cool.

In a large bowl, beat the egg whites until stiff, adding the remaining sugar gradually. Fold the cooled egg yolk mixture into the egg whites. Whip the cream and fold it in as well.

Roll the vanilla wafers into fine crumbs. Butter 8-10 individual serving dishes and spoon in some of the crumbs, twisting the serving dishes around so that a good layer of crumbs gets caught in the butter. Reserve some of the crumb mixture for topping. Spoon the cooled lemon cream into the serving dishes, being careful not to disturb the crumb coating, and top off with the reserved crumbs. Garnish with more whipped cream and/or a very thin slice of lemon, slit from skin to centre and twisted.

Serves 8-10.

When the peach season is in full swing, I try to make Crusty Peach Cobbler at least once.

Crusty Peach Cobbler

3 cups	fresh peaches	750 mL
¼ cup	sugar	50 mL
1 tsp.	almond extract	5 mL
1 tbsp.	lemon juice	15 mL
1 tsp.	lemon rind	5 mL
1½ cups	flour	375 mL
½ tsp.	salt	2 mL
3 tsp.	baking powder	15 mL
1 tbsp.	sugar	15 mL
⅓ cup	shortening	75 mL
½ cup	milk	125 mL
1	egg	1
2 tbsp.	sugar	30 mL

Grease an 8x8″ (2 L) pan. Scald, skin and slice the peaches. Arrange them over the bottom of the prepared pan. Mix the ¼ cup sugar, almond extract, lemon juice and lemon rind, and sprinkle over the peaches. Turn oven on to 400°F (200°C) and put the peaches in while preparing the shortcake topping.

In a bowl, mix together the flour, salt, baking powder and 1 tbsp. sugar. Cut in the shortening until the mixture resembles coarse crumbs. Mix together the milk and egg and add all at once to the crumb mixture. Stir only until the flour is barely moistened. Remove the peaches from the oven and spoon the batter on top. It will cook more evenly if you drop the batter over the surface, leaving spaces for the syrup to bubble up during the cooking.

Sprinkle the 2 tbsp. sugar over the batter and return to 400°F (200°C) oven for about 40 minutes or until the centre of the cake batter tests done.

Serves 4-6.

Notes and Variations

Every now and then, someone will remark, "We haven't had a good bread pudding for a long time." Well, there are bread puddings and bread puddings, some that would never be missed and others that manage to combine that good old fashioned taste with a slightly new twist ... like Elsie's Rhubarb Bread Pudding.

Elsie's Rhubarb Bread Pudding

3 cups	diced raw rhubarb	750 mL
1 cup	sugar	250 mL
3 cups	cubed dry bread	750 mL
½ cup	milk	125 mL
¼ cup	butter	50 mL
½ cup	sugar	125 mL
2	eggs	2
1 tsp.	vanilla	5 mL
optional	cinnamon, coconut	optional

Butter a large casserole dish.

Clean the rhubarb and slice into small pieces. Mix with the 1 cup sugar. Set aside.

Cube the dry bread and pour milk over. Set aside.

In a fairly large bowl, cream the butter and sugar and add eggs, beating well. Add vanilla. Fold in the bread and milk mixture as well as the rhubarb and sugar mixture.

Pour into prepared pan and sprinkle with cinnamon and/or coconut, if desired. Bake in 350°F (180°C) oven for about 40 minutes or until custard is done.

Pineapple squares turn up at just about every community potluck dinner, and well they might! They're a lovely dessert.

Pineapple Squares

2½ cups	crumbs	625 mL
½ cup	melted butter	125 mL
½ cup	butter	125 mL
1½ cups	icing sugar	375 mL
2	eggs, unbeaten	2
1 cup	whipping cream	250 mL
1 large can	crushed pineapple	1 large can

To make the crumbs, use vanilla wafers, graham wafers or arrowroot cookies. Roll fine and mix with the melted butter. Press into a baking pan 9x13" (3.5 L), reserving ½ cup for topping. Bake for 15 minutes and cool.

Cream the remaining butter and add icing sugar and eggs. Beat until light and then spread on the cooled crumb mixture.

Whip cream until stiff. Drain the pineapple as well as possible and then add to the whipped cream. Spread on top of the egg mixture. Top with reserved crumbs. Chill for at least 6 hours. Cut in squares.

Serves 18-24.

Breadcrumbs browned in butter enhance all kinds of dishes—including some dessert dishes like the Apple Brown Betty to follow.

Apple Brown Betty

2 cups	bread crumbs	500 mL
3-5 tbsp.	melted butter	50-60 mL
3-4	apples	3-4
1 tbsp.	lemon juice	15 mL
½ tsp.	grated lemon	2 mL
½ cup	brown sugar	125 mL
⅓ cup	hot water	75 mL

Grease a square baking dish or large casserole.

Using a heavy skillet, brown the bread crumbs in the melted butter, using the larger quantity of butter if the crumbs are very dry. Place ⅓ of the crumbs in the greased baking dish.

Pare, core and slice the apples. Arrange half of the apples over the crumb layer. Sprinkle with half the lemon juice, grated lemon rind and brown sugar. Place another ⅓ of the crumbs over the apples. Then layer the rest of the apples, the lemon juice, rind and sugar. Cover with remaining crumbs. Pour hot water over top and bake in a 375°F (190°C) oven for 30-40 minutes.

Serves 6-8, and is particularly good with a warm lemon sauce, like the one which follows.

Lemon Sauce

¼ cup	butter	50 mL
½ cup	sugar	125 mL
2 tbsp.	flour	30 mL
dash	salt	dash
1	lemon, juice of	1
1 cup	boiling water	250 mL
dash	grated nutmeg	dash

If fresh lemon juice is not available, use 1½ tbsp. bottled lemon juice.

In a small saucepan, melt butter, add sugar, flour and salt, blending well. Add the lemon juice and boiling water. Stirring constantly, bring to a boil over low heat and stir until clear and thick. Place over hot water to keep hot. Add grated nutmeg when ready to serve.

Notes and Variations

Desserts

The English Trifles we made at the restaurant were never the same twice, but they were always popular with guests. The recipe is a bit vague, but the combinations always seem to work out.

English Trifle

cake, enough to make several layers
a rich cream custard (page 189)
fresh fruit, if possible, and if not, then jam
sherry, enough to flavour the cake layers, or
fruit juice
lots of whipped cream
icing sugar to sweeten the cream

Cut cake into fingers or cubes to fit the curves of the bowl. If using jam and not fresh fruit, spread one side of each piece of cake with jam — strawberry and raspberry work well. Speaking of cake, a very pretty trifle can be made with slices of jelly roll which are already spread with jam or jelly. Cut into thin slices and arrange around the base of the bowl so that the swirls show through.

Soak the cake with sherry, or fruit juice if a non-alcoholic dessert is preferred.

If you are using fresh fruit, layer the fruit on top of the sherried cake. Keep making layers of cake, sherry, fruit until the bowl is nearly ¾ full.

Then pour the rich custard over the layers, gently inserting a knife here and there to be sure the custard is seeping through to the bottom layer. Chill well to allow the custard to set.

Whip the cream, sweeten with icing sugar and spread thickly over the top of the bowl.

Decorate with whole berries, if using fresh fruit, or candied cherries, almonds or angelica.

Rice, for a dessert, can be hot or cold, plain or elegant, terrific or more terrific. This is a plain version of rice but one that most people remember with pleasure ... rice pudding.

Our first livestock purchase when we moved to Driftwillow was a wonderful Jersey cow called Buttercup. Some of her cream when tested had the highest percentage of butterfat ever recorded in our local district — 52%. Needless to say, Buttercup's milk and cream made wonderful rice puddings.

Rice Pudding in Honour of Buttercup

½ cup	regular rice	125 mL
4 cups	whole milk	1 L
½ cup	sugar	125 mL
½ cup	raisins	125 mL
¼ tsp.	nutmeg	1 mL
½	lemon or orange	½

Grease a large baking dish or casserole.

Wash the rice in several waters. You should be using plain rice — not the converted or instant kind. Mix washed rice with milk, sugar, raisins and nutmeg. Grind rind from ½ lemon or orange. Add to the rice mixture. Pour into prepared dish.

Bake at 300°F (150°C) about 2 hours, stirring several times. If rice is still hard, add a little more milk and continue baking another half hour.

Serve with lots of Buttercup's cream or the equivalent thereof.

You never know what's going to turn up in a torte these days! The following recipe dresses rice up so you'd barely know her, but you'll want to!

Rice Torte with Fresh Fruit

½ cup	converted rice	125 mL
2 cups	milk	500 mL
⅓ cup	candied fruit	75 mL
2 tbsp.	kirsch or brandy	25 mL
1½ tbsp.	gelatine	10 g
2 tbsp.	cold water	25 mL
2 cups	whipping cream	500 mL
⅓ cup	sugar	75 mL

sponge cake, whipped cream, fresh fruit

Cook the rice in milk until the milk is completely absorbed and the rice is tender.

While the rice is cooking, marinate the candied fruit in the kirsch or brandy. Soften gelatine in the cold water.

When rice is cooked, add the sugar, gelatine and marinated fruits and allow to cool completely. Whip the cream and fold in.

Line bottom of 9″ (3.5 L) spring form pan with a layer of sponge cake cut about ½″ (1 cm) thick. If desired, sprinkle the cake with more kirsch or brandy. Fill the pan with the rice mixture and allow to set for at least an hour.

Carefully remove from ring, decorate with more whipped cream, fresh peach slices or strawberries or raspberries or whatever fresh fruit you have burning a hole in your frig.

Notes and Variations

Desserts

The two desserts served at the Wild Game Dinner were Saskatoon Souffle and Maple Syrup Mousse. Both met with complete approval; in other words, there were no leftovers!

Saskatoon Souffle

1 tbsp.	gelatine	1 pkg. (7 g)
¼ cup	cold water	50 mL
¼ cup	boiling water	50 mL
1	lemon, juice and rind	1
¾ cup	sugar	175 mL
1 cup	saskatoons	250 mL
1 tbsp.	Cointreau	15 mL
3	egg whites	3
⅓ tsp.	salt	2 mL
½ cup	whipping cream	125 mL
1 tbsp.	Cointreau	15 mL

Note: Blueberries may be used in place of saskatoons.

Soak gelatine in cold water and then add both to the boiling water, stirring to dissolve the gelatine.

Grate the rind of the lemon and add to the sugar. Add both to the gelatine mixture and stir to dissolve the sugar.

Squeeze lemon for juice and add 3 tbsp. (50 mL) of juice to the first mixture. Crush the saskatoons slightly and add. Finally, add the Cointreau and mix well. Chill until partly stiff and then beat until frothy.

Whip the egg whites and salt until stiff. Fold into the gelatine mixture. Set in individual molds or larger molds.

To serve, whip the cream and fold in the Cointreau. Put a generous spoonful on each serving. Should serve 4.

Maple syrup, they say, is as Canadian as Pierre Berton. Thus, for an all-Canadian, all wild game dinner, we had to end with Maple Syrup Mousse.

Maple Syrup Mousse

1 cup	maple syrup	250 mL
4	egg yolks, beaten	4
2 cups	whipping cream	500 mL
more whipping cream and grated maple sugar		

Pour the maple syrup into a saucepan and stir in the beaten egg yolks. Heat until thick, stirring constantly to prevent burning. Remove from heat and let chill.

Whip the cream, fold gently into the maple syrup mixture, turn into a mold and chill.

Serve with a dollop of additional whipped cream topped with grated maple sugar (or maple sugar candy).

Rhubarb crisp was always a favourite whenever it was served at banquets or at home. The following recipe can be increased to suit the occasion and the numbers.

Good Old Reliable Rhubarb Crisp

5 cups	cut up rhubarb	1.25 L
¾ cup	sugar	175 mL
1 tbsp.	cornstarch	15 mL
¾ cup	flour	175 mL
1 tsp.	baking powder	5 mL
¼ tsp.	salt	1 mL
½ tsp.	cinnamon	2 mL
3 tbsp.	butter, margarine	50 mL
¾ cup	sugar	175 mL
½ cup	cornflakes	125 mL
¼ cup	flaked coconut	50 mL
½ cup	milk	125 mL
½ cup	orange juice	125 mL

whipping cream or pouring cream for the final touch

Note: You can use either cornflakes or bran flakes or a combination thereof.

Grease an 8″ (2 L) square pan or casserole dish. Cut up rhubarb and arrange on the bottom of the pan. Mix together the ¾ cup (175 mL) sugar and cornstarch and sprinkle over the rhubarb.

In a small bowl, mix together the flour, baking powder, salt and cinnamon.

In a larger bowl, cream the butter or margarine with the second ¾ cup (175 mL) sugar. Crush the cornflakes or bran flakes and add along with the coconut. Add dry ingredients alternately with the milk.

Drop dough on top of rhubarb and spread over pan. Heat the orange juice to boiling and pour over the topping. Bake at 350°F (180°C) for 45 minutes or until cake is baked and rhubarb is tender.

Serve warm with pouring cream, whipped cream or ice cream.

Notes and Variations

What do you do when you've got a small country restaurant and a clientele that seldom reserves ahead?

For one thing, you rely on ice cream in the dessert department, but I couldn't bear to serve up ice cream in the usual uninteresting way—with a scoop here and an ice cream wafer there. So I came up with a whole series of ice cream cocktails, a combination of vanilla ice cream and various liqueurs.

The Polar Bear Parfait was the first, a combination of one scoop of ice cream, creme de menthe and creme de cacao. Pretty soon, we added other liqueurs, then we had to offer two scoops of ice cream and then three, creating the Grizzly Bear and the Kodiak Bear.

The waitresses had a longer and longer list to rhyme off, especially after we began offering different sundae toppings as well. It got to be one of the attractions of the restaurant, to see if the waitress could actually rhyme off all 50 choices, or however many there were that night!

To make similar ice cream parfaits in advance, just scoop out ice cream, make a hole in the middle with the handle of a wooden spoon, pouring as much liqueur as you wish to use into the hole. Fill in with a bit more ice cream and freeze in paper baking cups set in muffin tins. To serve, put into stemmed glasses, top with whipped cream and a cherry.

Eventually, we began offering banana splits as well, made with a banana cut lengthwise in two, three different kinds of ice cream piled on the banana, three different sundae toppings piled on the ice cream, whipped cream piled on that and a cherry to top it all off.

As if that weren't enough, some people ordered what we called Suicide Sundaes.

Suicide Sundaes

> **seven scoops of ice cream**
> **seven different sundae toppings**
> **whipped cream, nuts and cherries**

If a customer ate two Suicide Sundaes in one sitting, any more he or she wanted that night were on the house. The ladies' record was topped at three—remember that's 21 scoops of ice cream with as many sundae toppings! The men's record went up to four, or 28 scoops of ice cream.

Another record of sorts must have been made when a young man ate two Suicide Sundaes just after he had finished a full course meal that included a 24 ounce porterhouse steak.

He's still alive and well and able to tell the story.

Ice cream bombes are also good choices for do-ahead desserts. Choose different ice cream flavours for their taste and colour compatibility, keeping the richest and most colourful for the centre.

The Only Good Bombe

8 cups	maple walnut ice cream	2 L
5 cups	mint ice cream	1.25 L
2 cups	strawberry ice cream	500 mL
¼ cup	maraschino cherries	50 mL
¼ cup	raisins	50 mL
¼ cup	chopped pecans	50 mL
¼ cup	macaroon crumbs	50 mL

Note: The amounts given above are enough to make the bombe pictured on page 161. The bowl used to mold that particular bombe was 9″ (22 cm) across. If your container is bigger or smaller, make adjustments in the amounts.

Whatever mold is to be used, line it with strong strips of parchment paper, wax paper or double strength foil paper in order to be able to lift the bombe out. Do not depend on warm cloths or warm water to get the bombe out. Cut the lining strips long enough so that there are good sturdy ends sticking out, the better to get a handle on the bombe when the time comes.

Press the maple walnut ice cream into the lined mold first, completely lining the bowl with an even layer about 1½″ (4 cm) thick. Let freeze firmly in place.

Layer on the mint ice cream next, again making a layer of about 1½″ (4 cm). Let freeze firmly.

Chop the maraschino cherries, the raisins, if they're big, pecans and macaroons. Add to the strawberry ice cream. Fill the centre of the bombe and freeze once again.

When the time comes, unmold the bombe with the aid of the paper strips, invert onto a serving plate and decorate with whipped cream and various garnishes. The cream may be tinted in ice cream shades of pink, yellow or green, using food colourings or liqueurs. Candied fruit, angelica and/or chocolate curls can also be added for garnish. Return to freezer until ready to serve.

When serving, be sure to cut through all layers so that everyone gets the total effect.

Notes and Variations

Desserts

I once had mincemeat pie topped with chocolate ice cream, and it gave me the idea for a superquick and easy dessert.

Mincemeat and Chocolate Ice Cream

2 cups   mincemeat   500 mL
apple juice and/or rum to dilute mincemeat
chocolate ice cream, enough for 4-6 servings

In the top of a double boiler, warm the mincemeat over hot water. If it's very thick, dilute with several tablespoons apple juice and/or rum.

Scoop chocolate ice cream into stemmed sherbet glasses (or more ordinary ones, if that's what your cupboard produces). Top with hot mincemeat mixture.

Cookie Clowns were always made for the children who came to our country restaurant, a quick and easy idea that could be used for birthday parties or special occasions of whatever sort.

Cookie Clowns

flat cookies, about 4″ (10 cm) across
soft butter icing, enough for a name
ice cream cones, the pointed kind
ice cream, pink, white or chocolate
chocolate chips, raisins, nuts, cherries

Load an icing tube or bag with soft icing and write the child's name around the outside of the large cookie.

Fill a cone with a rounded scoop of ice cream, invert it on the cookie so that it looks like a head with a clown hat on. Add clown features with chocolate chips, raisins, nuts, and cherries and make a ruffle around the neck with whipped cream or icing.

Has anybody here seen a Railroad Cake?

I've run across references to railroad cake in several different places. Nellie McClung, Western Canada's great lady, casually mentioned in one of her books that she had enjoyed railroad cake at a community picnic. A local history book in Saskatchewan also had a fleeting reference to railroad cake.

But that's where it ends. I cannot seem to track down a likely recipe. Joan sent me one she'd seen in a New York restaurant, a rather complicated arrangement of almond paste, apricot preserves and slivered almonds. It did not sound like something Nellie McClung's mother would have taken to a picnic.

Melva turned up a recipe for Railway Cake in a 1915 Five Roses Cookbook, but it only added to my puzzlement. The recipe called for butter and lard, 2 eggs, cream of tartar, carbonate of soda, caraway seeds and candied peel, all of which were to be unmixed. The instructions said, "This cake requires no beating. Put in quick oven at once and bake one hour."

Somehow, I think there's something missing.

I even wrote to Pierre Berton, thinking he of all people would know about railroad cake, what with his expertise in history and things connected to the railroad. "It's the first time I've ever heard of it," he wrote back.

As I said at the beginning of this ... has anybody here seen a railroad cake?

Recipes illustrated overleaf

CAKES
& FROSTINGS

One of my earliest recollections is of helping my mother bake cakes, and being allowed to eat the little "try" cake as she called it. It never occurred to me to ask why she always baked a small sample of the batter before trusting it to the regular pan. Perhaps her mother had always done so as a test for oven temperatures in the days when there were no oven thermometers, perhaps it was her way of avoiding baking mistakes but whatever the reason, I appreciated and remembered those little "try" cakes.

One of my greatest pleasures in more recent years has been the annual "Cake Bake", a weekend in October when a number of old friends get together somewhere in Canada and jointly make our Christmas cakes. We produce two kinds of cake—light and dark—and enjoy good fun and fellowship at the same time.

Dark Christmas Cake

4 oz.	slivered almonds	125 g
16 oz.	candied cherries	500 g
8 oz.	chopped mixed peel	250 g
2 cups	raisins	500 mL
1 cup	currants	250 mL
1 cup	chopped dates	250 mL
½ cup	brandy	125 mL
½ cup	flour	125 mL
2 cups	flour	500 mL
½ tsp.	baking soda	2 mL
1 tsp.	cloves	5 mL
1 tsp.	allspice	5 mL
1 tsp.	cinnamon	5 mL
½ tsp.	salt	2 mL
1 cup	butter	250 mL
2 cups	brown sugar	500 mL
6	eggs	6
1 cup	apple juice	250 mL
½ cup	molasses	125 mL

Prepare two large cake tins, lining them with at least two layers of well greased brown paper.

Blanch the almonds if not done so already, and cut into slivers. Chop and peel remaining fruit and nuts, and assemble together in a medium sized bowl. Add a bit of chopped preserved ginger, if desired. Splash with the brandy and dredge lightly with the ½ cup flour.

In another bowl, mix together the 2 cups flour, baking soda, cloves, allspice, cinnamon and salt. Put aside.

Recipe continues overleaf

In a very large bowl, cream the butter with the brown sugar and add the eggs, one at a time. In a smaller bowl or measuring cup, mix together the apple juice and molasses. Then add the dry ingredients alternately with the liquid (four dry and three liquid additions), combining lightly. Finally, fold in the floured fruit.

Pour into prepared cake tins and bake in 350°F (180°C) oven. Time will vary according to the size of pan used. If you are using the three tin set often used for wedding cakes, and if each tin is filled about 2-3″ (5-8 cm) deep, then the small size would require about 1-1½ hours, the medium sized 2-3 hours and the largest 3-5 hours. By weight, a 2½ pound cake will take about 3 hours, over 5 pounds at least 5 hours. For added moisture, put a pan of water in the oven for the first hour or two of baking.

Test with a straw or cake tester to be sure cake is cooked in the centre. Cool on a rack for about ½ hour, then remove from pans and carefully remove the baking papers. Continue to cool until no warmth can be felt. At this stage, dip a triple thickness of cheesecloth into brandy and wrap around the cakes. Finish with a wrap of heavy duty foil.

If the cakes are to be used within a few months, they can be safely stored without freezing if kept in a cool, dry place. For longer periods of storage, freeze.

To make the white fruit cake, we need as many willing hands as possible. That's why some of the husbands have found themselves grating coconut and trying to watch a fall football game at the same time.

White Fruit Cake

1 lb.	light raisins	500 g
1 lb.	candied cherries	500 g
¾ lb.	candied pineapple	375 g
¼ lb.	citron peel	125 g
¼ lb.	orange peel	125 g
½ lb.	grated coconut	250 g
½ lb.	blanched almonds	250 g
½ lb.	chopped pecans	250 g
½ cup	flour	125 mL
2½ cups	flour	625 mL
1½ tsp.	baking powder	7 mL
¾ tsp.	salt	3 mL
1½ cups	soft shortening	375 mL
1½ cups	white sugar	375 mL
2¼ cups	unbeaten eggs	550 mL
⅔ cup	orange juice	150 mL

Note: ½ lb. of fruit or nuts should measure approximately 1½ cups.

Also note: 2¼ cups unbeaten eggs generally requires about 9 eggs.

Prepare 2 large cake tins, lining them with at least two layers of well greased brown paper.

Prepare the fruit, chopping up what needs to be chopped, blanching the almonds if need be, grating the coconut if you have a fresh one. Dredge fruit mixture lightly with ½ cup flour and set aside.

In another bowl, mix together the 2½ cups flour, baking powder and salt.

In large bowl, cream the shortening (you can use butter but it will color the cake slightly; shortening keeps it lighter) and the sugar. Add unbeaten eggs. Mix well. Stir in orange juice. Add dry ingredients and floured fruits.

At this point, everyone involved in the process should take a turn at the long wooden spoon, giving the batter a quick mix for good luck all round. Then the batter is poured into the prepared pans and baked according to the same directions as given above in Dark Christmas Cake. When cakes are cooled and ready for storage, be sure to label the foil package "light" or "dark".

Each of the fruit cakes will make 2 large (10″ tube pan or 9x5x3 loaf pan or 2 L pan) cakes or will fill the usual wedding set of three different sized pans. The recipes can be doubled if you have oven space to bake them all at once.

Carrot cakes have enjoyed a revival in the past few years. Again, you can find many variations but after trying several, this is the one we selected as the best at The Flying N. The icing also added to its reputation, especially after we started using the icing to suggest icicles and snow and added Christmas trees.

See page 178 for the cream cheese frosting and page 179 for a picture of the finished product, iced to suit any season.

Prize Winning Carrot Cake

1 cup	cooking oil	250 mL
2 cups	sugar	500 mL
4	eggs	4
1 tsp.	vanilla	5 mL
2¾ cups	flour	675 mL
½ tsp.	salt	2 mL
1 tbsp.	baking powder	15 mL
1 tbsp.	baking soda	15 mL
1 tbsp.	cinnamon	15 mL
1 cup	raisins	250 mL
1 cup	walnuts	250 mL
4 cups	grated carrot	1 L

Combine oil and sugar and beat until smooth. Add eggs one at a time, beating well after each addition. Add vanilla.

In another bowl, mix together the dry ingredients, add the raisins and walnuts. Add both to the creamed mixture. Fold in the grated carrots.

Bake in a greased 9x13″ (3.5 L) pan or in a bundt pan at 350°F (180°C) for approximately 1 hour or until firm and springs back when touched.

My dad preferred what he called "soggy" cakes, cakes with substance ... like the Tomato Soup Cake or the Prince of Wales Cake.

Tomato Soup Cake

4 tbsp.	shortening	50 mL
1 cup	sugar	250 mL
2	egg yolks	2
1 can (10 oz.)	tomato soup	1 can (284 mL)
1/3 cup	water	75 mL
2 cups	flour	500 mL
2 tsp.	baking powder	10 mL
1 tsp.	salt	5 mL
1 tsp.	allspice	5 mL
1 tsp.	nutmeg	5 mL
1 tsp.	cinnamon	5 mL
1 cup	raisins	250 mL
1 cup	chopped nuts	250 mL

Grease a large cake pan, 9x13″ or 3.5 L.

Combine the shortening, sugar, egg yolks, tomato soup and water. Mix together the dry ingredients and add to the first mixture. Fold in the raisins and nuts. Pour into greased cake pan and bake at 350°F (180°C) for 35-40 minutes or until done.

This would be good iced with the cream cheese frosting page 178.

Prince of Wales Cake

2 cups	raisins	500 mL
2½ cups	water	625 mL
1 cup	butter or oil	250 mL
2 cups	brown sugar	500 mL
2	eggs	2
1 tsp.	vanilla	5 mL
2½ cups	flour	625 mL
2 tsp.	baking soda	10 mL
1 tsp.	baking powder	5 mL
2 tsp.	cinnamon	10 mL
2 tsp.	nutmeg	10 mL
1 tsp.	salt	5 mL

Grease and flour a large 9x13 pan or 3.5 L pan.

Simmer the raisins and water for 10 minutes. Cool and drain, reserving the liquid.

Mix together the butter or oil, sugar, eggs and vanilla. Add the water in which the raisins had been simmered. Sift the dry ingredients together and add to the first mixture. Stir well. Fold in the raisins.

Pour into the prepared cake pan and bake at 350°F (180°C) for about 40 minutes or until a cake tester comes out clean when inserted into the centre of the cake.

When cool, frost with Dimple Icing on page 178.

Queen Elizabeth Cake

Use the recipe for the Prince of Wales Cake as above, except use 1 cup (250 mL) raisins and 1 cup (250 mL) chopped dates instead of the 2 cups (500 mL) raisins. Follow instructions as given.

Frost with a broiled icing like the one which follows:

Brown Sugar Broiled Icing

5 tbsp.	brown sugar	60 mL
3 tbsp.	butter	50 mL
2 tbsp.	cream	25 mL
½ cup	shredded coconut	125 mL

Mix ingredients together in a small saucepan and boil lightly for 3 minutes. Pour over the hot cake just fresh from the oven and return to the oven until the frosting browns and bubbles.

Gingerbread is another old-time favourite. I particularly like it served with applesauce made from the first green apples of the season, topped with whipped cream and perhaps a bit of chopped crystalized giner.

Hot Water Gingerbread

¼ cup	butter	50 mL
¼ cup	lard	50 mL
½ cup	brown sugar	125 mL
2	eggs	2
½ cup	molasses	125 mL
1½ cups	flour	375 mL
1½ tsp.	baking soda	7 mL
dash	salt	dash
1½ tsp.	ground ginger	7 mL
½ cup	boiling water	125 mL

Grease an 8″ or 9″ square pan (2 L or 2.5 L).

In a fairly large bowl, cream the butter and lard, add sugar and beat well. Beat the eggs separately and then add to the creamed mixture. Add molasses.

In a smaller bowl, mix together the dry ingredients. Add to the creamed mixture. Stir in the boiling water last.

Pour into prepared pan and bake at 325°F (160°C) for 25-30 minutes.

Cakes & Frostings

When The Flying N closed, liquor regulations required that all liquor stocks be removed from the premises. Since we used so many liqueurs in our ice cream parfaits and in the house specialty, The Flying Hen drink, we had to dispose of quite a few cases of opened bottles, so these we transported to the ranch, piling them up temporarily just inside the front door.

The winter was a cold one and the nearby creek froze solid to the bottom, causing an enormous problem to the towns downstream that depended on it for their water supply. The provincial government got involved, sending out teams of experts to try to solve the problem.

The first day the experts arrived, one of them came to my door to explain the whole situation. I answered his knock, opening the door wide without thinking about the sea of booze surrounding me. I must give the gentleman credit. Other than a very strange look on his face (and goodness knows what must have crossed his mind in those few minutes), he just stated his business and left. I wondered afterward if he thought perhaps I might have contributed to the shortage of liquid in the creek, or whether indeed I might not just have the solution to the dry spell.

Needless to say, I got busy and moved the bottles to a more suitable storage place. I also figured out ways to use up bits and pieces of liquor, as with the Bacardi Rum Cake.

Bacardi Rum Cake

1 box	yellow cake mix	1 box
1 cup	chopped nuts	250 mL
3	eggs	3
1/3 cup	cooking oil	75 mL
1/2 cup	water	125 mL
1/2 cup	rum	125 mL
1/2 cup	butter	125 mL
1/4 cup	water	50 mL
1 cup	sugar	250 mL
1/2 cup	rum	125 mL

Use the cake mix which claims to have pudding in it as well. Use either walnuts or pecans but chop them finely. Whole ones look nice but make cutting the cake very difficult.

Grease heavily (butter gives the best flavour for this cake) and flour lightly a large bundt cake pan or a 10″ (3 L) tube pan. Sprinkle the chopped nuts evenly over the bottom of the pan.

Mix the cake mix with the eggs, oil, water and rum. Pour the batter carefully over the nuts and bake in a 325°F (160°C) oven for about 1 hour or until tester comes out clean.

Cool completely and turn out onto a platter or deep plate, deep enough to allow glaze to be poured over the cake and overflow in spots.

To make the glaze, melt the butter, water and sugar in a small saucepan. Boil 5 minutes, stirring constantly as it will want to boil over. Remove from heat and stir in the 1/2 cup rum (light or dark—doesn't matter).

Prick top and sides of cake lightly with a fork or toothpicks and pour glaze over it slowly, letting it soak into the cake. Repeat until glaze is used up, spooning extra glaze up from the plate or platter. Chill well.

A spectacular cake for special occasions is the famous Black Forest Cake. This is not the time to cut corners or use pre-mixes or cream substitutes. This is not the time to diet either; this is the time to go all out.

There is no comparison between a true German Black Forest Cherry Torte and the chocolate cakes with cherry pie filling between the layers that are sometimes passed off on unsuspecting victims as the real thing. What follows is the real thing.

Black Forest Cherry Torte

9	large eggs	9
1 tbsp.	water	15 mL
1 cup	sugar	250 mL
¾ cup	dry breadcrumbs	175 mL
½ cup	ground almonds	125 mL
⅓ cup	cocoa	75 mL
½ cup	sifted flour	125 mL

Cherry filling … see below
Chantilly cream … also below
unsweetened chocolate, red glaceed cherries
Kirsch … optional but nice

Grease and flour a 10″ (3 L) tube pan or use a 9″ round cake pan but be sure it has high edges. The tube pan is safest.

Crush the dry breadcrumbs until fine. Put aside. Blanch the almonds if necessary, and grind them. It's easier by far to buy them that way.

Separate 8 of the eggs, putting the yolks into a fairly large bowl and the whites into a high narrow bowl to be beaten later. Beat the egg yolks and add the remaining whole egg and 1 tbsp. water. Gradually add the sugar, beating all the while. Add breadcrumbs and ground almonds. Mix well.

Sift the cocoa with the flour, add to the first mixture and mix well.

Beat the egg whites until they stand in stiff peaks and fold into the first mixture.

Pour batter into prepared pan and bake in 350°F (180°C) oven for about 40 minutes or until tester comes out clean. Cool the cake in the pan for 5 minutes, then turn out on a rack to finish cooling.

Now, comes the interesting part. When the cake is completely cooled, split it into three thin layers and begin the assembly process.

Assemble the cake in this order: bottom layer of cake, layer of cherry filling (all of it), layer of Chantilly Cream (about ¼ of it), another cake layer, more Chantilly Cream (another ¼ of the total) and the final cake layer. Cover the top and sides of all layers with the remaining Chantilly Cream, finishing with rosettes of cream put through a decorating bag, if that's your bag. Top each rosette with a cherry.

Use a vegetable parer to shave chocolate curls from a square of unsweetened chocolate. Sprinkle the curls on the sides and in the centre of the cake.

Cherry Filling

2 cups	fresh red cherries	500 mL
2 tbsp.	water	25 mL
¼ cup	sugar	50 mL
1 tbsp.	cornstarch	15 mL
dash	salt	dash
⅛ tsp.	almond extract	1 mL

Pit cherries and put with the water into a small saucepan. (For canned cherries, see below). Cover and cook over low heat for 10 minutes or until cherry juice has formed in the pan. In a small bowl, mix together the sugar, cornstarch and salt. Add to the cherries. Increase the heat slightly, stirring and cooking until the juice is clear and has thickened with no trace of raw starch. Add almond extract and cool.

Use for the Black Forest Cherry Torte or as filling for small tart shells.

Cherry Filling from Canned Cherries

1 can (14 oz.)	canned cherries	1 can (398 mL)
2 tbsp.	cornstarch	30 mL
¼ cup	water	50 mL
dash	salt	dash
⅛ tsp.	almond extract	1 mL

Pit the cherries, if necessary.

Put the cherries and juice into a small saucepan. Heat. In small bowl, mix the cornstarch with the water and salt. Add a bit of the hot cherry liquid and then pour the entire cornstarch mixture into the hot cherries. Stir constantly until mixture bubbles, thickens and clarifies. Add flavouring. Cool.

Chantilly Cream

2 cups	whipping cream	500 mL
3 tbsp.	icing sugar	50 mL
flavouring to taste—vanilla or rum or brandy or Kirsch or		
Cointreau or other liqueur		

Whip the cream until stiff and add sugar and flavouring.

To set the whipped cream, you could mix 1 tsp. (5 mL) gelatin in 1 tbsp. (15 mL) water, stirring over hot water until the gelatin dissolves. Begin to whip the cream and when it's partially set, add about ¼ cup (50 mL) to gelatin mixture and then pour the combined mixture back into the partially whipped cream. Continue whipping until the cream holds its shape. Then add the sugar and flavouring. This method will hold whipped cream together for up to 12 hours or more.

Whipped cream is also good the following way and is a nice variation for Black Forest Cherry Torte. If you use it for the cake instead of Chantilly Cream, sprinkle the cake layers with a little additional Kirsch.

Whipped Cream with Almonds and Kirsch

2 cups	whipping cream	500 mL
½ cup	icing sugar	125 mL
dash	salt	dash
3 tbsp.	shredded almonds	50 mL
3 tbsp.	Kirsch	50 mL

Blanch almonds, if necessary, and cut up into fine pieces.

Put the whipping cream, sugar and salt into a bowl and whip until soft peaks form. Fold in almonds and Kirsch. Makes about 3 cups.

Jelly rolls aren't served as much as they used to be. I wonder if this is so because there isn't a mix available to turn out these marvelous thin sponge cakes rolled around jam or jelly fillings.

Ladies of the Meadow Creek district near Driftwillow published a cookbook a few years ago, full of recipes that are ideal for everybody but especially good for those of us at higher altitudes. A jelly roll that I tried from that book has been very popular. Many customers have asked for the recipe—a sure sign of approval.

Hazel's Pumpkin Cake Roll

¾ cup	flour	175 mL
1 tsp.	baking powder	5 mL
dash of	salt	dash
2 tsp.	cinnamon	10 mL
½ tsp.	nutmeg	2 mL
1 tsp.	ginger	5 mL
3	eggs	3
1 cup	sugar	250 mL
⅔ cup	cooked pumpkin	150 mL
1 tsp.	lemon juice	5 mL
1 cup	chopped walnuts	250 mL

Grease and flour a jelly roll pan, about 10x15″.

Mix together the flour, baking powder, salt and spices. Set aside.

In a fairly large bowl, beat the eggs for 5 minutes or until very thick. Gradually add the sugar, beating all the while. Stir in the pumpkin and lemon juice. Finally, fold in the prepared dry ingredients.

Spread in the prepared pan and sprinkle the chopped walnuts over the top of the batter. Bake about 15 minutes at 375°F (190°C) or until cake springs back when touched. Spread a teatowel with icing sugar and turn the hot jelly roll out onto the towel—carefully—nut side down. Roll cake up in the towel and allow to cool.

Make cream cheese filling (see below). Carefully unroll the cake and spread with filling. Reroll and chill well before serving. This can be topped with a rosette of whipped cream or ice cream—vanilla, coffee or even the pumpkin flavoured ice cream that is sometimes available in the fall months.

Note: To make tidy slices, this jelly roll should be made and filled well in advance as the cream cheese filling needs to be thoroughly chilled.

Cream Cheese Filling for Roll Cake

¾ cup	cream cheese	175 mL
4 tbsp.	butter	50 mL
1 cup	icing sugar	250 mL
½ tsp.	vanilla	2 mL

Note: This amount of cream cheese is equivalent to 1½ small size pkgs. (the 125 g size).

Have the cream cheese at room temperature. Cream it together with the butter. Add icing sugar gradually, beating well after each addition. Beat in vanilla.

When cake mixes were first introduced, the idea was often better than the finished product. Gradually, however, they have been improved until now it's quite possible to get a very good cake from a mix . . . especially if you add a bit as I did in this meringue cake.

Baked-In Meringue Cake

small size	white cake mix	small size
2	egg whites	2
1 cup	brown sugar	250 mL
1 tsp.	cornstarch	5 mL
½ tsp.	baking powder	2 mL
½ tsp.	cinnamon	2 mL
½ cup	chopped nuts	125 mL

Use a single cake mix or a small size as mentioned in the ingredients above. Either a plain white or white with pudding in the mix will work well.

Grease a 9″ square pan (2.5 L) and fit with a square of wax paper on the bottom of the pan, or thoroughly grease a 9″ (3 L) tube pan (sometimes the best bet because this cake can rise quite high).

Make the cake according to the instructions on the box and pour into the prepared pan.

Beat the egg whites until stiff but not dry. Mix the dry ingredients together and gradually beat them into the stiff egg white mixture. Finally, fold in the nuts.

Spread the mixture over the top of the cake batter, making sure it goes right to the edges of the pan. Using a broad-bladed knife, work the meringue mixture into the cake by cutting through the meringue and the cake batter with a swirling motion. This will have the effect of marbling the cake while leaving enough meringue on top to form a self-frosting.

Bake in 350°F (180°C) oven for about 45 minutes or until tester comes out clean. Let cake cool completely in pan before cutting.

For variety, make this cake with a mixture of almonds and maraschino cherries instead of chopped nuts. Or use white sugar in the meringue and then tint it pale green or pink — whatever color suits your fancy and the occasion! Coconut may also be used.

Through the years at the restaurant, we made birthday cakes in every possible flavour, size and shape—trying always to reflect the interests of the "birthday child", whatever the age of the celebrant! Some birthday cakes were not cakes at all. Dad liked apple pie so one year that is what he got with "Happy Birthday Dad" spelled out on the top crust with thin strips of pastry.

Shirley indulged her daughter's preferences and yearly made this wonderful torte.

Shirley's Chocolate Torte Royale

2	egg whites	2
¼ tsp.	salt	1 mL
½ tsp.	vinegar	2 mL
½ cup	sugar	125 mL
¼ tsp.	cinnamon	1 mL
1 cup	chocolate chips	250 mL
2	egg yolks, beaten	2
¼ cup	water	50 mL
1 cup	whipping cream	250 mL
¼ cup	sugar	50 mL
¼ tsp.	cinnamon	1 mL

Cover a cookie sheet with a piece of heavy brown paper. Draw an 8″ circle in the centre—use the bottom of your 8″ round cake pan as guide.

Beat the egg whites, salt and vinegar until soft peaks form. In a small bowl or cup, lightly mix the sugar and cinnamon and add to the egg whites, beating until very stiff peaks form and all sugar has been dissolved. Now use this mixture to make the shell.

Spread the egg white mixture within the circle, making the bottom ½″ (1 cm) thick and mounding up the edge until it's at least 2″ (5 cm) high. Use the back of a teaspoon to shape this rim and to form decorative ridges on the outside edge.

Bake in a very slow oven—275°F (140°C)—for 1 hour; then turn off the heat and let dry in the oven, without opening the door, for about 2 hours. Peel from the paper.

When the shell is ready, begin the filling. Melt the chocolate chips over hot (not boiling) water. Cool slightly, then spread 2 tbsp. (25 mL) of the soft chocolate over the bottom of the cooled meringue shell. To the remaining chocolate, add the beaten egg yolks and water. Blend well and chill until the mixture is thick.

Combine the whipping cream, sugar and cinnamon. Whip until stiff. Spread half of the whipped cream over the chocolate in the shell; fold the remainder of the cream into the chocolate-egg mixture and spread over the top, making the final layer. Chill several hours or overnight.

To serve, trim with more whipped cream and top with whole pecans.

If you'd like something on a slightly smaller scale, try the classic Madeleines, the tiny scallop shaped cakes that supposedly helped Marcel Proust create the seven volumes of "Remembrance of Things Past."

Madeleines remind me of my mother's "Try cakes" which she baked in fluted tart tins and which a spoiled daughter got to eat, warm and buttery, straight from the oven. My mother who avoided what she called "fussy" recipes would have been surprised to discover that her humble little "Try cakes" were very much like the famous French tea cake—the Madeleine.

Madeleines

1¼ cups	cake flour	300 mL
½ tsp.	baking powderr	2 mL
dash	salt	dash
3	large eggs	3
1 tsp.	vanilla	5 mL
⅔ cup	sugar	150 mL
2 tsp.	lemon rind, grated	10 mL
¾ cup	butter	175 mL
sifted icing sugar		

Melt the butter and set aside to cool. Don't use a substitute for butter. Only the real thing will do.

Melt a bit of extra butter and use to grease the madeleine pans or small tart tins or muffin tins.

Sift the flour, baking powder and salt together. If you don't have cake flour, use regular flour but decrease the amount to slightly over 1 cup. Set the dry ingredients aside.

In a large mixing bowl, beat the eggs until light and lemon coloured. The mixture should be thick enough to stick to the beaters. Add vanilla. Gradually beat in the sugar and continue beating until the volume has increased to four times the original amount.

Gradually fold in the flour mixture and the lemon rind. Stir in the melted butter. Spoon 1 tbsp. (15 mL) of batter into each shell (or as much as is necessary to fill the container ⅔ full). Bake in 350°F (180°C) oven for 8-12 minutes or until a toothpick inserted into the centre comes out clean.

Remove the cakes from the pans and cool on racks. Dust tops with sifted icing sugar.

Makes about 36 small Madeleines. For variety, try grated orange rind in place of the lemon rind.

Do you consider cheesecake a cake, a pie, or do you simply play it safe and call it dessert? Since I prefer the baked kind to the ones set with gelatine and chilled, I consider it a cake and the best ones I ever had were eaten at deli counters in Toronto years ago, after night school courses on Bloor Street near Spadina.

Cheesecakes are a food with a long history as is evidenced by the story involving Socrates and his bad-tempered wife. Apparently, an admirer sent Socrates a cheesecake and his wife was so cheesed off by the gesture that she not only snatched it away, she even trampled it into the ground. All that Socrates was left with was the consoling thought that if he could not enjoy the gift, neither could his shrewish wife.

The cheesecakes I recall enjoying particularly had crusts of crushed zwieback rusks. The following recipe doesn't have a zwieback crust, but you could substitute one. I chose the recipe for the filling which may have been similar to those of ancient Greece.

Sesame Honey Cheese Tart

	rich pastry to fill 10″ (25 cm) pie plate	
1 lb.	cream cheese	500 g
½ cup	heavy cream	125 mL
½ cup	honey	125 mL
⅓ cup	sugar	75 mL
½ tsp.	nutmeg	2 mL
3	egg yolks	3
2 tbsp.	sesame seeds	30 mL
3	egg whites	3

Make up recipe for rich pastry (page 201), roll out and place in large pie plate (10″ or 25 cm). Flute the edges so that the edge extends approximately ½″ or 2 cm above the rim. Chill while preparing the filling. As mentioned above, you could also use a zwieback crust here.

Before starting the filling, lightly toast the sesame seeds in a moderate oven. Set aside.

Have the cream cheese at room temperature. In a medium size bowl, beat the cream cheese until smooth, add the cream and honey. Mix the sugar and nutmeg together and add to the first mixture, stirring well. Beat the egg yolks and add to the cream cheese mixture. Fold in the toasted sesame seeds.

Beat the egg whites until they stand in stiff peaks and fold into the first mixture. Pour into prepared pie shell and bake in preheated oven 350°F (180°C) oven for about 45 minutes.

Notes and Variations

Cakes & Frostings

A double boiler and a portable electric beater are all you need to make a great variety of cake frostings based on the basic Seven Minute Frosting.

Basic Seven Minute Frosting

2	egg whites	2
1½ cups	sugar	375 mL
1½ tsp.	light corn syrup	7 mL
⅓ cup	cold water	75 mL
dash	salt	dash
1 tsp.	vanilla	5 mL

You can use ¼ tsp. (1 mL) cream of tartar in place of the light corn syrup.

Place all ingredients except the vanilla in the top of a double boiler over hot water. Cook, beating constantly with electric or hand beater until mixture forms stiff peaks – about 7 minutes. Remove from heat, add vanilla, and beat until mixture reaches spreading consistency.

Variation #1 ... Caramel Frosting

Replace the light corn syrup with 2 tbsp. (25 mL) burnt sugar syrup.

To make this burnt syrup, melt ½ cup (125 mL) white sugar in a heavy iron skillet over low heat until it gets dark brown and smooth. Remove from heat, add ½ cup (125 mL) boiling water. Sugar may harden. Return to heat and stir until the sugar is melted and the resulting mixture is like molasses.

Variation #2 ... Chocolate Frosting

Melt 3 squares (1 oz. each) of unsweetened chocolate over hot water. Allow it to cool and add to the frosting just before spreading it on the cake. Fold in gently. Rather than beat it in evenly and decrease the fluff, let the chocolate create a marbled effect.

Variation #3 ... Brown Sugar Frosting

Replace white sugar with brown sugar, reduce water to ¼ cup (50 mL) and do not use the corn syrup.

Variation #4 ... Coffee Frosting

Omit the vanilla. Instead, add 2 tsp. (10 mL) instant coffee and ⅛ tsp. (1 mL) cinnamon.

Variation #5 ... Peppermint Frosting

To the finished icing, add a few drops of either pink or pale green food colouring and ¼ to ½ tsp. (1-2 mL) peppermint extract. These vary in strength so taste and add more if needed. Creme de menthe liqueur may also be used, green or white, depending on the colour you want.

Variation #6 ... Pineapple Frosting

Substitute juice from canned pineapple for the water used in the recipe. Omit the vanilla and use 1 tsp. (5 mL) grated lemon rind. Use the drained pineapple for garnish.

And now for something entirely different — one of my favourites ... Grape Seven Minute Frosting and Grape Filling.

Grape Seven Minute Frosting

1	egg white	1
¾ tbsp.	white sugar	10 mL
½ tsp.	light corn syrup	2 mL
3 tbsp.	grape juice	50 mL

In a double boiler over boiling water, mix the ingredients and beat constantly until peaks form. Remove from heat and continue to beat until thick and beginning to cool.

If a bit more colour is needed, use pink food colour a drop at a time. Blue or grape colours will not work — they tend to turn the icing an unappetizing muddy grey.

Grape Filling

3 tbsp.	cornstarch	50 mL
½ cup	water	125 mL
½ cup	sugar	125 mL
½ cup	grape juice	125 mL
dash	salt	dash
4 tbsp.	lemon juice	50 mL
1 tbsp.	butter	15 mL

Mix first five ingredients together and cook in double boiler over hot water until thick and smooth, about 30 minutes, stirring occasionally. Remove from heat and add lemon juice and butter. When cool, spread between layers of white or lemon flavoured butter cakes, sponge cakes or angel food. Ice with Grape Seven Minute Icing.

If you're out of icing sugar, you can make a reasonably good substitute by putting 1 cup (250 mL) granulated sugar into the blender and blending at highest speed until it is reduced to a powder.

And speaking of emergencies, the following makes a good chocolate frosting that stays soft and smooth and doesn't need icing sugar.

Cooked Chocolate Frosting

½ cup	granulated sugar	125 mL
1½ tbsp.	cornstarch	20 mL
1 square	unsweetened chocolate	1 square
dash	salt	dash
½ cup	boiling water	125 mL
1½ tbsp.	butter	20 mL
½ tsp.	vanilla	2 mL

In a double boiler over hot water, or in a heavy pot, mix together the sugar and cornstarch. Grate the chocolate and add along with the salt. Add boiling water and cook until the mixture thickens, stirring constantly. Be sure to cook until there's no taste of raw starch. Remove from heat, add butter and vanilla, and spread over cake while still hot to give a glossy finish.

Carrot cake which gets ever more popular should be frosted with a mixture that includes cream cheese. I like this one because you can still taste the cream cheese.

Cream Cheese Frosting

1 large pkg.	cream cheese	1 large pkg. (250 g)
¼ cup	butter	50 mL
2 cups	icing sugar	500 mL
dash of salt		
1 tbsp.	cream, if needed	15 mL

Be sure both the cream cheese and butter are room temperature.

Whip the softened cream cheese and butter with electric beater and add the sugar gradually, blending well. Add salt. If the mixture looks too stiff for easy spreading, add the cream.

Ice the cake and chill slightly before serving.

There is no doubt which recipe is the favourite in our family as far as icing is concerned. It's a fudge-like topping that often mysteriously disappears off the top of the cake. Our neighbor Eva named it because it "dimples" while it cooks.

Eva's Dimple Icing

2 cups	packed brown sugar	500 mL
¾ cup	cream	175 mL
1 tbsp.	butter	15 mL
1 tsp.	vanilla	5 mL

You can use either sweet or sour cream.

In a fairly heavy pot, mix sugar and cream together. Bring to a boil, stirring all the while, and continue cooking for about 8-10 minutes until the soft ball stage is reached (236°F on a candy thermometer or that stage when a bit of the mixture forms a soft ball when dropped into cold water). Remove from heat, add butter and vanilla. Beat well until sticky but still shiny. Take care—this can harden quickly. Spread over the cake before it hardens completely.

If you've been overly generous with the cream or find the icing does not want to turn creamy and thick for whatever reason, gradually add some sifted icing sugar until the mixture is of spreading consistency. The flavour won't be quite as wonderful, but nearly.

Notes and Variations

Wedding guests must have wondered sometimes just what was going on in the kitchen.

Wedding cakes are generally iced with what's called Royal Icing, a mixture of egg whites and sugar that gets rock hard. It holds the decorations nicely, it is true, but it's like cement when it hardens.

I have vivid recollections of trying to slice up a cake, quietly, in the kitchen, while the tearful speeches and serious toasts were being made out front. Sometimes, we were lucky and a good strong arm and a heavy knife was all that was needed.

But other nights, we'd have to resort to hammer, cleaver or mallet, just to get a knife through. Of course, most of the icing was wasted and guests were treated to the sounds of massacre in the kitchen.

It's no wonder that I think styrofoam cakes are just fine, as long as there are real ones in the kitchen, waiting to be sliced and brought on in all their proper glory.

Recipes illustrated overleaf

PIES & PASTRIES

Once upon a time, there were only a few people who could afford the lard and flour needed to make two crusts on a pie. Consequently, they became known as the "upper crust."

The rest of the folks simply had their pie and ate it too — right out of the bottom crust, I suppose!

Which brings me to the matter of perfect pie crusts.

The most consistently perfect pastry I have ever eaten is made by Evelyn with whom I share some grandchildren. She does it the original way with shortening, flour and ice water, adding just enough brown sugar and baking powder until experience tells her it is just right.

I have better luck with the never fail pastry, and ever since Blanche gave me my first version of the recipe, I've never taken a chance on the old way.

Basic Pastry Recipe

5½ cups	all-purpose flour	1.4 L
2 tsp.	salt	10 mL
1 lb.	lard	454 g
1	egg	1
1 tbsp.	vinegar	15 mL
water added to egg and vinegar to make 1 cup liquid		

Pastry flour may be used in place of all-purpose flour. Use 6 cups instead of the 5½ of the all-purpose.

In a large bowl, combine flour and salt. Cut in lard with pastry blender or quick fingers until the mixture resembles coarse crumbs.

In a measuring cup, beat egg and vinegar lightly and add water to make 1 cup liquid. Add to the dry mixture and blend quickly, mixing just until dough forms a ball. If more liquid is needed since flours do vary, add a few drops of water.

Use immediately, rolling out on a slightly floured surface. Use a light hand in the rolling stage. If it tears or needs a patch, just dampen lightly and apply the necessary repairs.

The pie dough can also be frozen, either whole or in portions big enough to make one crust when needed.

Variations of Basic Pastry

For a slightly sweeter dough, add 3 tbsp. (50 mL) brown sugar. Add 1 tsp. (5 mL) baking powder for a crust that rises slightly. Substitute milk for the water in the basic recipe and you'll have a different look to the finished product. Decrease the flour to 4 or 4½ cups and you'll have a very rich short pastry.

Early homesteaders often found substitutes for scarce items. If you lived 50 miles from the nearest lemon, you used vinegar instead and if you were half a continent away from apples, you used soda crackers. And you turned out remarkably good pies!

Apple Pie without Apples

pastry for a double crust pie

2 cups	soda crackers	500 mL
2	eggs	2
1 cup	sugar or honey	250 mL
1 cup	milk	250 mL
3 tsp.	nutmeg	15 mL
2 tsp.	cinnamon	10 mL

grated lemon rind from half a lemon

Prepare the pie crust and line a standard size pie plate.

Break up the soda crackers and mix with the beaten eggs. Add sugar or honey and milk. Add spices and lemon rind. Mix well and pour into bottom pie crust. Top with crust and bake in 325°F (160°C) oven for about 40 minutes.

Best served warm with ice cream.

Lemon Pie without Lemons

pastry for single crust standard size pie

2 tbsp.	butter	25 mL
½ cup	sugar	125 mL
⅓ cup	flour	75 mL
2 tsp.	cinnamon	10 mL
½ tsp.	cloves	2 mL
½ tsp.	allspice	2 mL
2 tbsp.	cider vinegar	25 mL
1 cup	water	250 mL

Prepare the pastry and line a standard size pie plate.

In the top of a double boiler, cream butter and sugar together. Mix flour with spices and add to the creamed mixture. Stir in vinegar and water. Cook over boiling water until thick. Pour into prepared pie shell and bake at 350°F (180°C) for 30-40 minutes.

This recipe is included for historical interest mostly. There were many versions of the Vinegar Pie. Nellie McClung, western author and activist, described in one of her books how her mother used to make up half a dozen vinegar pies to take to a community gathering. Hers included molasses, butter, bread crumbs, vinegar and cinnamon. If she had an egg to spare, she'd put on a meringue topping.

If you make this pie and if you have some ice cream or whipped cream to spare, I'd suggest including it.

Pies & Pastry

In the margin of my most battered cookbook, on the page that includes Sour Cream Raisin Pie, is written one word … "Swell!"

Sour Cream Raisin Pie

pastry for a single crust standard size pie

1 cup	sugar	250 mL
¼ tsp.	nutmeg	1 mL
½ tsp.	cinnamon	2 mL
¼ tsp.	cloves	1 mL
¼ tsp.	salt	1 mL
3	eggs, separated	3
1 cup	sour cream	250 mL
1 cup	seedless raisins	250 mL
1 tbsp.	flour	15 mL
½ cup	sugar	125 mL
½ tsp.	cinnamon	2 mL

Prepare the pastry and line the bottom of a standard size pie plate.

In a bowl, mix together the sugar, spices, salt, egg yolks and sour cream. (If you have access to unpasteurized farm cream turned sour, grab it. Otherwise, commercial sour cream will do nicely.)

Sprinkle the raisins with the flour and add to the sour cream mixture. Pour into the prepared pie shell and bake in a 350°F (180°C) oven until the custard is set — about 25 minutes. Check the custard by inserting a silver knife. If it comes out clean, the custard is done.

Just before the pie is done, prepare the meringue by beating the egg whites until stiff peaks form. Mix 2 tbsp. of the remaining sugar with cinnamon and add to the egg whites, beating together until glossy and stiff. Fold in the balance of the sugar. Spread over the hot custard, return to the oven and brown lightly.

Notes and Variations

Pies & Pastry

For those who have trouble choosing between sour cream raisin pie or pumpkin, here is the solution ... a combination.

Pickaway Pumpkin Pie

pastry for bottom crust of standard size pie plate

1 cup	sugar	250 mL
2 tbsp.	pumpkin pie spice	30 mL
1 tbsp.	flour	15 mL
½ tsp.	salt	2 mL
3	eggs	3
1½ cups	pumpkin	375 mL
1 cup	sour cream	250 mL
½ cup	raisins	125 mL

Prepare pastry and line the bottom of a standard size pie plate.

If you don't have pumpkin pie spice, make up 2 tbsp. of a combination of cinnamon, nutmeg, allspice, mace, ginger and cloves.

In a small bowl, mix together the sugar, spice, flour and salt.

In a large bowl, beat eggs slightly; blend in pumpkin, sour cream and raisins. Stir in the sugar mixture. Pour into the prepared pie shell.

Bake in a 400°F (200°C) oven for 50 minutes or until a knife inserted in the centre comes out clean. Garnish with whipped cream.

When my dad was working on the CNR on runs through northern Ontario, he used to buy wild blueberries from various entrepreneurs along the way. They made incomparable pies, and I sometimes have fits of nostalgia over those blueberries. However, that doesn't stop me from making a very good pie from the commercially grown blueberries available nowadays.

Aunt Agnes' Blueberry Pie

single pastry shell already baked

4 cups	blueberries	1 L
¾ cup	sugar	175 mL
2	eggs	2
2 tbsp.	flour	30 mL
2 tbsp.	lemon juice	25 mL
dash	salt	dash
¼ cup	sugar	50 mL

Prepare pastry, line a standard size pie plate and bake until nicely browned. Cool.

In a medium sized pan, cook the blueberries with the sugar for 5-10 minutes. Separate the eggs, set the whites aside for the meringue. To the yolks, add the flour, lemon juice and salt. Add to the hot berries. Lower the heat and cook a few minutes longer until thickened and clear. Cool slightly, then pour into the baked pastry shell.

Beat the egg whites until stiff. Gradually add the sugar and continue beating until glossy and smooth. Spoon over the blueberries and brown lightly in 350°F (180°C) oven.

Rhubarb leads the list of things you are offered from friends' gardens. I often use it in a recipe that comes from one of my most battered books and includes the long-ago notation, "Best one."

Rhubarb Lattice Pie

pastry enough for bottom crust and lattice strips

1 cup	sugar	250 mL
3 tbsp.	flour	50 mL
1 tsp.	grated orange peel	5 mL
1 tbsp.	butter	15 mL
2	eggs, beaten	2
3 cups	cut up rhubarb	750 mL
2 tbsp.	butter	25 mL

Prepare pastry and line bottom of a standard size pie plate. Reserve enough for lattice topping.

In a small bowl, mix together the sugar, flour, orange peel and butter. Add the eggs and beat until smooth.

Cut up the rhubarb and spread over the bottom of the pie crust. Pour the egg mixture evenly over it, and dot with the remaining butter. Cut lattice strips and arrange over the pie.

Bake at 450°F (230°C) for 10 minutes; then reduce to 350°F (180°C) for about 30 minutes more.

Rhubarb and Saskatoon Pie

If you're lucky enough to live near saskatoon bushes, try making the above pie with 1½ cups rhubarb, 1½ cups saskatoons. The combination makes the most of both.

Notes and Variations

Pies & Pastry

I learned to appreciate saskatoons after moving to Alberta, but I brought with me from Ontario an enduring passion for blue Concord grapes. Once a year, I spend the money and time to make a grape pie.

Blue Concord Grape Pie

pastry enough for bottom crust and lattice topping

3 cups	concord grapes	750 mL
1 cup	sugar	250 mL
3 tbsp.	flour	50 mL
dash	salt	dash
½ tsp.	grated lemon rind	2 mL
2 tbsp.	butter	25 mL

Prepare pastry and line a standard size pie plate. Reserve enough dough for lattice strips.

Slip the skins from the grapes. Reserve skins for later. In a fairly large saucepan, bring the pulp to a boil so that the seeds will more easily separate. Remove from heat and press through a sieve, reserving the grape pulp and discarding the seeds. To the seedless pulp, add the skins.

Mix sugar, flour, salt and lemon rind. Add to the pulp.

Pour into pastry lined pan, make a lattice top and bake in 450°F (230°C) oven for 10 minutes, then a 350°F (180°C) oven for 30 minutes. When the pie is removed from the oven, cut butter into small pieces and put between lattice strips on the hot pie.

One year, I happened to have a lot of Italian blue plums at the same time I was making my annual Concord grape pie. Looking at the colours, I wondered what a mixture would produce.

Concord Grape and Plum Pie

Cut plums into grape size pieces and substitute for half of the grapes called for in the above recipe. In other words use 1½ cups grapes, 1½ cups plums. Complete the recipe as above.

The finished product is a wonderful marriage — the plums cut down the intense flavour of the grapes and the grapes give the plums a needed lift!

I sometimes extend the grape/plum pie season by making several batches of the filling and pouring it into foil lined pans, rather than pastry lined pans. I freeze the fillings in the pans, then lift them out of the pans and keep them until the urge comes on me for a taste of summer. All I have to do then is line a pie plate with pastry, slip in the frozen (or thawed filling) and bake. If thawed before baking, use the regular baking times. If still frozen when put in the oven, extend the time by about 20 minutes.

When fresh fruit is plentiful, I am always tempted to buy in bulk, and generally do, much to the despair of my family and friends. During one such shopping binge, I bought peaches. In the ensuing baking spree, I discovered Peachy Praline Pie.

Peachy Praline Pie

pastry for bottom crust for standard size pie

4 cups	fresh peaches	1 L
¾ cup	sugar	175 mL
¼ cup	flour	50 mL
1½ tsp.	lemon juice	7 mL
⅓ cup	brown sugar	75 mL
3 tbsp.	flour	50 mL
3 tbsp.	butter	50 mL
½ cup	chopped pecans	125 mL

Prepare pastry and line bottom of standard size pie plate.

Scald, peel and slice peaches. Mix with the sugar, flour and lemon juice.

To make the praline mixture, mix the brown sugar and flour together in another bowl. Cut in the butter until the mixture resembles coarse crumbs. Add pecans.

To assemble the pie, sprinkle ⅓ of the praline mixture over the bottom crust. Cover with the peaches and top with the rest of the praline mixture.

Bake in a 400°F (200°C) oven until peaches are tender—about 40 minutes.

Wonderful as is, but out of this world with the addition of whipped cream or butter pecan ice cream!

Notes and Variations

Pies & Pastry

This is one of the best fresh strawberry pies I've ever made because it uses absolutely no added water. All the flavour comes from the berries. It's the berries, as they say!

Ida's Fresh Strawberry Pie

1 baked pie shell, not pricked
icing sugar to sprinkle over pie shell

4 cups	fresh strawberries	1 L
1 cup	sugar	250 mL
3 tbsp.	cornstarch	50 mL
1 tbsp.	lemon juice	15 mL

whipping cream as garnish

Note: Save the paper from the lard used in the pastry. It can be used to shape the crust.

Prepare a pie shell. Cut a piece of wax paper or lard paper to fit into the bottom of the pie plate and up the sides. Place it on top of the pie dough. Cover the paper with dried beans or uncooked rice and bake. That way, the pie shell will keep its shape. Take out the beans and/or rice as soon as you remove from the oven. Normally, you prick the pie shell to keep it flat during baking but for this pie, you want a baked pie shell without prick holes.

The rice and beans trick works for tarts and other pies as well. Sometimes pricking isn't that effective.

Now, back to the pie proper.

Sprinkle icing sugar over the bottom of the baked pie shell.

Pick over the berries, picking out 2 cups (500 mL) of whole very nicely shaped berries and 2 cups (500 mL) of not-so-nice berries. Put the whole best berries into the bottom of the pie shell, pointy ends up. Arrange in circles or squares or whatever.

Coarsely chop the remaining berries and put into a small saucepan. Mix sugar and cornstarch together and add to the chopped berries, cooking slowly until mixture is thick and clear. Remove from heat and add lemon juice.

Pour sauce over the berries in the pie shell. And that's all there is to it! Chill.

Top with whipped cream, more berries and a mint sprig or two, if you should be so lucky as to have both fresh strawberries and fresh mint!

Notes and Variations

I remember one friend to whom the word "pie" was synonymous with "banana cream". Whenever you saw his cattle truck parked outside a truck stop or restaurant, you knew they must have good banana cream pie!

Basic Cream Pie Recipe

pastry enough for bottom of standard size pie plate

⅓ cup	flour	75 mL
⅔ cup	sugar	150 mL
dash	salt	dash
2 cups	milk, scalded	500 mL
3	egg yolks, beaten	3
2 tbsp.	butter	25 mL
½ tsp.	vanilla	2 mL
3	egg whites	3
⅓ cup	sugar	75 mL

Prepare pastry, line pie plate and bake until nicely browned. Set aside to cool.

In the top of a double boiler, mix together the flour, sugar and salt. Scald the milk and add to the dry ingredients, stirring constantly until thick. Add a small amount of this hot mixture to the beaten egg yolks, mix well and then return to the remaining hot mixture. Cook about 2 minutes longer. Remove from heat, add butter and vanilla and allow to cool.

Make the meringue by beating the egg whites until they stand in stiff peaks and gradually adding the sugar.

Pour the cream mixture into cooled shell, cover with meringue and bake in 350°F (180°C) oven for 10-15 minutes until meringue is lightly browned and set.

Fun with Basic Cream Pie

Variations on the basic cream pie are limited only by your imagination, the state of your frig and the stock in your cupboards! One trick is to make up one or two basic pies without adding the meringue. Use the egg whites for something else, and turn into a short order cook. That is, turn the basic pie into banana cream, strawberry, coconut, pineapple, date, peach, apricot, whatever. Slice or sprinkle the selected topping over an individual piece of pie and then top with lightly sweetened whipped cream. Save one whole berry or a slice or a sprinkle for garnish.

Another way of varying the basic cream pie is by turning it into Butterscotch Cream Pie, another favourite with truckers and just about everybody else! Simply substitute 1 cup brown sugar (250 mL) for the ⅔ cup white sugar called for in the recipe above, and increase the butter to 3 tbsp. (50 mL).

Pies & Pastry

Another kind of cream pie is the Open Sesame Cream Pie, a creation that combines dates and sesame seeds in a way that honors both.

Open Sesame Pie

4 tbsp.	sesame seeds	50 mL
1 cup	flour	250 mL
½ tsp.	salt	2 mL
⅓ cup	shortening	75 mL
3-4 tbsp.	cold water	50 mL
1 envelope	unflavoured gelatin	1 envelope
¼ cup	cold water	50 mL
1 cup	milk	250 mL
2	egg yolks	2
¼ cup	sugar	50 mL
dash	salt	dash
¾ cup	whipping cream	175 mL
1 tsp.	vanilla	5 mL
1 cup	dates, cut fine	250 mL
2	egg whites	2
2 tbsp.	sugar	30 mL
grated nutmeg for final garnish		

To make the shell, begin by toasting the sesame seeds in a pie plate at 325°F (160°C) until light brown. Remove from pan to mixing bowl and add flour and salt. Cut in the shortening until particles are the size of small peas. Gradually sprinkle 3-4 tbsp. cold water over mixture, stirring lightly with a fork. Form into a ball, roll out and fit into standard size pie plate. Crimp edges and secure over the rim of the pan. Prick with a fork and bake at 450°F (230°C) for 10-12 minutes or until golden brown. Cool.

(Note: Any pastry recipe could be used for the crust as long as the toasted sesame seeds are added and rolled out with the pastry.)

To make the filling, soften gelatin in cold water. Set aside.

In the top of a double boiler, mix together milk, egg yolks, sugar and salt. Cook over hot water, stirring constantly, until mixture coats a metal spoon. Add softened gelatin and stir until dissolved. Chill until almost set, stirring occasionally.

Whip the cream. Fold into the chilled mixture. Also add the vanilla and chopped dates.

Beat egg whites until soft mounds form. Add sugar gradually, beating after each addition. Fold the meringue into the date mixture. Pile into cooled shell and chill until firm. Just before serving, sprinkle with nutmeg.

Another favourite pie filling starts with cooked pumpkin, readily available all year round in cans. At traditional times of the year—like Thanksgiving—everyone seems to prefer a traditional form of Pumpkin Pie.

Traditional Pumpkin Pie

pastry enough for bottom crust of standard size pie

1½ cups	canned pumpkin	375 mL
¾ cup	sugar	175 mL
½ tsp.	salt	2 mL
½ tsp.	ginger	2 mL
¼ tsp.	nutmeg	1 mL
1 tsp.	cinnamon	5 mL
¼ tsp.	cloves (optional)	1 mL
3	eggs, beaten	3
1¾ cups	evaporated milk	425 mL

Note: The milk may also be a combination of 1 cup heavy cream, ¾ cup regular milk. The sugar may be all white, all brown or a combination. Instead of canned or cooked pumpkin, you may use baked winter squash, mashed sweet potatoes or cooked, mashed carrots. Decrease the sugar slightly for sweet potatoes or carrots. Prepare pastry and line the bottom of a standard size pie plate.

In a large bowl, mix together the pumpkin, sugar, salt and spices. Use the ground cloves if you want a dark spicy filling. Beat the eggs slightly and add with the milk to the pumpkin mixture. Blend well.

Pour into pie shell and bake in 450°F (230°C) oven for 10 minutes, then in a 325°F (160°C) oven for about 50 minutes, or until a knife blade inserted in the centre of the pie comes out clean. Garnish with whipped cream.

A hot oven for the first ten minutes of a pie's life should avoid a soggy bottom crust. So will an unbaked pie filling like the Pumpkin Chiffon Pie.

Pumpkin Chiffon Pie

pastry or crumb crust for bottom of standard pie plate

2 cups	canned pumpkin	500 mL
1 cup	brown sugar	250 mL
2 tsp.	cinnamon	10 mL
½ tsp.	ginger	2 mL
½ tsp.	nutmeg	2 mL
¼ tsp.	mace	1 mL
½ tsp.	vanilla	2 mL
2	eggs, separated	2
½ cup	cream or half & half	125 mL
1 envelope	plain gelatin	1 envelope
2 tbsp.	cold water	25 mL
2 tbsp.	sugar	30 mL

Prepare pie shell of your choice. Bake, if needed, and set aside.

In top of a double boiler, mix together the pumpkin, sugar, spices, vanilla, egg yolks and cream. Cook over hot water for 15 minutes.

Dissolve the gelatin in cold water and melt over hot water. Add to the pumpkin mixture. Stir well and cool.

When the mixture begins to set, beat the egg whites until stiff and add the sugar gradually. Fold into the chilled pumpkin. Pour into prepared pie shell and chill.

Millie, one of my cake baking friends, found this recipe for a wonderfully sweet pie.

French Mint Pie

pastry, crumb crust or meringue shell for 9" pie

1½ squares	unsweetened chocolate	1½ squares
1 cup	icing sugar	250 mL
½ cup	butter	125 mL
2	eggs	2
1 tbsp.	creme de menthe	15 mL
or 1 tsp.	artificial mint flavour	5 mL

Prepare crust, baking if necessary. Cool.

Melt chocolate over hot water. Let cool.

Beat sugar and butter until smooth. Add eggs, unbeaten, one at a time, beating until smooth. Add cooled chocolate and mint flavouring, tasting as you go since both the artificial and the creme de menthe liqueur vary greatly in intensity.

Spread into prepared pie shell. Chill.

For people with a whole set of sweet teeth, there is another kind of pie filling that brings smiles of delight at their very mention — maple syrup pie, sugar pie, pecan pie, even Shoo Fly pie. Very sweet and doubly rich, they all need (in my opinion) to be served with hard frozen ice cream. The cold chills your taste buds so you can savour the syrupy sweetness of the pies.

Maple Syrup Pie

pastry enough for bottom crust of standard size pie

1 cup	brown sugar	250 ml
1½ cups	maple syrup	375 mL
½ cup	milk	125 mL
4	eggs, separated	4
2 tbsp.	butter	25 mL
dash	grated nutmeg	dash

Prepare the pastry and line the pie plate. Set aside.

Separate the eggs and beat the yolks lightly.

Mix together the brown sugar, maple syrup, milk, egg yolks and butter. Beat the egg whites until stiff but not dry. Add the nutmeg and fold into the sugar mixture.

Pour into pie shell and bake at 350°F (180°C) for 25-30 minutes.

Pecan pie, Southern or otherwise, is probably the best known of this group of rich sweet pies. There are as many variations as there are written recipes. However, the basic syrup-egg proportion remains the same in most of them, and the spices can be varied to suit your own tastes.

Pecan Pie

pastry for bottom crust of standard size pie		
3	eggs, beaten	3
1 cup	corn syrup	250 mL
½ cup	brown sugar	125 mL
3 tbsp.	melted butter	50 mL
dash	salt	dash
¼ tsp.	nutmeg	1 mL
½ tsp.	cinnamon	2 mL
¾ tsp.	allspice	4 mL
½ tsp.	grated orange rind	2 mL
1 tsp.	vanilla	5 mL
1 cup	chopped pecans	250 mL
1 tbsp.	flour	15 mL

Prepare pastry and line bottom of a pie plate. Set aside.

Mix all ingredients except the pecans and flour. In a smaller bowl, mix together the chopped pecans and flour and add them to the first mixture. Pour into prepared crust, and bake in 400°F (200°C) oven for 10 minutes, then in a 350°F (180°C) oven for an additional 35 minutes. To test, insert a silver knife into center. If it comes out clean, the pie is done. The filling will set further as it cools.

Top with whipped cream and pecan halves just before serving.

To make a slightly different version of this pie, you can also use ½ cup (125 mL) chopped pecans, ½ cup (125 mL) raisins.

When it comes to tarts, my mother's butter tarts top the list. She made hers with currants but chopped raisins or pecans or a mixture of dried fruit and nuts may also be used.

Mom's Butter Tarts

pastry enough to line tart forms, about 12 total		
½ cup	butter	125 mL
1 cup	brown sugar	250 mL
1 tsp.	cornstarch	5 mL
dash	salt	dash
1	egg, lightly beaten	1
⅓ cup	water	75 mL
1 tsp.	vanilla	5 mL
1 cup	currants	250 mL

Prepare pastry and line tart shells. Set aside.

Cream butter with sugar, cornstarch and salt. Add egg, water, vanilla and currants. Spoon into pastry lined tart shells, filling about ⅔ full.

Bake in 350°F (180°C) oven for 25 minutes or until set.

Variations: Cream cheese pastry is particularly good in this recipe. See page 201. Also, you may substitute milk or cream for the water in the recipe.

My mother-in-law, a native of London, England, used to make the most delicious morsels called Cheese Tarts. However, I was never able to get the recipe from her because she had been sworn to secrecy, and she kept that promise fiercely. Thus, I've spent many an hour trying to duplicate her Cheese Tarts, sometimes coming close but never quite achieving the original. In the process, however, I came up with Viennese Tarts and Maids of Honour.

Viennese Tarts

rich pastry to line 12 deep or 24 shallow tart shells

6 tbsp.	butter	75 mL
⅓ cup	berry sugar	75 mL
1	egg, beaten	1
1 tsp.	grated lemon rind	5 mL
½ tsp.	vanilla	2 mL
1 cup	pastry flour	250 mL
1 tsp.	baking powder	5 mL
dash	salt	dash
1 tbsp.	lemon juice	15 mL
1 tbsp.	milk	15 mL

thick jam to fill bottom of each tart shell

Prepare pastry (there's a good rich one on page 201), line tart shells and set aside.

Instead of berry sugar, you can use the same amount of white sugar. Instead of 1 cup (250 mL) pastry flour, you can use ⅞ cup (220 mL) all purpose white flour.

Cream the butter and gradually blend in sugar. Add beaten egg, grated lemon rind and vanilla.

Mix together the flour, baking powder and salt. Add ⅓ of the flour mixture to the creamed mixture, add the lemon juice and blend well. Add the next ⅓ of the flour mixture to the creamed mixture with the milk. Blend well. Add remaining flour mixture.

In the bottom of each pastry lined tart shell, place a dollop of thick jam—plum, apricot, raspberry or strawberry, for example. The size of the dollop depends on whether you're making good sized or tea sized tarts, somewhere between a teaspoon and a tablespoon. Over the jam, drop a spoonful of the tart batter, filling each tart about ⅔ full.

Bake in 400°F (200°C) oven for 8 minutes; reduce heat to 350°F (180°C) and bake 12-15 minutes longer or until pastry and batter are cooked.

Some Viennese Tarts call for a sprinkle of coconut just before baking.

Maids of Honour were supposedly created by Anne Boleyn to please Henry VIII, an effort that was apparently successful since she went from Maid of Honour to Queen.

Maids of Honour

rich pastry to line 16 large, 24 small tart shells

1/3 cup	soft bread crumbs	75 mL
dash	salt	dash
1 1/4 cups	milk, scalded	300 mL
1/2 cup	butter	125 mL
2 tbsp.	sugar	30 mL
2	eggs, well beaten	2
1	lemon, grated	1
3/4 cup	ground almonds	175 mL

Prepare pastry (there's a good rich one on page 181). Line the tart shells, leaving rim of pastry above the shells. Prick well with a fork and bake in a 450°F (230°C) oven until set—about 5-6 minutes. If you want to keep a good tart shape, line the pastry with wax paper and fill with rice or beans. When the tart shells are baked, remove the paper containing the rice or beans and you should have a shapely tart shell without undue bumps or shrinking. Cool.

Add the bread crumbs and salt to the hot milk. Let stand 10 minutes. Then add the remaining ingredients, mixing all together thoroughly. Spoon this mixture into the baked tart shells, filling each one about 2/3 full.

Bake in 300°F (150°C) oven for 20 minutes or until custard is set.

Instant biscuit mix produces one of the easiest pies to come down the pike in a long time! For many years, I made Buttermilk Pie in the traditional time consuming way. Not any more. I now use the blender.

Buttermilk Pie

1 cup	buttermilk	250 mL
1/3 cup	butter, melted	75 mL
3	eggs	3
1 tsp.	vanilla	5 mL
1 1/2 cups	sugar	375 mL
1/2 cup	instant biscuit mix	125 mL

Grease a large pie plate.

Put all ingredients into a blender and beat on high for 30 seconds (or 1 minute with a hand mixer). Pour into prepared pie plate.

Bake at 350°F (180°C) for 30 minutes or until knife inserted in centre comes out clean. Cool for 5 minutes before serving to give the bottom crust time to form. Top with fresh fruit, if desired.

Forgotten Pie is another easy one. It's actually a meringue shaped into a crust and put into the oven, there to be forgotten until the next day.

Forgotten Pie

4	egg whites	4
⅛ tsp.	cream of tartar	1 mL
1 cup	sugar	250 mL
1 tsp.	vanilla	5 mL
½ cup	chopped nuts	125 mL

cream filling enough to make the pie unforgettable!

Grease and flour a deep pie plate.

Beat egg whites until foamy. Add the cream of tartar and continue beating until stiff but not dry. Add the sugar very gradually, beating until the mixture stands in stiff peaks. Fold in vanilla and chopped nuts. (Use walnuts, pecans, almonds, macadamia, etc.)

Spoon into the prepared pie plate, making sure the bottom is well covered and sides are high enough to hold whatever filling you choose.

Put into a 275°F (140°C) oven for 40 minutes; then turn off the heat without peeking inside, and leave the pie overnight.

Fill with basic cream filling (page 189) or maple syrup souffle (page 156) or fresh berries or whatever time and taste dictates!

There's more to cracker crumb crusts than graham wafers! Cousin Doris uses digestive biscuits, my mother used to prefer vanilla wafers, and I've used a whole variety of crumbs, everything from zwieback to fine dry breadcrumbs, cornflakes to granola.

The Formula for Crumb Crusts

For each cup (250 mL) of crumbs, use ¼ cup (50mL) melted butter or margarine. Add sugar (brown is best) according to the sweetness of the crumbs used — about ⅓ cup (75 mL) is needed to sweeten not-so-sweet breadcrumbs, for example. Vanilla wafers, cornflakes or granola would require less.

Depending on the filling to be used, you may also add a dash of cinnamon or nutmeg.

Mix well and press into bottom and up sides of pie plate or baking dish. Bake at 350°F (180°C) for 10 minutes, and then chill before filling.

Being named one of Canada's ten best restaurants in 1972 and 1973 was something of a mixed blessing.

It was wonderful, of course, to be given such an honour. But it also meant such crowds of people. And because we were located in the country, people somehow didn't believe it would be necessary to make a reservation.

I'd be rich if I had a nickel for every disappointed customer who, upon being turned away, would say, "But we've driven all the way from Calgary."

One woman didn't believe me when I told her we couldn't possibly take any more people. She sat in the lobby with a notebook and counted people as they came in. Finally, she admitted to me, "You really are full."

Recipes illustrated overleaf

The following Chocolate Coconut Crust is perfect for people who love chocolate and easy desserts!

Chocolate Coconut Crust

2 squares	unsweetened chocolate	2 squares
2 tbsp.	butter	25 mL
2 tbsp.	hot milk or water	25 mL
⅔ cup	icing sugar	150 mL
1½ cups	unsweetened coconut	375 mL

Use the medium shred coconut or you'll have trouble cutting the crust later on.

Grease a large pie plate and set aside.

In the top of a double boiler over hot water, melt the chocolate with the butter. Add hot milk or water and icing sugar, stirring well. Add the coconut and mix well.

Spread on the bottom and sides of prepared pie plate. Chill until firm.

The crust can be frozen and used to create quick and easy desserts when emergencies dictate. Just fill with ice cream or cream filling or chiffon type filling.

If you want to get really spectacular, try the Mauna Loa, a flaming dessert that's easier than it looks! (No one needs to know!)

Mauna Loa or Flaming Volcano Pie

1 recipe for Chocolate Coconut crust, see above		
8 cups	ice cream	2 L
3	egg whites	3
½ cup	sugar	125 mL
macadamia nuts, if desired		

Prepare the Chocolate Coconut Crust as above.

Use vanilla ice cream and add macadamia nuts, if you want to be Hawaiian about this. Otherwise, use whatever ice cream pleases your family—maple walnut is good since it already has nuts added or black walnut.

Let the ice cream soften slightly and pile into the crust, shaping it up into a high peak in the centre ... like a volcano.

Beat the egg whites until stiff; then add the sugar gradually and beat until stiff and dry. Spoon the meringue over the ice cream, also building it into a volcano shape. Make sure the meringue covers the ice cream completely, sealing it well to the crust.

Fit a small metal cap into the crater at the top of the volcano or fashion a small cup from foil. This is to hold the flame eventually.

Keep in freezer until ready to serve. Then bring it out, brown lightly in a 475°F (240°C) oven for 2-3 minutes, watching all the while. Warm a few tablespoons of sherry or brandy, pour carefully into the crater and ignite. Dim the lights and bring on the flaming dessert, and don't admit that it wasn't all that complicated!

Pies & Pastry

We never really had swans on our Willow Creek behind the house, but we made hundreds of Willow Creek Swans for the restaurant through the years. They are made of choux paste, otherwise known as cream puff dough, and they taste as good as they look.

Choux Paste

2 cups	water	500 mL
1 cup	butter	250 mL
dash	salt	dash
2 cups	flour	500 mL
8	eggs	8

In a large heavy saucepan, mix water, butter and salt. Bring to a boil, making sure the butter is completely melted and mixed. Remove from the heat and add all the flour at once, beating vigorously with a wooden spoon. Return to the heat and cook, stirring continuously, until the mixture comes away from the sides of the pan and forms a very stiff ball.

Remove from the heat once again and add the eggs one at a time, beating each one until completely absorbed by the dough before adding the next one.

Willow Creek Swans

Make up a batch of choux paste, see above.

Use most of the dough to make regulation size cream puff shells. Reserve just a bit to form the swan necks.

Put the reserved dough into a piping bag or cookie press and press out an "S" shape. Use ungreased pans.

Bake cream puffs in a 400°F (200°C) oven for 10 minutes; then in a 350°F (180°C) oven for an additional 25 minutes. Bake the necks for the first 10 minutes only. Both the shells and the necks should be firm to the touch, not damp in any way. Turn off the oven and leave them to dry a bit longer, if need be.

To assemble the swans, cut off the top third of each cream puff and then cut that piece in half lengthwise. Put aside to form the wings when the time comes to fly.

Fill the bottom of the cream puffs with sweetened whipped cream or Chantilly Cream (page 170). Fit the "S" pieces into the front to form the neck and head. Put the two wing pieces in place. Sprinkle with icing sugar and float on a mirror if you're feeling fancy. Otherwise, float on a serving plate and watch them disappear.

Notes and Variations

If you like puff pastry but hate the bother of making it, try this easy version.

Sour Cream Pastry Tarts

1 cup	butter	250 mL
1½ cups	flour	375 mL
½ cup	sour cream	125 mL
½ cup	thick jam	125 mL

water and sugar to sprinkle over finished product

Cut butter into flour until it resembles coarse crumbs. Add sour cream, mixing it in gently with a fork. Shape into two balls and chill at least 8 hours or overnight.

When ready to bake, roll dough out thinly and cut into desired shapes, at least two of every shape. Put the first layer on an ungreased baking sheet, cut an opening in the second one and lay it on the first. Fill the opening with a half teaspoonful of thick jam, your choice. Brush tops lightly with water and sprinkle with sugar.

Bake at 350°F (180°C) for about 20 minutes or until sugar has melted into a glaze and pastry is lightly browned. Cool on wire rack.

Makes about 2 dozen.

For a change from regular pastry, try one based on cream cheese.

Cream Cheese Pastry

1 small pkg.	cream cheese	1 small pkg. (125 g)
5 tbsp.	butter	60 mL
1 cup	flour	250 mL

Using a pastry blender (or your fingertips), lightly mix cream cheese, butter and flour. When well mixed, form into a ball, wrap in wax paper and chill for at least one hour.

Particularly good for tart shells. Will make 12-18, depending on tart size.

Pies & Pastry

COOKIES, BARS & CANDIES

Shortbread is my first choice in cookies—perhaps it is my Scottish background showing up. I just wish some of those ancestors had been peering over my shoulder when I made a tremendous batch for a Christmas banquet at The Flying N one year and quadrupled everything but the flour. The result was a giant lace cookie, which disintegrated at the touch of a spatula. Mind you, we had a lot of desserts with a delicious buttery crumb base for the next few weeks and didn't waste a drop. It's better in the long run, I decided, to stick with the rule—Never ever double a recipe. It is no saving.

True Shortbread

1 lb.	butter	500 g
1 cup	sugar	250 mL
4 cups	flour	1 L

Cream the butter until soft. Add the sugar gradually, blending until very light and creamy. Add the flour gradually, again blending carefully.

Pat the dough out on a lightly floured board, shape as desired and place on baking sheet. The traditional shortbread is shaped into circles, about 8″ across, pinched on the edges and pricked on the top. Bake 375°F (190°C) for about 5 minutes, then lower the oven to 300°F (150°C) and continue baking for 45-60 minutes. Shortbread should be golden but not brown when done. Cut into wedges while still warm.

Variations on True Shortbread

Although true shortbread contains only three basic ingredients, these three can be altered somewhat. For instance, fresh unsalted butter can be used instead of the regular butter; it makes a very delicate shortbread. Brown sugar or powdered sugar may be used. As for the flour, substitute one cup of rice flour for one cup of regular flour, or use ¾ cup cornstarch in place of one cup of regular flour. Whatever you do, do not add eggs or vanilla or nuts or cherries. You'll be making a good cookie or bar, but it will not be true shortbread.

Not to be confused with traditional Christmas shortbread, my cousin Betty makes Cheese Shortbread. These were served at the first Art Show and Auction of the Stockmen's Foundation, and had the art work disappeared as quickly as the goodies, the auction would have set a world record.

Betty's Cheese Shortbread

4 oz.	sharp cheese	125 g
4 tbsp.	berry sugar	50 mL
1 cup	butter	250 mL
2 cups	flour	500 mL

Use the soft crumbly cheese, the kind that comes in a round red box.

Mix the four ingredients together well, form into rolls about 1½″ (4 cm) across, wrap in wax paper or foil and chill overnight.

When ready to bake, slice thin and bake at 350°F (180°C) for 10-12 minutes.

A very easy nibble for after dinners, or any time for that matter, is one my Aunt Agnes used to make.

The Agnes Nibble

1 cup	whole almonds	250 mL
⅓ cup	sugar	75 mL
¼ cup	water	50 mL

Use whole unblanched almonds. They have the best flavour.

In a heavy skillet over medium heat, toss the almonds, sugar and water. Keep them moving with a fork and in a few minutes, the almonds will have absorbed the water and will have a lovely sugared coating.

Quick, easy and delicious for an impromptu snack.

It used to be a bit of a chore finding (or making) dipping chocolate, but ever since the homemade chocolate boom, it's been readily available in many stores. I have tried not only the dark or milk chocolate but also the white and pastel colours. My favourite of all is Whole Dipped Strawberries.

Whole Dipped Strawberries

milk chocolate, melted
whole perfect strawberries, stems on
liqueur to be injected into berries

Choose large perfect strawberries. Wash carefully so that the stems remain. Marinate in a liqueur like kirsch or Grand Marnier, or inject a squirt into each berry. There is a special syringe made for this purpose. The berries are also fine as is.

Melt the chocolate. Holding the berries by the stem, dip them in until about ⅔ of the bottom of the berry is covered with chocolate. Place on wax paper to harden. Serve as soon as possible. They do not keep overnight, but they can be made during the afternoon and still be perfect for an after-dinner treat.

My friend Jesse comes from Texas and when he returns from family visits, he brings along pecans picked from his family's groves. Believe me, I don't just throw them into any old recipe that calls for chopped nuts. They are saved for special dishes where they are shown off to best advantage — like in Mary Cartwright's Pecan Kisses.

Mary Cartwright's Pecan Kisses

2	egg whites	2
¾ cup	light brown sugar	175 mL
½ tsp.	vanilla	2 mL
2 cups	chopped pecans	500 mL

Keep some whole pecans for garnish.

Beat the egg whites until stiff and add the sugar gradually. Add vanilla. Do not underbeat. Fold in chopped pecans and drop by teaspoonfuls on well greased cookie sheet or lined pie plates. Top each with a whole pecan.

Bake at 250°F (140°C) for 30 minutes, then turn off oven and leave for another 30 minutes without opening the door.

Makes 24 cookies. Will freeze well.

Speaking of goodies that freeze well, I used to find in my freezer a pan of squares that I particularly liked but could never get the recipe for. Whenever I asked my friend Helen for the recipe, she would just say, "I'll make them for you", and she was as good as her word. But she finally relented for this book and here is the recipe for Helen's Birthday Surprise Squares.

Helen's Birthday Surprise Squares

36 (1 pkg.)	coconut cookies	36 (1 pkg.)
¼ cup	butter	50 mL
2 squares	semi-sweet chocolate	2 squares
¼ cup	butter	50 mL
1½ cups	icing sugar	375 mL
1 tsp.	vanilla	5 mL
1	egg, beaten	1
1 cup	walnuts, chopped	250 mL

Dad's Cookies work well for this recipe. Crush the cookies, melt the first ¼ cup (50 mL) butter and mix together. Pat ⅔ of the mixture into a 9x9″ (2.5 L) pan and bake for 5 minutes at 300°F (150°C).

Melt the chocolate and second ¼ cup of butter over hot water. Add the icing sugar, vanilla, beaten egg and walnuts. Spread over the crumb layer and sprinkle with remaining crumbs. Refrigerate. Cut in squares when chilled.

For the ultimate in richness, however, Irene's Caramel Squares are first in place. Following her instructions, I always make a double batch because, as she says, "What can you do with a half can of Eagle brand condensed milk?" Thus, the following recipe has already been doubled and needs a big pan.

Irene's Caramel Squares

1 cup	flour	250 mL
½ cup	brown sugar	125 mL
½ cup	butter	125 mL
1 cup	butter	250 mL
1 cup	brown sugar	250 mL
4 tbsp.	golden syrup	50 mL
1 can (cup)	Eagle brand milk	250 mL
12 oz. pkg.	chocolate chips	375 g

To make the shortbread base, combine the flour and ½ cup brown sugar. Mix in the ½ cup butter with a pastry cutter or by hand until the mixture resembles crumbs. Then pack into a 12x9″ pan (3.5 L) and bake in a 350°F (180°C) oven until light brown, about 12-15 minutes.

In a saucepan with a good heavy bottom, melt the 1 cup butter, add sugar, syrup and sweetened condensed milk. Cook 5 minutes, stirring constantly. Pour over the shortbread base and allow to cool thoroughly.

Melt the chocolate chips over hot water and spread over the cooled caramel mixture. Refrigerate to set. Cut into squares or bars. It turns out like old fashioned caramel candy and Scottish shortbread combined, with chocolate thrown in for good measure. Don't try to count the calories. Just enjoy.

Over the years, I haven't had a lot of good to say about rice cereal and the various cookies and bars made with the cereal ... which is why I thought I should include the following. It's remarkably good and I take back some of my unkind words.

How to Say Sorry to a Rice Krispie

1 cup	butter	250 mL
½ cup	white sugar	125 mL
½ cup	brown sugar	125 mL
1	egg, beaten	1
1¼ cups	flour	300 mL
½ tsp.	baking powder	2 mL
½ tsp.	salt	2 mL
1 tsp.	vanilla	5 mL
1 cup	oatmeal	250 mL
1 cup	rice krispies	250 mL
½ cup	coconut	125 mL
½ cup	chopped nuts	125 mL

Cream butter, gradually add sugars and mix well. Add beaten egg and beat until fluffy.

Mix together the dry ingredients and add to the creamed mixture. Stir in vanilla.

Add the remaining ingredients. Drop onto greased cookie sheet. Bake in 375°F (190°C) oven for 12-15 minutes or until light brown.

Cookies & Candy

The chocolate fudge of my early days was a pretty unreliable process largely dependent upon luck. The following version is a bit more involved but much more reliable. Flexible too since it can be turned into six different versions.

Basic White Fudge

³⁄₄ cup	evaporated milk	175 mL
3 cups	granulated sugar	750 mL
3 tbsp.	butter	50 mL
³⁄₄ cup	water	175 mL
³⁄₄ tsp.	salt	3 mL
1¹⁄₂ tsp.	vanilla	7 mL
³⁄₄ cup	marshmallow cream	175 mL
¹⁄₃ cup	chopped nuts, fruit	75 mL

Mix the first five ingredients in a large saucepan and heat to the boiling point, stirring continually. Maintain a full rolling boil, stirring all the while, until a candy thermometer registers 236°, or a soft ball forms when a bit is dropped into cold water. Remove from heat and cool to room temperature, without stirring, until mixture registers 110° on the thermometer or lukewarm to the hand.

Add vanilla at this point and beat until the mixture holds its shape. Add marshmallow cream and the optional chopped nuts or fruit. Beat again until the mixture loses its shine and is stiff. Spread quickly in 8x8" (2 L) buttered pan.

The following variations all use the above basic recipe—just the names and tastes are changed.

Chocolate Fudge

Follow the basic recipe as above until the soft ball stage is reached or until the candy thermometer registers 236°. To make chocolate fudge, add 12 oz. (375 g) chocolate chips while the mixture is still very hot, stirring just enough to make a marbled effect or stirring until an even color is achieved. Allow to cool, then stir until the mixture holds its shape. Add the marshmallow cream, nuts if desired, and once again, beat until the shine is gone and the mixture is stiff.

Lemon Fudge

Make the basic white fudge as described above but omit the vanilla and fruit or nuts. Add 1¹⁄₂ tsp. (7 mL) grated lemon rind and 8 drops of yellow food coloring just before adding the marshmallow cream.

Orange Fudge

Make the basic white fudge as described above but omit the vanilla and fruit or nuts. Add 1¹⁄₂ tbsp. (20 mL) grated orange rind and both yellow and red food coloring—to make a total of 8 drops—before adding the marshmallow cream.

Coffee Fudge

Make the basic white fudge as described above but add 3 tsp. (15 mL) instant coffee to the first five ingredients before cooking. Follow the rest of the recipe as outlined. Cut into squares or form into rolls, coat the rolls with chopped nuts and slice when firm.

Maple Walnut Fudge

Make the basic white fudge as described above but omit vanilla and fruits. Use ¾ tsp. (3 mL) imitation maple extract instead of the vanilla, and add chopped walnuts or pecans.

I was an only child until I was ten years old, and although I filled my time as well as I could with reading (under the covers with a flashlight when necessary), there were still moments when I needed something to do. To be allowed to make a batch of candy was my favorite solution to this problem of "What to do?"

When I moved to Alberta, I quickly learned to make my Aunt Dorothy's Sour Cream Orange Fudge, partly because it tasted so good but also because Buttercup gave us unlimited supplies of cream.

Aunt Dorothy's Sour Cream Orange Fudge

3 cups	brown sugar	750 mL
1 cup	sour cream	250 mL
¼ cup	orange juice	50 mL
pinch	salt	pinch
¼ cup	soft butter	50 mL
1	orange, grated	1
1 cup	nuts, chopped	250 mL

Butter an 8x8″ (2 L) pan. Grate the orange and reserve the grated rind for later in the recipe. Also, because fresh orange juice is best, squeeze the orange you've just grated and keep until required.

Over medium heat in a fairly heavy pan, cook together the brown sugar, sour cream and orange juice, stirring until the mixture comes to the boiling point. Then continue boiling without stirring until mixture reaches 240° on a candy thermometer, or until it forms a soft ball when dropped in cold water — a process that should take some 8-10 minutes.

Remove from heat and add salt, butter and orange rind. Beat until the mixture thickens and loses its shine. Add the chopped nuts, if desired, and pour into the buttered pan. Allow to cool and cut into fairly small squares. The candy is very rich.

If you're not keen on a strong orange flavour, substitute 1 tsp. vanilla for the grated orange rind.

Notes and Variations

A good friend, Rhea, who lives in a beautiful home overlooking Hood Canal off the west coast of Washington, brings this wonderful Almond Roca along when she and her husband come to Alberta on hunting trips. I also enjoy it when we go to Hood Canal to fish for salmon.

Wonderful Almond Roca

1 lb.	butter	500 g
2¼ cups	sugar	550 mL
1 cup	whole almonds	250 mL
4 squares	sweet chocolate	4 squares
½ cup	chopped walnuts	125 mL

In a heavy pan over high heat, using a long handled spoon, stir the butter until it is melted. Add the sugar and stir continuously until foamy and doughy; then turn to low and cook another 5 minutes, stirring occasionally. Add almonds, turn heat to high until the nuts spit two or three times (about 3 minutes) and then turn to low again for 10 minutes. Total cooking time should be no more than 20 minutes.

Pour out onto an ungreased cookie sheet — best to use one with edges. Let cool.

In the meantime, melt the chocolate over hot water (or in a microwave). Spread half the chocolate over the cooled roca and then press half the chopped walnuts into the chocolate. When completely cooled, flip the roca slab over into the original pan or have a slightly larger one handy, if flipping's not your thing. Spread the rest of the chocolate on this side of the roca, press the remaining nuts into the chocolate. Cool and break into pieces.

DRINKS

We used to have two punchbowls, one for the alcoholic punch and one for the juice punch. To distinguish them, my friend Clarence carved two faces on wooden planks which were hung behind the appropriate punch bowl. They were identical except for one small thing—in the centre of the forehead of one of the faces was a large nail. This was the "spiked" bowl ... get it?

The word "punch" is said to have come from a Hindustani word meaning "five". And sure enough, when British soldiers discovered punch, among other things, in India in the 16th century, they found it contained five things: one sweet, one sour, one bitter, one weak and one of fermented spirits. They quickly got the hang of the thing and invented rum punch which has been popular ever since.

Our most popular non-alcoholic drink at the restaurants was undoubtedly hot apple cider. We served lakesful ... until the manufacturer discontinued that particular kind of apple juice. We then served up lakesful of a combination of apple juice and cranberry juice.

Hot Fruit Cider

Mix 1 can apple juice with one big jar cranberry juice. Heat in a large container. Add 2 whole cinnamon sticks, 2 baked apples and 2 whole oranges stuck with whole cloves. Keep on the simmer until served.

Some people have lovely punch bowls with matching cups and cute little ladles. Then again, some don't ... but do not despair!

Punch Bowls with a Difference

A large watermelon can double for a fruit punch bowl. Cut lengthwise, removing the top third of the watermelon and keeping the other ⅔ for the container. Scoop out the meat and use in fruit salads or use some in a ring mold—see above. Mix the punch in another container and pour into the watermelon.

Bowl shaped ice containers can also be concocted. Try fitting a smaller bowl inside a bigger one. Fill the space in between the two with water and freeze. To use, stand in more ice and hope for the best.

Try freezing some of the juice that goes into the punch in ice cube trays. Add to the punch at the last minute. Put a sprig of mint into each cube.

The sky's the limit when it comes to punch ... in more ways than one!

When I was growing up in Toronto, Ontario, there was no going down to the nearest convenience store for a handy cold drink. Instead, my mother kept a jar of Boston Cream in the icebox, a lovely cool refreshing drink.

When I had two thirsty kids of my own, I wrote to mom asking for the recipe. Fortunately, she found it in an old cookbook put out by the ladies of Danforth Avenue Baptist Church in Toronto many years ago.

Boston Cream

2 cups	sugar	500 mL
4 cups	water	1 L
2 tbsp.	tartaric acid	30 mL
1 tsp.	vanilla	5 mL
1	egg white	1
ice water and baking soda		

Notes: Tartaric acid is available in the spice sections of most supermarkets. Otherwise, it's available in drug stores.

Boil sugar in the water until dissolved. Allow to cool. Add the tartaric acid and vanilla. Beat the egg white until it holds stiff peaks and add. Keep in a covered jar in the frig.

To serve, put 2 tbsp. (25 mL) of the mixture in a tall glass. Fill ⅔ full with ice water. Add ¼ tsp. baking soda per glass and stir briefly. The action of the baking soda and acid will cause the mixture to bubble up and over, thus creating an illusion of cream.

It's very refreshing – not too sweet and fun to watch!

Soda fountains have gone the way of many old pleasures. I know I can get the same thing by adding a carbonated drink to ice cream but I miss the tall glasses, the soda jerk behind the counter, the whole atmosphere.

However, I discovered some years ago that non-alcoholic eggnogs have a soda fountain look and taste, especially made this way with ice cream.

Orange Ice Cream Eggnog

3	eggs	3
3 tbsp.	sugar	50 mL
2½ cups	ice water	625 mL
1 large can	orange juice concentrate	1 large can (355 mL)
¼ cup	lemon juice	50 mL
2 cups	ice cream	500 mL
1½ cups	ginger ale	375 mL

Beat eggs and sugar together until light and lemon coloured. Add the water, orange juice concentrate and lemon juice.

In a fairly large bowl or punchbowl, place scoops of the ice cream. Pour juice mixture over the ice cream. Add ginger ale for sparkle just before serving.

Enough for 10 servings.

I always tried to provide two punches—one with alcohol and one without, and generally I tried to make them look somewhat similar so that neither the drinkers nor the non-drinkers needed to feel self conscious about their choices. This is what we served to approximate champagne.

Mock Pink Champagne

½ cup	sugar	125 mL
1½ cups	water	375 mL
2 cups	cranberry juice	500 mL
1 cup	pineapple juice	250 mL
½ cup	orange juice	125 mL
2 cups	lemon/lime pop	500 mL

Notes: The lemon/lime pop may be any carbonated soft drink with the flavour of lemon or lime.

Boil the sugar and water together until the sugar is dissolved. Cool. Add cranberry juice, pineapple juice and orange juice. Chill well. Just before serving, add the carbonated beverage.

The non-alcoholic version of the popular drink known as Slush is this one called Banana Crush.

Banana Crush

4 cups	sugar	1 L
6 cups	water	1.5 L
5	oranges	5
2	lemons	2
5	bananas	5
1 large can	pineapple juice	1 large can (1.36 L)
carbonated water to complete the drink		

Note: Carbonated water is the best thing to add to this slush because it doesn't add any calories—just fizz. However, you can also use a fruit pop or ginger ale.

Make a syrup by boiling the sugar and water together for 3 minutes. Cool.

Squeeze juice from oranges and lemons. Crush the bananas. Add the pineapple juice. Mix up together and stir in cooled syrup. Freeze.

To serve, beat the frozen mixture with a spoon and fill glasses half full of mixture. Fill the rest of the way with carbonated water to give the drink its fizz.

Makes about 30 glasses (12 oz. each).

Drinks

Any punch, alcoholic or otherwise, looks particularly nice with a floating ring of ice instead of the ubiquitous ice cubes.

Floating Ring of Ice

> boiled water to fill a ring mold
> fruit such as strawberries, raspberries, kiwi, peach slices
> leaves such as mint, strawberry tops, flower petals

Fill a ring mold about ⅓ full of boiled water — boiled water doesn't have as many bubbles. Let sit for awhile, stirring occasionally to remove any remaining bubbles. Then arrange the fruit, leaves and/or flower petals in the water, remembering that the ring will be floating with the bottom side up so put the best parts facing toward the bottom. Freeze. Then fill with more boiled water.

Add to punch bowl after the punch is assembled so that it can float up top, showing off its lovely bottom.

A basic fruit punch is a handy thing to have in case of family reunions, community picnics, you name it.

Basic Fruit Punch

1 small can	orange juice concentrate	1 small can (178 mL)
1 large can	limeade concentrate	1 large can (355 mL)
1 large can	pineapple juice	1 large can (1.36 L)
2 cups	cranberry cocktail	500 mL
4 cups	cold water	1 L
8 cups	chilled ginger ale	2 L
2 cups	chilled club soda	500 mL
ice cubes or fruited ice ring		

Notes: The small cans of frozen juice concentrate are 6 oz. (178 mL). The large cans are 12.5 oz. (355 mL). Both the orange juice concentrate and the limeade concentrate should be frozen. The large can of pineapple juice is 48 oz. (1.36 L).

Put frozen concentrates, pineapple, cranberry juice and water into a large container. Let stand until the frozen juice is thawed — just a few minutes. Pour mixture into a punchbowl and add enough ice to keep it very cool.

Just before serving, gently pour in ginger ale and club soda. Garnish with fruit ring or fancy ice cubes.

Notes and Variations

Drinks

The first restaurant out in the country was never licensed to sell alcoholic drinks but when we moved to The Flying N nearer town, we became a fully licensed outlet. Once this was bestowed upon us, we decided we should have a house specialty.

Thus we hit upon the plan of using one of our nicknames— the Flying Hens— and turning it into a unique mixed drink. With such a name, the drink would naturally have to include an egg.

You have no idea— until you try it— how hard it is to work an egg into a drink. The taste of the egg kills the flavour of practically everyting else so it took many weeks of experimenting with various combinations of liquors, liqueurs and mixers before we finally hit on the right one ... the now famous Flying Hen.

The Flying Hen Drink

1 oz.	white rum	30 mL
1 oz.	Galliano	30 mL
½ oz.	apricot brandy	15 mL
1-2 oz.	orange juice	30 - 60 mL
1-2 oz.	pineapple juice	30 - 60 mL
1	egg	1

orange, lemon or lime slices, cherries, strawberries

Measure out the rum, Galliano·and brandy. Pour into a blender. Add juices (amount depends on the strength of drink desired). Add egg. Blend for about 30 seconds.

Prepare a large brandy snifter by half filling with ice cubes. Don't used crushed ice since it melts too quickly and dilutes the drink. Pour contents of blender over the ice.

Arrange fruit garnishes on a long plastic or wooden pick and place across the glass.

To make more than one Flying Hen, premix the liquor and liqueur. Then just add the juices and the egg.

The most Canadian of mixed drinks includes one portion of sweet, one of sour and one of strong. Once assembled, it's one powerful drink!

The Most Canadian Cocktail of All

1 oz	rye whiskey	30 mL
1 oz.	pure maple syrup	30 mL
1 oz.	fresh lemon juice	30 mL

Mix ingredients, shake with ice and sip with respect.

Drinks

The Scandinavian Glogg is a popular after skiing drink, often served around a roaring fire with friends and snacks nearby. Legend has it that glogg was originally heated by daring souls who grabbed hot pokers right out of the fire and applied them to the drink. Certainly more exciting than the modern method which uses tame old stoves!

Glogg, Otherwise Known as Great

3 bottles	red wine	3 bottles
10 slices	orange	10 slices
whole cloves to use with the orange slices		
15	whole cardamom seeds	15
2 bottles	aqvavit	2 bottles
20	sugar cubes	20
2 cups	blanched almonds	500 mL
2 cups	seedless raisins	500 mL

Place wine in a non-metallic pan, preferably an enamelled saucepan. Stud orange slices with whole cloves. Add to the wine mixture along with the cardamom seeds. Simmer—do not boil—for 10 minutes.

Heat aqvavit in a separate enamelled pan.

When everything is hot, pour the wine mixture into a sturdy punchbowl. Place a metal grate over the bowl. Moisten sugar cubes with a bit of the aqvavit and place on the grate above the hot wine mixture. Ignite remaining aqvavit and slowly pour over sugar until all sugar is melted and gone into the wine. Add any remaining aqvavit.

To serve, put a few almonds and raisins into each punch cup or metal stein and ladle hot liquid over them. Serves 35-40.

While glogg may be perfect for long winter evenings, slush is more what's needed for long summer evenings.

Slush in the Summer

8 cups	water	2 L
4 cups	sugar	1 L
6	lemons	6
5	oranges	2
2	bananas, mashed	2
1½ cups	lemon juice	375 mL
48 oz.	grapefruit juice	1.36 L
26 oz.	vodka	750 mL
lemon/lime carbonated soft drink		

Notes: Use unsweetened grapefruit or pineapple juice. Any carbonated soft drink will do at the end but lemon/lime is the best.

Boil the water and sugar together for 15 minutes. Then add the juice and pulp of the lemons and oranges. Mash the bananas and add. Add remaining ingredients and mix well.

Put into the freezer and stir occasionally. It won't freeze hard but will remain slushy—which is the whole idea!

To serve, fill glasses ⅔ full and add a carbonated lemon/lime drink.

Drinks

One year, we decided to have a big community barbecue and ask the oldtimers in the district to come and share their memories. So many people came that the local Mounties came out to see why so many cars were turning off at the Pulteney Corner, normally a pretty slow spot!

From that grew the Willow Creek Historical Society, the meetings of which became my favourite fringe benefit since the members met first at the Driftwood Room and later at The Flying N. Each year, we chose a different group of people to honour—cowboys, Indians, the RCMP, writers, anyone who had made an impact on our local history. Then I got busy and created a meal suitable for that group.

Because our district had begun as one big open range, we made our boundaries for the society the same way. It was north to Mosquito Creek, south to the Oldman River, west to the Porcupine Hills and east to the Little Bow River.

The success of the historical society points to a fact I see demonstrated over and over again—people are interested in their roots. We all want to know where we've been.

Back before big round oak tables became collectors' items, I bought three at country auctions to use in the restaurant. We knew which table came from which family. Whenever members of those families would come to the restaurant, they'd ask to sit at "Grandma's table" ... the Lineham table or the Flitten table or the Ramage table.

See what I mean? We like reminders of "the way we were".

Recipes illustrated overleaf

Most recipes for eggnog suggest that it's best if mixed at least 24 hours ahead and allowed to mellow in a covered container in the frig. This is supposed to remove the eggy taste. One such recipe is actually called Overnight Eggnog. It's also an overnight success!

Overnight Eggnog, Instant Success

12	eggs, separated	12
1½ cups	bourbon, rum or brandy	375 mL
¾ cup	sugar	175 mL
4 cups	milk	1 L
4 cups	whipping cream	1 L
1 tsp.	nutmeg	5 mL

Separate eggs and put whites away in the frig, covered. Beat the yolks until thick and lemon coloured.

Slowly add bourbon, rum or brandy, an ounce at a time. Add sugar and milk and beat well. Cover and set in frig overnight. (Empty ice cream pails work well for this.)

Just before serving the next day, beat egg whites stiff and fold into the egg yolk mixture. Beat whipping cream until stiff and add the nutmeg to the whipped cream. Pour over mixture in the punch bowl.

Ladle into cups so that each cup gets its fair share of whipped cream and nutmeg.

Serves 30.

I have tried my hand at making wine at home with varying degrees of success. My brother Gordon has had better luck, although his wines aren't always what they're intended to be! For instance, on one of my visits, I enjoyed an excellent golden brown sherry that began its life as a white wine. Or so Gordon thought.

Chokecherry Wine

Pick and wash fully ripe chokecherries. Some people claim a touch of frost helps. Grind through meat grinder to break about half the pits. Let pulp stand for 3 days.

Transfer pulp to a large pot and measure the total pulp in the process. To each gallon of juice, add 1 gallon boiling water. Simmer 10-15 minutes. Strain and measure again.

To each gallon of juice this time, add 2 cups raisins and 2 cups brown sugar. Let stand in a warm place for about 3 weeks, to ferment. This process will go faster if you add ¼ tsp. (1 mL) of yeast per gallon of juice. One way to accomplish this is by spreading the yeast on a piece of bread and floating it on the fermenting juice.

When fermentation is over, strain, bottle and age. The only way to know when a wine has aged enough is to keep testing. Happy wine making!

Drinks

Speaking of wine, sangria has become very popular in the last few years. Essentially, it's a mixture of red wine, orange and lemon juice and sparkling water. However, since you can buy it ready made at liquor stores now and since some of us prefer white wine, here is my recipe for White Wine Sangria.

White Wine Sangria

1	whole orange	1
1 bottle	dry white wine	1 bottle
2 slices	lemon	2 slices
2 slices	lime	2 slices
1 oz.	cognac	30 mL
2 tbsp.	sugar	30 mL
1 piece	stick cinnamon	1 piece
8	large strawberries	8
6 oz.	iced club soda	170 mL

Peel the orange but do it with this difference — try to get the entire orange peeled in one continuous strip. Begin at the stem end and continue the spiral to the other end. Take a healthy swath — you want to expose the orange flesh. When you manage this feat, leave the peel attached to the orange bottom so that it may hang in the wine mixture.

Pour wine into a large pitcher. Add lemon and lime slices, the cognac, sugar and cinnamon. Remove stems from strawberries, halve them and add to the wine. Stir to dissolve the sugar.

Carefully place the orange in the pitcher, draping the top of the peel over the top of the pitcher. Let mixture marinate at room temperature at least 1 hour.

To serve, add soda and about 1 tray of ice cubes. Stir.

Draw lots for the orange after the sangria is all gone. Serves 6.

SPECIAL MENUS, SPECIAL FOOD

— edited by Nancy Millar

It's ironic that the meal Jean Hoare remembers best after all her years in the restaurant business is one so simple that any one of us could almost manage it. We might have a bit of trouble with a whole pit roasted buffalo, I grant you, but beyond that, the meal included beans, coleslaw, pickles, biscuits and carrot pudding. Nothing that could be categorized as gourmet and/or out of reach.

Therefore, it wasn't the food that was memorable; it was the spirit with which the food was served. And that, I think, is an important concept when we talk about Jean Hoare's accomplishments in the food preparation business.

In 1980, Alberta was 75 years old as a province. The southern part of the province got a jump on celebrations by planning a special party for January 1, 1980, the very first day of the big year. The location of the party? The Flying N.

Somehow, the idea of the celebration caught on in Claresholm. Some 80 volunteers came forward to help with food and arrangements. Three bands volunteered to play and took turns doing so. Some of Jean's neighbours hitched up their teams of horses and oldfashioned wagons and brought all the guests from the gate of the airport to the restaurant. Others came with food. Just about everybody dressed up in costumes reminiscent of 75 years ago. Just about 350 people came.

An oldtimer of the district, born January 1, 1905, cut the first slice out of the big birthday cake.

It was a marvelous party all round, Jean says now, and the food never tasted so good. The menu included:
— cold moose milk and hot mulled sweet cider
— Alberta cheddar cheese and crackers from a barrel
— Burton buffalo
— baked beans with beef
— crocks of salad and barrels of pickles
— biscuits hot from the griddle with honey and butter
— carrot pudding
— Willow Creek coffee from freshly ground beans
— dried fruit, oranges and whole nuts

As simple as the food was, it tasted so good because it was served and eaten in a spirit of cooperation and friendship, something like the atmosphere of oldfashioned work bees. And that, I think, is one of the chief reasons for Jean Hoare's success. She was not the cook on one side of the door, unapproachable and removed from the customers on the other side of the door. She was (and is) always on both sides of the door, and the better the relationship between the two, the better the food. Just like the memorable 75th birthday.

Special Menus

When the provincial organizers came back at the end of the 75th year and suggested a wind-up party, Jean put another of her strengths to work. She loves a challenge, some new way of presenting food, so she came up with the idea of a meal that could be served 75 years hence, in the year 2055.

The ingredients would all have to be Alberta made, she decided, and fairly basic so that they'd still be around 75 years in the future.

Thus, the menu included:

—Lobsters Lougheed, the lobsters coming from a fish ranch in Red Deer with a good chance of being around in 75 years, the Lougheed name coming from the premier of the province who won't likely be here in 75 years although Albertans do tend to stick with one political party for a long time!

—Game Bird Casserole, with the game birds coming from a Didsbury farm, the champagne from a little further afield!

—Mineral water from local bottlers in Nanton

—Prime Ribs of Beef with Dowling Dumplings … again the beef will likely last but the politician may not.

—Porcupine Hills potatoes from a nearby Hutterite colony

—Tomatoes from a Claresholm hydroponic greenhouse that has already gone into other produce, but tomatoes will always be around one way or another.

—Mosquito Creek mushrooms from a Nanton grower.

—Country Cheese board with cheese from Faith Farms in Red Deer and Glenwood Cheese factory.

—And finally, an Alberta birthday parfait with ice cream from the Anderson Bros. Creamery in Claresholm.

The futuristic theme was continued through Star Wars decorations, characters and music. R2D2 came and so did Darth Vader. It cost Jean $45.00 just to buy batteries for all the Star Wars toys that paraded around that night.

But again, it was fun. And the food was good even though it was not heavy duty gourmet.

Which is not to suggest that Jean Hoare didn't get into heavy duty gourmet. She did and enjoyed that too. I am just trying to make the point that good food alone is not enough. There's another element, and that is the spirit with which the food is presented and received. That is an element of successful restaurants that can't be measured and can't be duplicated.

One of the most popular features of the restaurant was a Gourmet Club organized by Jean to accomplish two things: present meals that were out of the ordinary and therefore lots of fun for her to organize and make, and secondly, allow the serving of liquor. The first country restaurant was not licensed and could serve liquor only if a special permit were granted. Special permits were granted in those days to non-profit organizations … so the Gourmet Club was born.

Aloha From the Alberta Foothills

Theme meals were featured—things like a Danish smorgasbord or a Robert Burns dinner or a Hawaiian Luau, the most popular of all!

Perhaps the reason for the popularity of the Hawaiian evenings was not all in the food, although that has to be given most of the credit. The thing is that southern Alberta is a long way from Hawaii, especially in the middle of winter, and sometimes a reminder of warmth and flowers was just what everyone needed. One memorable winter night, the band almost missed the whole affair. In a snowstorm, they missed the turnoff and were well on their way into the Porcupine Hills before they realized their mistake. Fortunately, the dancing girls had not yet changed into their grass skirts.

Guests were invited to dress for the occasion as well, and most did, making it a happy evening all round.

Now, for the food, just in case you want to try a luau sometime.

The meal started with Hawaiian appetizers and dips ... trays of cut up pineapple, banana and papaya dipped into a mixture of mayonnaise, maraschino cherry juice and pineapple juice. Or use this tangy dip.

Dip for Fruit Cubes

1 cup	mayonnaise	250 mL
2 tbsp.	fruit chutney	25 mL
½-1 tsp.	curry powder	2-5 mL

Blend ingredients well and chill.

Buy shrimp chips in specialty stores. They can be deep fat fried, according to package instructions, in just minutes and are worth the extra trouble. Make a dip of mayonnaise, cream cheese, fresh pineapple cut into small pieces or canned crushed pineapple, drained well.

A shrimp salad was often served after the appetizers.

Shrimp Great and Beautiful

salad greens to line individual salad bowls
avocado halves, one per serving
lemon juice to prevent avocados browning
giant shrimps, as many as you can afford per serving!
papaya seed dressing, page 69.

Wash and crisp salad greens. Line salad bowls. Cut avocados in half, brush with lemon juice and arrange on the lettuce. Pile as many shrimps on as you'd like and top everything with the papaya seed dressing.

Fruit boats were also served, either individually in pineapple halves or generally in watermelon boats. See page 7 for ideas and instructions about fruit boats.

The maluna Coconut Curried Shrimp was so popular with guests, it was made many times afterwards for smaller parties. The recipe is very adaptable — use it for an intimate dinner of two or expand it to 20. Use the basic curry sauce in this recipe or try it with lobster, chicken or meat. You can bake it in a coconut shell or pineapple shell or plain old casserole. It gets around very well, believe me!

Basic Curry for Maluna Coconut Curried Shrimp

½ cup	clarified butter	125 mL
2 tbsp.	curry powder	30 mL
2 cloves	garlic, minced	2 cloves
1	onion, chopped fine	1
3 stalks	celery, chopped	3 stalks
1	green pepper	1
1	apple	1
3 cups	broth	750 mL
2 tbsp.	sherry	25 mL
2 tbsp.	soy sauce	25 mL
1 tsp.	sugar	5 mL
salt and freshly ground pepper to taste		
2 tbsp.	cornstarch	30 mL
4 tbsp.	water	50 mL

Note: To clarify butter, melt the butter over low heat and remove. Let milk solids settle to the bottom and then skim off the clear butter. Broth may be meat or chicken broth, home prepared or canned.

In a large skillet or wok, melt butter and warm curry powder in it. Add garlic, onion, celery and chopped green pepper. Saute until onion is clear but not brown. Peel and chop apple. Add to the butter mixture and cook for about 3 minutes, until apple is soft. Add broth, sherry, soy sauce, sugar, salt and pepper. Mix well and bring to a boil.

If being used at once, mix the cornstarch with the water and add to the hot curry mixture. Cook until it's clear and raw taste gone. Otherwise, if you're not using it immediately, reduce the heat and simmer the curry for several hours until it thickens on its own.

Maluna Coconut Curried Shrimp

1 recipe of basic curry, above
as much shrimp as you need for your party
coconut shells, pineapple shells or casserole dish
chopped green onions or scallions for garnish

Note: You can use shrimp, chicken or cooked meat in this recipe. Allow about ⅓ to ½ lb. (175 to 250 g) per person.

Add the basic curry to shrimp, put into coconut shells or casserole dish and bake in 350°F (180°C) oven for 30 minutes. If using pineapple shells, heat the shrimp and curry together and then put into the pineapple shell, just warming the shells briefly before serving since they don't hold up under heat too well.

Sprinkle with chopped green onions or scallions on top.

Serve with hot boiled rice and condiments.

Condiment Ideas

Individual bowls of: fresh grated coconut, chutney (see page 134), sliced bananas with yogurt or lemon juice, diced green peppers, raisins, cashew nuts, toasted sesame seeds, watermelon rind pickles (see page 129).

Native Drums Chicken is done Polynesian style with a buttered fruit sauce.

Native Drums Chicken

1 leg and thigh piece of chicken per serving		
flour and seasoned salt		
1 cup	butter	250 mL
1 cup	orange juice	250 mL
2 tbsp.	lemon juice	25 mL
½ cup	brown sugar	125 mL
1 tbsp.	cornstarch	15 mL
1 tbsp.	soy sauce	15 mL
1	fresh pineapple	1
1	fresh papaya	1
chopped green pepper and toasted sesame seeds		

Season the chicken by shaking in a bag of flour and seasoned salt.

Melt the butter in a baking dish or casserole. Arrange chicken pieces in it, spooning the melted butter up over each piece. Bake about 50 minutes at 350°F (180°C) or until chicken is nicely browned and juice runs clear when pierced by a fork in the leg joint.

While the chicken is baking, combine the orange juice, lemon juice, sugar, cornstarch and soy sauce in a sauce pan, mixing well until all lumps are worked out. Bring to a boil, stirring constantly. When clear and thickened, remove from heat.

Cut open the pineapple and papaya and remove the fruit. Remove the core in the case of the pineapple. Cube the fruit into small pieces.

Add cubed fruit to the sauce and pour over the baked chicken. Bake 10 minutes longer.

Serve garnished with green pepper and sesame seeds.

Pork is often served for Hawaiian meals, anything from a whole roasted suckling pig to something as easy as Butterflied Pork Chops.

Butterflied Pork Chops

1 recipe of buttered fruit sauce, above
pork loin chops, cut double

Get the butcher to cut a pork loin into double chops, about 1½" (4 cm) thick. From the fat side of the chop, have them sliced almost through, leaving them attached at the bone side. Open out — like a butterfly — and brown each side on a grill or over open coals. Finish cooking in the oven, covered at 350°F (180°C) for about 40 minutes.

Serve one "butterfly" to each guest, spooning a serving of fruit sauce between the wings.

Pork is good in stir fried combinations as long as the meat is cut into small cubes and cooked long enough to remove all traces of pink.

Number One Girl Sweet-Sour Pork

1 lb.	boneless pork	500 g
1	egg, beaten	1
¼ cup	cornstarch	50 mL
¼ cup	flour	50 mL
1½ cups	chicken broth	375 mL
½ tsp.	salt	2 mL
cooking oil for deep fat frying		
1	green pepper	1
½ cup	chopped carrot	125 mL
1 clove	garlic, minced	1
2 tbsp.	oil	25 mL
½ cup	sugar	125 mL
⅓ cup	red wine vinegar	75 mL
2 tsp.	soy sauce	10 mL
2 tbsp.	cornstarch	30 mL
¼ cup	cold water	50 mL

Cut the pork into small 1″ cubes.

In a bowl, mix egg, ¼ cup (50 mL) cornstarch, flour, ¼ cup (50 mL) of the broth and salt, beating until smooth. Dip pork cubes into this batter and fry in deep hot oil at 365°F (185°C) for 5-6 minutes or until golden brown. Drain and keep warm.

In wok or skillet, cook chopped green pepper, carrot and garlic in 2 tbsp. (25 mL) oil until they're tender but not brown. Add remaining broth, sugar, vinegar and soy sauce. Bring to a boil and cook 1 minute.

Blend together the cornstarch and cold water. Stir into vegetable mixture and cook, stirring constantly until it's thick and bubbly and all taste of raw starch has gone. Add pork cubes and heat them through.

Serve with hot fluffy rice.

This is a delicious way to roast pork whether it's to be served hot or cold. Any that's left over can be shredded and used as a topping for other dishes such as chow mein or fried rice.

Sweet Roast Pork

1½ lbs.	boneless pork	750 g
3 tbsp.	brown sugar	50 mL
¼ cup	honey	50 mL
⅓ cup	water	75 mL
1 tsp.	soy sauce	5 mL
1 tbsp.	white wine	15 mL
1 tbsp.	red food colouring	15 mL
½ tsp.	salt	2 mL
½ tsp.	MSG (Accent)	2 mL
⅛ tsp.	allspice	1 mL
3 tbsp.	red bean curd sauce	50 mL

Note: The boneless pork should be about 1½″ (4 cm) thick. Also note, the red bean curd sauce is optional.

Rub brown sugar into the pork. Let stand for 5 minutes. Combine remaining ingredients, pour over pork and marinate overnight in the frig. When ready to roast, drain the marinade and reserve it for basting. Place the meat on a rack in a pan over hot water and roast at 350°F (180°C) for 1 hour, turning the meat after the first 30 minutes. Baste with reserved marinade.

Roast another 30 minutes, thus making a total roasting time of 1½ hours.

The highlight of a genuine Hawaiian luau is a whole roasted pig. Instructions are included for pit barbecuing the pig as well as the more conventional oven method. Granted, very few people have pits for barbecuing beef or pork, but it seems that more and more are interested in trying it. So here goes.

Genuine Kalua Pig, Apple and All

Driftwillow Ranch has a pit that is used mainly for beef and buffalo but it could be adapted to Kalua Pig without much alteration.

The pit was dug in a level spot near the creek, large enough to hold a heavy iron screen about 3x6′. (Check local scrap metal yards for screens that might work.) The screen was then suspended at each corner from iron rods that rest on the surface, across the narrow end of the pit. The chains can be adjusted so that the meat can be put on the screen and lowered into the pit, or brought back up to the surface.

To cook a dressed pig of at least 100 lbs., heat up about 100 fist sized smooth rocks. (Test these first to make sure they don't explode when heated.) Get them red hot over the logs in the open pit. Cut slits in the pig skin at the neck and hindquarters and rub plenty of coarse salt (Hawaiian, if possible) into the slits and inside the cavity. Fill the slits and cavity with heated rocks and tie closed with heavy cord, tying all four feet together. Wrap pig in chicken wire.

Spread remaining hot rocks evenly in the bottom of the pit, making a depression to hold the pig. Line this depression with green banana leaves or ti leaves — available at specialty stores. Place pig in the leafy depression. Cover with additional leaves and wet clean burlap sacks. The moisture helps steam the pig as well as keep it clean. Shovel dry dirt over top of the pig, making sure no steam can escape. The meat is thus cooked from within by the hot rocks and from without by the remaining hot rocks.

According to Hawaiian instructions, a dressed pig of 100 pounds should cook in about 5 hours. Check pig when you take it out — there should be no sign of pink whatsoever. In fact, it should be falling off the bones.

Quick and easy next to that procedure is the oven roasting of a whole pig. The smaller ones that will fit into an oven have a very thin layer of meat so allow 1½ lbs. (750 g) per person. The pig may be partially boned but will require good stuffing and trussing. A 25 lb. (12 kg) pig will require about 20 cups of stuffing. Use a sage and onion bread stuffing or a rice, raisin and spice dressing.

If there is room in the oven, pull the front legs forward and the hind legs out to the back. If you don't have the room, tuck the legs under the body and tie in place. Put a wooden block in the mouth while roasting. This can be replaced when served with the traditional apple, lemon or cob of Indian corn.

Recipe continues overleaf

Make covers of double foil and place over the ears and tail as these parts will brown too quickly. If you have room and a large roasting pan, put the pig on a rack with water underneath to catch the drippings and prevent fat flare-ups or smoke.

Use a meat thermometer inserted into the thickest part of the leg and roast for 30 minutes to the pound, or until the thermometer registers 170°F (75°C). Every 15 minutes, baste with vinegar and water mixed half and half.

If the whole suckling pig is to be taken to the table, remove the wooden block and replace it with an apple or whatever. For a Hawaiian dinner, decorate the platter with ferns and place a lei around the neck. Cut in individual portions, carving along the backbone from head to tail. Remove the skin and if there's a very thick layer of fat, trim it away and discard. With each portion, serve a piece of the crisp skin, sometimes thought to be the best part of the roasted animal.

Ideas for a Scandinavian Meal ...

When planning the menus for that first restaurant, Jean stuck to meat and potatoes — fairly ordinary food that people would know and trust. She saved her flights of fancy for the gourmet dinners or special catered parties.

For instance, dinner "in the Scandinavian manner" included snitters, fiskefars, Norwegian meatballs in cream, sildesalat, rodgrod and aebleskivers.

Norwegian Meatballs in Cream

1 lb.	ground round beef	500 g
½ lb.	ground pork	250 g
1	egg, beaten	1
½ cup	mashed potatoes	125 mL
½ cup	dry bread crumbs	125 mL
½ cup	milk	125 mL
2 tsp.	salt	10 mL
¼ tsp.	cloves	1 mL
¼ tsp.	allspice	1 mL
¼ tsp.	ginger	1 mL
¼ tsp.	nutmeg	1 mL
freshly ground black pepper		
½ tsp.	brown sugar	2 mL
enough flour to dredge the meatballs		
2 tbsp.	cooking oil	25 mL
2 tbsp.	butter	25 mL
1 cup	heavy cream	250 mL

Combine the meats, egg, potatoes, bread crumbs, milk, salt, spices, pepper and brown sugar. Mix together well and shape into 24 meatballs. Roll in flour.

In a large skillet, heat the oil and butter. Brown the meatballs on all sides. Spoon into a baking dish or casserole and pour the cream over top. Cover and bake in a 325°F (160°C) oven for 40 minutes.

Red Fruit Combo

2 pkgs.	frozen raspberries	2 pkgs. (425 g each)
2 pkgs.	frozen strawberries	2 pkgs. (425 g each)
1/3 cup	cornstarch	75 mL
1/2 cup	water	125 mL
1 tbsp.	lemon juice	15 mL
1 tsp.	sugar	5 mL
1/3 cup	slivered almonds	75 mL
whipping cream, not whipped		

Note: 1 package of frozen berries weighs 15 oz. or 425 g.

Combine berries in a saucepan and bring to a boil, stirring occasionally. Strain through a fine sieve or puree in a blender. Put back into the saucepan.

Mix cornstarch with water to a smooth paste. Bring fruit back to the boiling point and add cornstarch. Cook about 3 minutes, stirring constantly until smooth and thick. Remove from heat and blend in lemon juice.

Pour into a glass serving dish and sprinkle top with sugar. Chill.

Before serving, decorate with slivered almonds. Serve with heavy unwhipped cream—just pour it on the berries. Serves about 6.

Other Scandinavian style dishes in the cookbook include aebleskivers, page 50; Glogg, page 214.

Claresholm Photo

Native Albertans, Sarcee Chief Clifford Big Plume (left) and Peigan Chief Nelson Small Legs (right) with Jean at Alberta's 75th Anniversary dinner.

Ideas for Dining in the French Style

Jean Hoare never tried anything easy! In the menu for dinner in the French manner, she tackled Aioli, the famous French garlic sauce that is used in so many dishes. She also presented a classic Quiche.

Classic Quiche

plain pastry for a standard size pie plate

4 slices	bacon	4 slices
1 tbsp.	bacon drippings	15 mL
1 cup	sliced onions	250 mL
1½ cups	cheese	375 mL
4	eggs, beaten	4
1 cup	milk	250 mL
1 cup	cream	250 mL
½ tsp.	salt	2 mL
¼ tsp.	nutmeg	1 mL
¼ tsp.	white pepper	1 mL

Note: Gruyere or Emmentaler cheese is best for Quiche Lorraine, but Swiss or cheddar may also be used.

Line pie plate with plain pastry (page 181) and bake in 350°F (180°C) oven for 5 minutes.

Fry bacon until crisp. Drain excess drippings from the frypan, keeping only 1 tbsp. (15 mL). In what's left, saute the sliced onions until they are transparent.

Crumble the bacon and put in the bottom of the pie shell. Grate the cheese and put it in. Finally, spread the onions over the cheese. Combine remaining ingredients and beat well. Pour over the other ingredients in the pie shell.

Bake in a preheated 450°F (230°C) oven for 10 minutes; then reduce heat to 350°F (180°C) and bake another 15-20 minutes or until a knife inserted into the centre comes out clean.

Once you have the hang of a classic Quiche, you can vary it all you like. Use ham instead of bacon, for instance. Or add a small can of shrimp, clams or crabmeat. Use shallots or leeks instead of onions. Add asparagus or cooked spinach. Have fun with it!

Aioli sauce is the basis for the next French dish. Once you have the sauce, you can use any manner of vegetables or seafood in the final dish.

Aioli Sauce

6-12 cloves	garlic, minced	6-12 cloves
4	egg yolks	4
1 tbsp.	boiling water	15 mL
salt and freshly ground pepper to taste		
1¼ cups	peanut oil	300 mL
1 cup	olive oil	250 mL
1 tbsp.	lemon juice	15 mL

Note: The number of garlic cloves used depends entirely on your preference. If you like lots of garlic, use 12. If you're not so keen, use 6.

Place the garlic in a large mixing bowl and add the egg yolks. Start beating with a wire whisk or beater. Or put everything in a blender and let it do the work. Add the rapidly boiling water, salt and pepper to taste. Then—while still beating—add the peanut oil, drop by drop, until more than half of it is added. The peanut oil and olive oil may then be added in increasing quantities. Finally, add the lemon juice.

Serve with any or all of the following to make up a classic French aioli.

French Aioli

Note: Aioli is a selection of seafood and vegetables served with the aioli sauce. Generally, all the ingredients are arranged on a platter and the sauce is applied before serving, or it can be served separately.

—Buy 2½ lbs. (1 kg) salt cod cut into 6 serving pieces. Soak for 24 hours, changing the water frequently. When ready to serve, cover with fresh cold water, add 4 whole cloves and simmer 10-15 minutes. Do not overcook. Let stand until ready to serve.

—Buy fresh or canned artichokes. If canned—no problem. Just heat them through and supply lots of aioli sauce. If fresh, cut away stems and rub heart with lemon to prevent it from discoloration. To further ensure the color, add ¼ cup (50 mL) flour to the water in which they're cooked. Cook for at least 30 minutes. Check for tenderness.

—Carrots for aioli should be cooked whole, if small, or cubed, if larger, until barely tender.

—Cauliflower for aioli should be broken up into flowerettes and simmered until just barely tender. Add flour (as with artichokes above) to keep the cauliflower white.

—Chick peas or garbanzos for aioli may be purchased in cans or cooked from the dried state. If working from dry beans, soak them overnight, and then simmer until tender the next day. Serve warm.

—Potatoes for aioli should be small tender new ones, if possible. Cook until just tender and serve hot.

—Tomatoes for aioli should be quartered and served cold.

—Eggs for aioli should be hardboiled, then chilled and peeled. Halve or quarter and arrange on the platter.

—Snails for aioli are easiest obtained in cans. Drain juice and all into a small saucepan, add 1 bay leaf, a pinch of dried thyme and simmer about 2 minutes. Drain and arrange on platter.

Crepes Suzette are the most distinctly French dessert. For years, we thought of this elegant dessert as something unapproachable, too hard for mere North Americans to tackle. Not so!

Crepes Suzette

1 batch of crepes, recipe page		
vanilla sugar with lemon and orange rind		
½ cup	butter	125 mL
½ cup	maraschino liqueur	125 mL
½ cup	curacao liqueur	125 mL
½ cup	kirsch liqueur	125 mL

Note: Other combinations of liqueurs can be used. Cointreau or Grand Marnier can be used instead of curacao, and apricot or peach brandy can be used in place of kirsch or the maraschino liqueur. Whatever the combination, you will need 1½ cups (375 mL) as outlined above.

Make crepes ahead of time according to instructions on page 51 and fold into quarters. Plan on 3 crepes per person.

Vanilla sugar is made by putting a vanilla bean, available at most supermarkets, into a small container of sugar. It gives the sugar a hint of vanilla. Several days before making the crepes, take 2½ tbsp. (40 mL) sugar out of the vanilla sugar container and add to it small pieces of lemon and orange rind cut in very fine strips. You want only the very outside of the fruits. Put this zest into the sugar and let stand 2-3 days. If you haven't time for the above, simply take about 4 large sugar cubes and rub them over a washed orange, trying to get as much of the oil out of the orange rind and onto the sugar cube as possible.

When the time comes to put the dessert together, place a chafing dish directly over burner (or use an electrically heated pan). Melt the butter in the pan. In a measuring cup, mix together the three liqueurs. When butter is melted, add ⅔ of the combined liqueurs. When they are warm, ignite. As soon as the flame dies down, add vanilla sugar and the strips of rind. Stir until the sugar is melted to a syrup. Put crepes into the syrup, turning each crepe once and coating them well with the mixture. Make sure they're heated through.

Add the remaining liqueur mixture and when warm, ignite again. Serve when flames burn out.

Ideas for an Irish Touch ...

For the St. Patrick's Day Gourmet dinner, Jean served up Mrs. Murphy's Chowder which, even without the overalls, is a hearty soup and then some.

Mrs. Murphy's Chowder

2 slices	salt pork	2 slices
1 tbsp.	butter	15 mL
1	large onion	1
4	medium potatoes	4
2 cups	water	500 mL
1 lb.	smoked haddock	500 g
1½ cups	milk	375 mL
salt and freshly ground pepper to taste		

In a large heavy saucepan or large skillet, fry the salt pork until the fat runs out. Add butter and sliced onion and cook 5 minutes. Peel potatoes, cut into fairly thick slices, and add to the salt pork mixture. Finally, add water and simmer for 15 minutes.

Cook the smoked haddock (sometimes known as finnan haddie) in milk for 20-30 minutes. Drain but keep the milk in which the fish cooked. Remove the skin and bones of the fish, and break into flakes. Add flaked fish and milk to the first mixture and simmer 5 minutes longer. Adjust seasonings.

The menu for St. Patrick's Day also included Corned Beef and Cabbage, page 113; Colcannon and its variations, on page 82.

Ideas to Please the Scots ...

The Scottish dinner for Robert Burns Day included haggis, page 112; clapshot, page 78 and stovies, page 77.

It also featured scones as made by Grandmother Patterson.

Soda Scones

4 cups	flour	1 L
4 tsp.	baking powder	20 mL
½ tsp.	baking soda	2 mL
½ tsp.	salt	2 mL
1 tbsp.	sugar	15 mL
1½ cups	buttermilk	375 mL

Note: Originally, this was made with farm buttermilk which had bits of butter floating in it. If you're using ordinary buttermilk bought in stores, add ½ cup (125 mL) butter. Add it to dry ingredients, using a pastry blender. Then add buttermilk.

Mix dry ingredients. Add buttermilk, mixing quickly and lightly. Turn dough out onto a floured board and pat lightly into two large circles about ½" (1 cm) thick. Bake as a whole with wedges just lightly marked on the dough, or cut into wedges and bake that way.

To do it the traditional Scottish way, bake on a surface griddle about 10 minutes a side on a fairly low heat.

Ideas from the Orient ...

The Japanese dinner included Sukiyaki, best known of stir fry dishes prepared at table. All ingredients must be prepared in advance and arranged on platters, starting with the beef and going on through mushrooms, onions, spinach, Chinese cabbage, snow peas, bamboo shoots, tofu and whatever else you'd like to include.

Sukiyaki

1½ lbs.	sirloin steak	750 g
½ lb.	beef suet	250 g
½ lb.	green onion	250 g
1	sweet onion	1
2	carrots	2
2 cups	shredded bok choy	500 mL
1 cup	bias cut celery	250 mL
1 can	water chestnuts	1 can
1 cup	fresh bean sprouts	250 mL
1 cup	canned bamboo shoots	250 mL
¼ lb.	snow peas	125 g
½ lb.	fresh spinach	250 g
½ lb.	fresh mushrooms	250 g
1 lb.	fresh tofu	500 g

for seasoning...MSG, sugar and broth (below)

In wok or suitable deep skillet, render the beef suet. That is, let it cook until fat is rendered out. Remove the brown bits and cracklings.

Cut beef in thin slices across the grain. This works best if meat is partially frozen. When ready to cook, it should be back to room temperature. Add slices of steak to the hot fat, one at a time, and sear quickly — about 15 seconds per side should be enough. Sprinkle with a little MSG (Accent), sugar and dashi broth (see below). Move meat to one side in the pan.

Cut the green onions into 1″ (2.5 cm) lengths. Slice the big onion, carrots, bok choy, celery and water chestnuts. Place in the centre of the hot skillet or wok and cook over high heat for 2 minutes, adding enough broth to keep the mixture moist. Push these vegetables aside.

Add drained bean sprouts and bamboo shoots. Prepare snow peas and chop up fresh spinach and fresh mushrooms. Add to pan. Cook these vegetables for 2 minutes at high heat, adding more broth if necessary.

Cut the tofu into 1″ (2.5 cm) cubes. Add to the meat and vegetables. Cook another 2 minutes.

Serve over hot rice.

Traditionally, the individual pieces of sukiyaki were dipped into beaten egg before eating. Provide some small bowls of beaten egg so that guests may try it that way too. Sukiyaki is known as a "friendship dish" so take your time over it, enjoying each individual portion.

Broth for Sukiyaki

6 cups	water	1.5 L
1 square	dried kelp	1 square
½ cup	dried bonito	125 mL
⅛ tsp.	MSG (Accent)	1 mL

Note: Dried bonito flakes (tuna flakes) and kelp are available in specialty food shops or oriental food shops. You only need a 1″ (2.5 cm) square of kelp.

Bring water, kelp and MSG almost to a boil. Remove the kelp. Add bonito and bring to a complete boil. Remove pan from heat and leave until the flakes of bonito sink to the bottom of the mixture. Strain the clear liquid and use in Sukiyaki, above.

Orange or lemon sponge is a nice light way to finish a Japanese meal, or any meal for that matter.

Orange or Lemon Sponge

¾ cup	sugar	175 mL
1½ tbsp.	butter	20 mL
1 tbsp.	grated orange rind	15 mL
3	eggs, separated	3
3 tbsp.	flour	50 mL
⅓ cup	orange juice	75 mL
1 cup	milk	250 mL

Note: To make a lemon sponge, substitute 2 tsp. (10 mL) lemon rind for the orange rind, and substitute ¼ cup (50 mL) lemon juice for the orange juice.

Butter 6 - 8 individual custard cups or 1 large casserole dish.

Cream the sugar with the butter. Add orange rind.

Separate the eggs. Set whites aside; beat the yolks and add to the creamed mixture. Stir in flour, orange juice and milk.

Beat the egg whites until stiff and fold into the yolk mixture.

Pour into the custard cups or the casserole dish. Set in a pan filled with 1″ (2.5 cm) water. Bake at 350°F (180°C) for 45 minutes for the smaller containers, an hour for the larger dish, or until set.

When the sponge bakes, it will separate into two layers; a spongey layer on top and a creamy jelly on the bottom. These are attractive if turned out of the cups and decorated with orange sections.

Ideas in the Spanish Style...

The Spanish meal started with gazpacho, see page 25. Sangria was served throughout, see page 218. Then it concluded with flan, the national dessert of Spain and Mexico. It's not like the flan served nowadays with fruit on top; it's a lemon and cinnamon custard baked in a caramel coated dish. Very tasty and unusual.

Spanish Flan

1 cup	sugar	250 mL
2 cups	evaporated milk	500 mL
sliced lemon rind to provide zest		
1	cinnamon stick	1
2	whole eggs	2
3	egg yolks	3
¼ tsp.	salt	1 mL
caramel flavoured whipped cream or fresh fruit		

Note: The traditional way of making this Spanish custard is to boil the milk down to half the quantity you started with, but you can save time by using canned evaporated milk. Do not dilute it.

In a heavy skillet, melt ½ cup (125 mL) sugar, stirring constantly. Warm the mold or souffle dish you plan to use for the flan, and pour the melted golden sugar into the bottom. Turn so that the bottom is coated evenly. Set aside.

Scald the milk. Slice a lemon very thinly, and add the thin strips and the cinnamon stick to the hot milk. Let stand for 15 minutes to infuse.

Beat eggs and egg yolks with the remaining sugar until thoroughly mixed, add salt. Remove the cinnamon stick from the hot milk and add the hot milk to the eggs, beating constantly.

Pour into prepared mold, set in a pan of hot water and bake in a 325°F (160°C) oven for about an hour or until knife inserted in the center comes out clean. Leave in pan and chill.

Just before serving, loosen the sides of the flan with a knife and turn out on a large flat serving dish (but choose one with a bit of a rim as the caramel runs down the side of the custard).

Serve with caramel flavoured whipped cream (add a bit of the caramel juice from the flan to whipped cream instead of sugar), or with fresh fruit. If using fruit and if you can get Spanish melon, cut this delicious pale gold melon in crescents and place around the unmolded flan with fresh lime wedges. Pass powdered ginger to sprinkle on the melon.

Ideas from Home...North American Food

One of the special meals featured foods native to the new world, foods that were not known in Europe and Asia until explorers took them back with them. In that line, Jean made up a Pemmican Pate, not completely authentic, but an approximation of the basic food that Indians, explorers and fur traders depended on so completely. See page 20. Also part of that meal was Pumpkin Soup, page 27, Cornbread Sticks, page 34 and Maple Sugar Pie, page 192.

Cornmeal, or Indian corn, was a staple of Indians and early settlers in North America. Teamed up with maple syrup in the following recipe, it's twice North American!

Johnny Cake with Maple Syrup

1 1/3 cups	flour	325 mL
2/3 cup	fine cornmeal	150 mL
4 tsp.	baking powder	30 mL
1/2 tsp.	salt	2 mL
2/3 cup	milk	150 mL
1/3 cup	maple syrup	75 mL
2	eggs, beaten	2
1/4 cup	melted butter or oil	50 mL

Grease a 9″ (2.5 L) pan.

Mix dry ingredients together, add milk, maple syrup, eggs and melted butter or oil. Don't overbeat. Pour into greased pan and bake at 375°F (190°C) for 25 minutes or until cake tests done. Serve hot with lots of butter and more syrup.

Ideas for a "Back to the Farm" Meal

Not all the special meals were based on exotic countries on the other side of the world. One of them came right back home. It was June and the gardens were at their very best, so a "Back to the Farm" meal was presented.

The menu included devilled eggs, page 21; Marj's Chicken, page 93; Famous Flying N Potatoes, page 76; Cranberry Relish, page 132; and Rhubarb Crisp, page 157. It also included Marj's Wilted Cucumber Salad.

Marj's Wilted Cucumber Salad

as many cucumber as you think you'll need
salt to sprinkle between the layers

1/2 cup	sour cream	125 mL
2 tbsp.	vinegar	25 mL
2 tbsp.	brown sugar	30 mL
1/4 tsp.	dry mustard	1 mL

sliced onions or chives

Note: You can use sweet cream for this recipe also — just increase the vinegar somewhat. Also, you may use lemon juice in place of the vinegar.

Completely peel the cucumbers, or if they happen to be young and tender, remove alternative strips from as many cucumbers as you think you'll need. Layer them in a glass or pottery bowl, sprinkling salt over each layer quite generously. Cover with a plate that fits down inside bowl as a light weight. Let stand at least 3 hours; overnight is better. An amazing amount of liquid will be drawn from the slices, taking with it the bitter taste and indigestible effect of cucumbers.

Drain, rinse to remove any salt that may remain, and drain again.

Mix sour cream, vinegar, brown sugar and dry mustard. Add the onions or chives to the cucumbers and then mix both with the dressing. Garnish with more chopped chives or fresh dill.

JEAN'S ALBUM

or: How I learned to love the kitchen but hate the piano... (by Jean Hoare)

I grew up in Toronto in a big house, the site of which is now a parking lot for the highrise buildings and hospitals on University Avenue, just below College Street.

The Toronto Conservatory of Music was just around the corner so it was decided that little Jean should be enrolled. Thus began an 8 year losing battle. I really only showed enthusiasm for the new clothes that had to be supplied for the recitals.

I much preferred to spend my after school time in the kitchen.

When we moved to the Avenue Road St. Clair district of Toronto, I was introduced to several households where the servants outnumbered the family and to my ten year old mind, that seemed a completely reasonable arrangement. Who else would look after the gardens and wash the "good" dishes and cutlery that were used as matter of course?

After watching and enjoying some of the fancier meals served up in my friends' houses, I went completely overboard at home. We should have butter in iced curls, I would argue, or I'd try to talk my mother into cutting off the crusts of the sandwiches she supplied for my dad's lunch.

Soon after this, I found an accomplice in this food mission of mine. Another ten year old was as interested as I was so we talked our folks into letting us prepare dinner every Friday night, After a frantic week of planning and shopping, we'd cook up this horrendous meal in our respective kitchens. She'd make the main meal, I'd make dessert or vice versa. Then, we'd serve all this simultaneously to our two households.

What appeared on the dinner table, I can only guess. But it served a very useful purpose — it taught us how to plan, shop and prepare whole meals and how to serve them in what we considered "elegant" ways.

Typically, once the meal was eaten, I lost interest in all things domestic — a failing I have never outgrown.

I graduated from high school at the peak of the great depression. Fortunately, I had taken several business courses along with my high school courses so I was able to get a job — in the buying office of the Hudson's Bay Company, an office that was tucked in beside the Royal York Hotel.

I began to learn how to stretch a salary. For one thing, we sometimes had access to sample clothing at greatly reduced prices and that kept me broke, besides which I had all of downtown Toronto to check out as far as restaurants and food were concerned.

Over and over again, I had buyers ask me to make dinner reservations for them at a little hotel in Niagara Falls called the Marigold. I could hardly wait to try it myself and when the day finally came, I said to myself, "If I ever have a restaurant, I want to serve dinners as they do at the Marigold."

Jean's Album

My memory of the hotel includes wide verandahs, tall columns and a great feeling of welcome. When you went into the dining room and were seated, a seemingly unending procession of food was offered for your selection. Nothing was hurried and the whole dinner, course after course, must have taken several hours but you were never aware of passing time. You always had something to eat or were in the process of getting the next dish.

It was the sense of welcome, and the continuous presentation of courses that most impressed me.

Marriage and Southern Alberta...

Wartime marriages were not elaborate affairs, and my own was an example of a compromise between what might have been and what had to be, what with rationing, schedules that continually changed and so on.

We set a June date. Then that had to be set back to April — or wait until the end of the war. At least, that's what we were told at the time. So my mother had to phone the guests (invitations had just been mailed), my aunt and uncle waved a wand (probably a green one) to get the Loft Room at the Old Mill for the reception and attendants finished wedding clothes in days, not weeks. Somehow, everything got speeded up and despite an unseasonable snowstorm on the morning of the wedding, all went smoothly.

After all the rushing, the Air Force changed plans again. We stayed in Ontario longer than we had expected, but then were to be transferred to Vancouver Island with a brief stay in Calgary enroute. I was to stay with relatives in southern Alberta until we found a place to live on the west coast. But that wasn't to be either. Stan was sent to India.

In the meantime, I was beginning to like what I saw in southern Alberta. Maybe we could live here after the war? So it was decided that I should stay on with my relatives and see whether the foothills of Alberta might be a good permanent home for us.

Fate stepped in at this point. My cousin married an English girl who came to Canada with other war brides to wait for the war to end. Betty arrived in Alberta about the time I returned for good and together we learned, the hard way, about life on an Alberta ranch.

We listened to the announcement of VJ Day over a barbwire telephone, carrying the news from a neighbour several miles away who had the only radio with a battery that was operating at the time. We had no direct phone to town which was 50 dirt miles away. Mail was brought out to mail boxes at the forks of the Willow Creek bridge, a 17 mile ride on horseback from the ranch.

Despite all the problems, I loved it and we decided to look for land in the area when the war was done.

In the spring of 1946, we made the big move, choosing a small spot on Willow Creek, not too far from town, with a huge old house and many outbuildings.

We knew practically nothing about such a life but were young and ready to try anything and everything. We got chickens, turkeys, pigs, a milk cow, horses, beef cattle, a crop of wheat and a bouncing baby boy.

Jean's Album

Then came the winter. The house was a mere shell with a wood stove and oil heaters. In spite of a few modern conveniences that I was lucky to have, I still felt like a pioneer woman, struggling with life on the great lone land.

Pack the Pig and Let's Go Camping...

Spring finally came, and with it some Eastern visitors. We must show them the scenic beauties of the Rockies. But how? We had no cash and no car.

Never mind. We put sides on the half ton truck, covered it with tarpaulin, and put our suitcases and camping gear in the top half of the truck box. In the bottom half, we put the pigs that were to be sold in Calgary to finance this trip.

Believe it or not, that was the best visit to Banff and Lake Louise that I've ever had. We camped when the weather was good, moved indoors when it was not, swam in the hot pools and dined in great style in both the Banff Springs Hotel and the Chateau Lake Louise.

When we drove up to the latter in the old pickup truck with its tarpaulin covered load, the parking attendant was a bit dubious but he pointed out a less conspicuous place for us to park and we were in.

That fall, Patricia was born. We now had our Pat and Mike, and the family was complete.

In the summer of 1956, the children and I visited friends and relatives in eastern Canada, and I couldn't help but make some comparisons. Not that I would have changed places with them for a minute but I did sense that a lot of improvements could be made to our house. Not only that, but there were signs of an illness that was eventually to make me the sole support of the family. It was time to reactivate the idea that had been simmering on the back burner all these years — time to try my hand at that nebulous dream — my own restaurant.

The story of first the Driftwillow Room and then The Flying N is told in other parts of this book. Suffice it to say here that I did start a country restaurant and I ran it for nearly 20 years.

At the end of that time, it was running me, so in 1975, I decided to sell.

Big News...Restaurant for Sale

I was used to the idea that people found The Flying N unique for various reasons, but it did come as a bit of a surprise when the story of its intended sale became a national news item. A picture of me, wearing a grin-and-bear-it look, my hair bedraggled, accompanied an article headlined, "Flying N proprietress tired, puts restaurant up for sale."

With that photo, the headline was redundant but the story was carried in newspapers from coast to coast. Several versions were mailed to me from as far away as the Maritimes.

In July of 1975, my son was married. Betty and Mike's reception was one of the last functions at The Flying N under its original owner. By August, I was retired and on my way to "eat my way around the world."

Jean Hoare and author Walter Stewart aboard Vancouver Island ferry enroute to the B.C. mainland for annual Christmas cake baking event.

Captain Arnott greets Jean as Wine and Food Society members arrive for cocktails aboard the QE 2, enroute to special Society dinner in London England.

Around the World in 80 Restaurants

I had joined the International Wine and Food Society, a group dedicated to the promotion of good food and wine throughout the world. For my first overseas trip, I was off to London to see the Queen, or at least to see as much of London and other parts of Europe as I could.

I nearly missed the plane what with all the excitement, and somehow got seated in the first class section of the plane. There, right across the aisle from me, was Mary Dover, another member of the I.W.&F.S. She was off to London to see roses, and buy more for her beautiful garden south of Calgary but when she learned this was to be my first visit to London, she arranged a day of sightseeing together. We visited the small bomb damaged church inside the medieval walls of the Inner Temple, burial place of the Knights Templar. We signed our names at Canada House and saw displays of roses that alone were worth the trip across the ocean.

And best of all, we had lunch at Simpsons-in-the Strand. I began to feel that I really was embarked on my dream of eating around the world.

There was the carver, all stiff upper lip in white, pushing the trolley from which the roasts of beef were served. There were the huge silver domes covering the meat. There were the famous menus that were printed daily to reflect the specials of the season.

I was sure I'd died and gone to heaven. The Flying N was far behind me. Then, the carver approached an adjoining table with the trolley containing the meat for the four people at that table. With due ceremony, he raised the cover and displayed what looked to my eyes like one small steak, about the size of one serving at The Flying N.

I couldn't help but remember The Flying N days when a visitor from England was served our standard porterhouse for one. She automatically assumed that such meat had to be for the whole table, and she carved it up to share with the rest.

Wouldn't you know it . . . I'm halfway across the world and thinking of The Flying N!

Jean's Album

Index

Index

Index

Index

Index

Index

Best Little Cookbook
General Store
Gift Ideas Galore!

The Best Little Cookbook

A special gift idea for Christmas, birthdays, new brides and old friends. Share Jean's Best Little Cookbook with family too! Twelve full page color photos capture Jean's wonderful world of down home cooking that anyone can create. Clear type and decorative section headings make these delicious recipes quick to find and easy to read. Order now!

$15.95

Keep in touch with friends!

Send a note on these illustrated antique woodstove notecards with one of Jean's famous recipes on the reverse of each design (Yukon Hot Cakes with Wild Rose Jelly, Sour Cream Raisin Pie). Printed on quality antique finish paper and folded to a handy 5¾″ x 7¼″, the notes come complete with envelopes in a set of 8 cards, 4 each of two designs. Suitable for framing or just saying hello to a friend, the famous Grand Jewel and McClary woodstoves are designed to convey warmth and good food memories.

$5.95

The Flying Hen Apron

Brighten kitchen chores and keep in the pink with this attractive strong pink cotton apron, specially designed for "Best Little Cookbook" fans. "Flying Hen" applique on bib adds extra sparkle. Sturdy long ties and halter will fit all sizes. An excellent gift for gourmet friends, favourite aunts, or … for yourself! Don't delay. Brighten your day!

$15.00

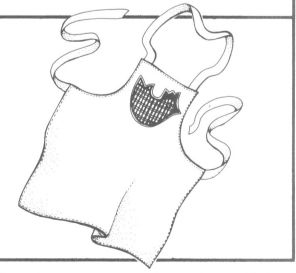

To order, complete form on following page, and enclose cheque or money order made payable to DEADWOOD PUBLISHING LTD.

Yes, I would like to order these special gifts from the Best Little Cookbook General Store

Gift Items		Price Per Item	Number Ordered	Total Cost
Best Little Cookbook	($15.95 plus $2.00 postage & handling)	$17.95		
Woodstove/Recipe Notecards	($5.95 plus $1.00 postage & handling)	$ 6.95		
Flying Hen Apron	($15.00 plus $1.25 postage & handling)	$16.25		
		TOTAL AMOUNT ENCLOSED ➤		

BONUS OFFER ✻ ✻ ✻

Order 3 or more of any of above items, or combination of items, and receive 1 package of woodstove notecards at no extra charge.
Send order to:

NAME _____

ADDRESS _____

CITY _____ PROVINCE _____ POSTAL CODE _____

Mail completed order form, with cheque or money order made payable to:

DEADWOOD PUBLISHING LTD.
Box 564, Station G
Calgary, Alberta
T3A 2G4

NOTE: Allow 4-6 weeks for delivery.
    Prices subject to change May 31, 1984.

◄ ◄

Yes, I would like to order these special gifts from the Best Little Cookbook General Store

Gift Items		Price Per Item	Number Ordered	Total Cost
Best Little Cookbook	($15.95 plus $2.00 postage & handling)	$17.95		
Woodstove/Recipe Notecards	($5.95 plus $1.00 postage & handling)	$ 6.95		
Flying Hen Apron	($15.00 plus $1.25 postage & handling)	$16.25		
		TOTAL AMOUNT ENCLOSED ➤		

BONUS OFFER ✻ ✻ ✻

Order 3 or more of any of above items, or combination of items, and receive 1 package of woodstove notecards at no extra charge.
Send order to:

NAME _____

ADDRESS _____

CITY _____ PROVINCE _____ POSTAL CODE _____

Mail completed order form, with cheque or money order made payable to:

DEADWOOD PUBLISHING LTD.
Box 564, Station G
Calgary, Alberta
T3A 2G4

NOTE: Allow 4-6 weeks for delivery.
    Prices subject to change May 31, 1984.